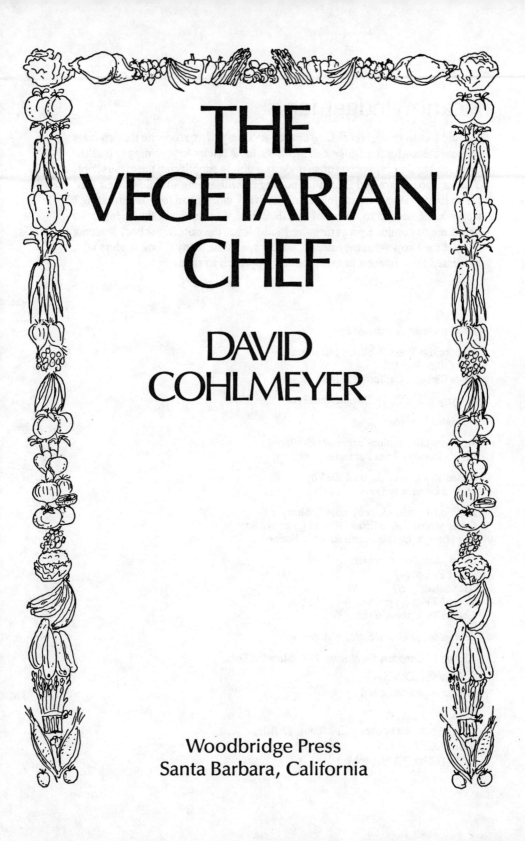

THE VEGETARIAN CHEF

DAVID COHLMEYER

Woodbridge Press
Santa Barbara, California

Acknowledgements

I would like to thank Nanci Lugsdin for encouraging me to write the originals of these menus for the *Globe and Mail*, Richard Teleky for deciding to publish them, and Sally Livingston for so understandingly simplifying the manuscript. Thanks also to Lara and Emma for putting up with seeing so little of their Dad for so long, and to Barbara for letting me work when I had to—and insisting I stop when I needed to. Most of all, though, I want to thank the clients who urged me to continue preparing the food I love, the cooking-school students who let me know what they needed to learn, and the many *Globe* readers who expressed their interest in this practical approach to food.

Published and distributed by

Woodbridge Press Publishing Company
Post Office Box 6189
Santa Barbara, California 93160

Copyright © 1985 by David Cohlmeyer

Additional illustrations copyright © 1986
by Woodbridge Press Publishing Company

Canadian edition published 1985 by
Oxford University Press

Additional illustrations by Lois Cohlmeyer
Cover photograph: Michael Kohn/Oyster Studio
Food design: Lucille Schur/Foods in Focus

Cover photograph recipes:
Apple Pie, p. 147
Rice Salad, p. 57
Zucchini Patties, p. 66
Grilled Vegetables, p. 63

Printed in the United States of America

Library of Congress Cataloging-in-Publication Data:

Cohlmeyer, David.
   The vegetarian chef.

   Includes index.
   1. Vegetarian cookery. 2. Menus. I. Title.
TX837.C57   1986   641.5'636   86-9121
ISBN 0-88007-159-1 (pbk.)

Contents

FALL MENUS

WINTER MENUS

Introduction

When I opened my restaurant, the Beggar's Banquet, in 1972, I deliberately avoided advertising that the food was vegetarian. The strategy worked: confirmed vegetarians found us anyway, but many more customers came on the merits of the food alone. I also decided to limit each day's offerings to a single meal of soup, salad, main course and dessert, because I knew the best way to ensure quality and an imaginative kitchen was to base the menu on whatever looked best in the market. I might design a meal around the first local asparagus or strawberries, a good deal on some pre-frost green tomatoes, or a shipment of carrots my favorite vendor assured me were "sweet like sugar." Sometimes the menu would celebrate the day itself: the first signs of spring (chives, mint and rhubarb), the hottest day of summer (all cold dishes) or a festive occasion such as Thanksgiving or Christmas. Other days the theme would be adaptations of traditional recipes from a particular country—Greece, Japan, India, Mexico, Sweden or Thailand (to name only a few). There was never any shortage of ideas.

Since selling the restaurant, however, I have devoted my time to running a catering business, teaching about vegetarian food, and writing a weekly column in the *Globe and Mail*. And I have discovered that many people who enjoy my professionally prepared vegetarian food find their own efforts disappointing. Judging from the questions asked by my customers, students and readers, the most common problem is menu-planning: without the traditional meat dish as a centerpiece, how do you design a complete and satisfying meal?

This book will provide some answers in menus with recipes for a wide range of occasions—from family outings to elegant dinner parties. In addition to providing nutrient complementation, they present appealing combinations of color and texture, and are designed to make the most efficient use of preparation time. The menu format will also spare you the frustration of deciding what dish to serve with what.

The menus are arranged by season, because any produce is naturally at its best at the height of its local growing period. You can follow them in sequence (especially in summer), but since these days almost every food seems to be "in season" all year round, you need not follow the seasonal recommendations too literally. And don't feel you have to save a recipe you like for the appropriate occasion—the Korean bindatuk pancakes suggested for a New Year's Eve party, for instance, also make a great mid-afternoon snack.

One of the most important questions people ask about a vegetarian diet is whether it will provide adequate nutrition. If you are now on a highly restricted diet, eat mainly processed foods with large amounts of refined sugars and fats, or have a serious metabolic problem, you should consult a reliable nutritionist or dietitian before attempting any change. But if you are basically healthy and eat a wide variety of unprocessed natural foods, you can count on getting all the nutrients you need from a vegetarian diet.

Most North Americans have been taught to be concerned about getting enough protein, even though such deficiencies are almost non-existent in this part of the world. As a result most of us, vegetarians included, take in entirely too much—excess protein is only converted into carbohydrates and any excess of these are then converted into fat and stored. How much protein do you need? The World Health Organization recommends about 35 grams per day, while the Canadian and American governments recommend about 45 grams. This is not very much—you will easily consume 45 grams of protein if you start the day with oatmeal porridge, milk and toast; have a sprout melt and a piece of fruit for lunch; a bran muffin for a snack; and for dinner a Caesar salad, some zucchini patties with sesame sauce, two steamed vegetables, and a slice of ginger loaf.

Everything we eat (except for refined sugars, starches and oils) contains a wide assortment of the amino acids that make up protein. Foods such as eggs, dairy products, soy beans and potatoes contain these in nearly the same proportions as our bodies use them. Grains and beans are also good sources of protein, but are slightly deficient in certain essential amino acids. Conveniently, the amino acids lacking in grains are abundant in beans, and vice versa. That is why nutritionists tell us to "complement proteins"—eat foods from both groups together in the same meal—in order to utilize all the amino acids.

Of more pressing concern for those following a vegetarian diet, particularly women and children, is iron deficiency. It's a good idea to monitor your levels with an annual blood test. Sea vegetables, dried fruit, dried beans, millet, sesame and sunflower seeds, leafy greens, peanut butter and potatoes are all good sources of iron. Eating these foods in combination with a source of vitamin C or E seems to improve iron absorption. (Using an old-fashioned cast-iron frying pan will also increase your intake of iron.)

Vegans (those who avoid all animal products, including eggs and dairy products) have additional dietary concerns. Since milk and cheese are the best sources of calcium, for instance, vegans should make a special effort to consume plenty of other foods that contain this important mineral: sesame seeds (tahini), sea vegetables and leafy greens (particularly those in the cabbage family). Vitamin B_{12}, primarily available from animal sources, is another food factor that vegans should pay attention to. The most reliable non-animal source is B_{12} fortified yeast, although tempeh, miso, sea vegetables, comfrey leaves and chickpea sprouts consumed in sufficient quantities may provide an adequate amount. Again, an annual blood test is the best safeguard against a deficiency.

Aside from these few specifics, the general dietary guidelines for vegetarians are the same as for anyone else. That is, make generous use of whole grains, dried beans, leafy greens, and fresh fruits and vegetables, and minimize your intake of oils and fats, concentrated sweeteners and synthetic ingredients. That way you can be sure of getting the maximum nutritional benefits from the food you eat.

By and large, North Americans enjoy a plentiful year-round supply of foods that are large in size and relatively cheap. Unfortunately this emphasis on quantity has often meant a loss in quality. And we have forfeited many pleasures: the excitement of the new asparagus crop, the opportunity to recognize the special character of countless apple varieties, the chance to appreciate the subtle nuances of an unpasteurized cheese. But real foods are still available if you shop carefully. "Organically" and locally grown fruits and vegetables are often of higher quality than others, since the seeds they come from are usually developed more for taste than ease of harvesting and length of shelf life, and the soils they grow in are less likely to have been depleted of the micro-nutrients required for rich flavor. Though such vegetables may cost more, you will probably be amply satisfied serving them simply steamed, without expensive and time-consuming sauces or condiments. But make sure they are fresh: tired "organic" foods can be just as unsatisfactory as tired "conventional" ones.

You should also make an effort to use ingredients that have been processed as little as possible. Even minimal processing—canning, drying, or freezing— results in considerable loss of flavor. In this book I have tried to avoid refined ingredients and limit the processing of foods to whatever can be done with ordinary home equipment—the fruit ice cream is made without artificial emulsifiers, the chocolate cheesecake contains only unprocessed, unsweet- ened chocolate, and the Romanian marzipan is crystallized with nothing more than unpasteurized honey.

One of the most common refined foods is cooking oil. If your corn oil doesn't smell like corn-on-the-cob, or your peanut oil like freshly roasted nuts, chances are they are refined. Try exploring the rich flavor possibilities avail- able from unrefined ("cold-pressed") oils—they will make all your meatless foods taste more exciting. Olive oil is the most readily available, but most natural food stores carry many other kinds. They may cost more than the refined versions, but you will probably use less, and you're bound to enjoy the foods cooked with them a great deal more. Experiment with almond oil in a Moroccan b'stilla, walnut oil in a Belgian endive salad, and palm oil in an African egasi stew.

Recipes are not sacred. Feel free to substitute cayenne for black or white pepper, tamari for soy sauce, or another starch for arrowroot. I prefer the mildly bitter flavor of sea salt, but the ordinary kind will do. Unsalted or sweet butter is more versatile and usually fresher than salted, but—except in pastries—you can sub- stitute oil. You could also use margarine in place of butter, though I don't because it is so highly refined. Soy milk can be substituted for animal milk in all recipes except those for cheese. But don't substitute Blackstrap molasses for the sweeter and milder light or Barbados molasses specified in the recipes. For those who choose to avoid wine, beer, liquor and chocolate (which can all be quite natural foods), I have tried to provide alternatives. However, I do suggest you use "organic" oranges and lemons—without dyes or fungicides—for zest (the aro- matic colored part of the skin), and unwaxed fruits and vegetables when you want to eat the skins. Finally, some of the recipes suggest a number of options for ingredients to include. Just remember that even if all the choices sound appealing, you should limit yourself to the recommended number; otherwise you could wind up with a disappointing hodgepodge.

For the sake of brevity, I have not always specified which recipe(s) in a menu should be prepared first. A quick glance at the timings should give you a good idea of where to begin. For main dishes that can be ready to serve within 30 minutes, start to finish, see the "Quick" section in the index; for dishes that can be mostly prepared some time in advance, then quickly completed at a moment's notice, see "Make-Ahead." You will save both time and money if you plan your meals in advance, a week at a time. Planning will not only permit you to shop more efficiently, but make it easier for you to prepare parts of tomorrow's meal while you are working on today's; you won't discard so much unused food, or have to rush so often to the costly convenience store to pick up missing ingredients. You will also find it easier to maintain a nutritionally balanced diet over the longer period, especially if you have some meals nearly ready to serve—you won't be forced to rely on the less nutritious and less satisfying "instant" kinds of food nearly so often. You may even find you have time to experiment with some exciting new recipes.

A Note on Using the Recipes

I have triple tested all the baking recipes at different times of the year and in different parts of the country. The recipes are balanced for the types of flours normally available in natural food stores. If you use the types found in supermarkets, you may have to increase the liquid measures slightly. For more consistent results in the more sensitive recipes, measure flour by weight. But when this is not practical, sift the flour (if specified) prior to measuring by volume. To prevent charring butter while frying, I recommend using clarified butter (see p. 60). If none is on hand, use oil or ½ butter and ½ oil. For convenience in measuring, the metric quantites specified in this book are not exact equivalents of the avoirdupois ones. Be sure to use one system or the other consistently throughout each recipe.

I'd Like to Hear from You

If you should have any difficulty finding ingredients or equipment recommended in the recipes, or encounter confusion or problems while preparing any of the recipes, please let me know. I will be happy to send you special suggestions or help. If you have any suggestions for future editions, I would love to hear. If you would like to learn how to obtain The Vegetarian Chef apron or audio cassettes of myself providing detailed instructions for preparing selected menus PLEASE WRITE The Vegetarian Chef, Woodbridge Press, P.O. Box 6189, Santa Barbara, CA 93160.

The Menus

End of Winter Blues

When winter seems to be going on too long, it sometimes helps to reminisce about warmer places. One of my best memories is of a barge-trip through the middle of Bolivia, from the headwaters of the Rio Grande to the town of Trinidad. The day before we were to arrive, we followed a narrow tributary to an old banana plantation, where I took the opportunity to taste many types of bananas—creamy and seedy, sweet and tart, aromatic and spicy, tender and chewy, large and small. In North America almost the only variety we ever see is the Cavendish. This is a fine banana—but if you ever see any others, be sure to try them.

Banana Ice Cream

about 1 quart (1 L)
10 minutes preparation
8 hours freezing

2 lb (6 medium) very ripe
  bananas (1 kg)
2 tbsp honey (25 mL)
1 tsp lemon OR lime juice
  (5 mL)
pinch salt
½ cup finely chopped nuts
  (optional) (125 mL)

OPTIONAL FLAVORINGS:
⅓ cup roasted carob powder
  (75 mL)
1 tsp freshly grated ginger
  (5 mL)
1 tsp ground anise (5 mL)

Is a sugar-free, fat-free, additive-free "ice cream" just what the doctor ordered? Frozen banana purée is the answer. You can use a blender, but a food processor makes a fluffier cream by incorporating more air.

Peel, slice and freeze bananas. When solid, blend in a food processor with the honey, lemon juice and salt. The flavor is fine as is, but you might like to stir in one of the optional flavorings. Fold in nuts and serve right away, as soft ice cream, or pack into containers and freeze until hard (about 8 hours).

Deep-Dish Spinach Pie

8 servings
25 minutes preparation
35 minutes baking

This pie has a crisp crust on the top rather than a soggy one on the bottom. For the best flavor use thick-leaved, bunched spinach.

To prepare filling, clean and chop the spinach (you can include tender stems and pink roots). Put onion, 2 tbsp (25 mL) water, stems and roots, and finally leaves in a large pot. Cover and cook on medium-high heat until wilted. Toss and drain well.

To prepare white sauce, melt butter on low heat in a saucepan. Blend in flour and cook, stirring, on low until it feels gritty (about 3 minutes). Raise heat to medium and whisk in milk. Whisk frequently until mixture thickens. Then stir in garlic, salt, nutmeg and pepper. Simmer gently 5 or more minutes and remove from heat.

Preheat oven to 350°F (180°C). In a buttered 3-quart (3-L) casserole, put layers of ⅓ spinach, ⅓ white sauce, ½ cheese, ½ bread crumbs and ½ egg slices. Repeat and finish with spinach and white sauce.

To prepare biscuit topping, sift together flour, baking powder, baking soda and salt. Cut in butter until pieces are the size of split peas. Toss in sesame seeds. Whisk together buttermilk, honey and egg. Fluff the flour-butter mixture as you slowly splash in the milk-egg mixture. Stir gently until mixed. Drop spoonfuls of batter on spinach pie.

Bake on middle shelf until biscuits brown and sauce is bubbling (about 35 minutes). Let cool slightly before serving.

FILLING:
2 lb (3 bunches) spinach (1 kg)
1 cup thinly sliced onion (250 mL)
1 cup diced Swiss cheese (250 mL)
1 cup fresh bread crumbs (250 mL)
4 hard-cooked eggs, sliced

WHITE SAUCE:
4 tbsp butter (60 mL)
4 tbsp flour (preferably soft white) (60 mL)
2 cups milk OR cereal cream (500 mL)
1 clove garlic, minced
¼ tsp salt (1 mL)
⅛ tsp freshly grated nutmeg (0.5 mL)
⅛ tsp ground white peppercorns (0.5 mL)

BISCUIT TOPPING:
2¼ cups sifted soft whole-wheat flour (550 mL)
2 tsp baking powder (10 mL)
1 tsp baking soda (5 mL)
¼ tsp salt (none if butter is salted) (1 mL)
⅓ cup butter, room temperature (75 mL)
1 tbsp roasted sesame seeds (optional) (15 mL)
1½ cups buttermilk OR milk with 3 tsp (15 mL) lemon juice or vinegar (375 mL)
¼ cup honey (50 mL)
1 lightly beaten egg

Maple Syrup

By the middle of March, the maple sap should be flowing. Celebrate with a jug of new syrup. I suggest buying the less expensive dark kind—it has a stronger maple taste.

Maple syrup can be enjoyed in more than just sweets. It's great over porridge, and a small amount in salad dressings and breads adds character. In fact, it makes an appearance in every course of the meal that follows: Quebec-style baked beans, glazed carrots and macaroons.

Fêves aux Pommes

6 cups cooked white (navy or kidney) beans (see p. 108) (1500 mL)
2 cups bean cooking liquid plus water (500 mL)
1 cup diced onion (250 mL)
¼ cup butter (50 mL)
½ cup maple syrup (125 mL)
4 cloves garlic, minced
1 tsp prepared mustard (5 mL)
½ tsp salt (2 mL)
3 cooking apples (Spy or Granny Smith), cored and cut in ½″ (1-cm) slices

8 servings
15 minutes preparation
4 hours baking

Preheat oven to 300°F (150°C). Slowly fry onion in butter until lightly browned. Stir fried onion, maple syrup, garlic, mustard and salt into cooked beans. Pour into a 3-quart (3-L) casserole and garnish with apple slices.

Bake uncovered until liquid turns thick and creamy (about 4 hours). Serve with freshly baked bread and a simple salad. Leftovers reheat well.

Glazed Carrots

4 servings
10 minutes preparation
20 minutes cooking

2 cups carrots, cut in finger-sized pieces (500 mL)
1 tbsp maple syrup (15 mL)
1 tbsp butter (15 mL)
salt and pepper to taste
1 tbsp freshly chopped parsley (15 mL)

Gently steam carrots with ¼ cup (50 mL) water in a heavy-bottomed pan. When softened (about 20 minutes), remove lid and turn up heat to high. Add syrup and butter. Toss until all water has evaporated and a shiny glaze has formed. Toss in salt, pepper and parsley. Serve promptly.

Macaroons

48 small cookies
10 minutes preparation
30 minutes baking

Most natural sweeteners are hydroscopic—they absorb moisture and become sticky—but maple products, being about 98% sucrose (table sugar), do not. For this reason maple syrup can be used in crisp cookies like macaroons.

Heat syrup in a small saucepan until it reaches 255°F (125°C) (don't let it foam over). Meanwhile whisk egg whites and lemon juice in a clean bowl until soft peaks form. Then beat as you slowly pour in the very hot syrup. Continue beating as mixture cools (about 5 minutes). Fold in ground nuts.

Preheat oven to 300°F (150°C). Cover a cookie sheet with parchment or buttered bond paper (waxed paper isn't sturdy enough). Drop on small spoonfuls of batter (or pipe on with a piping bag). Smooth with a moistened finger.

"Dry" in oven until lightly browned (about 30 minutes). Place cookies—still on paper—on a cake rack. When cool, turn paper over and moisten the bottom. In a few minutes the moisture will soak through and loosen the macaroons.

For crunchier cookies, put back on cake rack in a 150°F (65°C) oven with the door held ajar. Remove after 1 hour and store in a tightly sealed container.

½ cup maple syrup (125 mL)
3 egg whites
5 drops lemon juice
2 cups ground almonds, hazelnuts, OR coconut (500 mL)

Fire Pot

In many parts of the Far East, central heating is virtually unheard of. To keep warm through long winter evenings, families and friends gather in the middle of the room around a table, in the center of which is a pot with a chimney sitting over a charcoal fire. This "fire pot" serves the double purpose of keeping them warm and cooking their dinner.

In North America you can use an ordinary fondue or chafing dish, as long as you have one that uses electricity or alcohol—Sterno isn't hot enough. But for a more authentic atmosphere, consider buying a real fire pot (available, along with some of the more exotic ingredients, in Chinese or Japanese food stores).

Fire Pot

6 servings
40 minutes preparation
2¼ hours heating and cooling broth

In China, the dipping ingredients may be laid out on the table to form a design (perhaps the shape of a phoenix or dragon), interspersed with small bowls containing various dips.

BROTH:
3 cups soy bean OR mung
  bean sprouts (750 mL)
3 large pieces kelp (kombu)
½ cup dried black (shiitake)
  mushrooms (125 mL)
½ cup dried chestnuts
  (125 mL)
1 cup chopped green onions,
  mostly white parts (250 mL)
3 pieces orange zest, 1"
  (2.5-cm) squares
3 tbsp soy sauce (50 mL)
1" (2.5 cm) fresh ginger,
  peeled and thinly sliced
2 cloves garlic, crushed
3 pieces star anise OR
  1 tbsp fennel seeds
  (15 mL)
1 dried hot chili

BROTH FLAVORINGS:
2 tbsp rice vinegar (25 mL)
2 tbsp bean paste (miso)
  (25 mL)
2 tsp dark sesame oil
  (10 mL)
3 oz bean-thread noodles
  (100 g)

For the broth, put all ingredients in a large pot. Cover with 2 quarts (2 L) cold water. Heat slowly (it should take 1 hour to reach a simmer) and let simmer 15 minutes. Remove from heat. When liquid has cooled (about 1 hour), strain out flavorings. Broth is ready to use.

Make the mustard, sesame and bean-paste dips as directed below. In addition, prepare the following:

ASSORTED CONDIMENTS: soy sauce; hoisin sauce; Chinkiang (or Balsamic) vinegar; hot chili paste; roasted sesame seeds; roasted and crushed Szechuan peppercorns; chopped fresh coriander leaves; grated white radish.

ASSORTED DIPPING INGREDIENTS (10 cups/2.5 L): trimmed green onions; pickling cucumber slices; blanched carrot ovals; peeled water chestnuts; snow peas, stems removed; lettuce or spinach leaves; watercress sprigs; blanched broccoli flowerets; mushrooms; mung bean sprouts; hard-cooked quail eggs; Chinese red dates, plumped for 1 hour in hot water; pressed and diced tofu.

Just before serving, add broth flavorings (vinegar, bean paste and sesame oil) to the broth and bring to a simmer. Soak bean-thread noodles in cold water to cover. Arrange dips and condiments on table in small bowls. Place dipping ingredients either in mounds directly on the table or on serving platters.

Seat guests around the table, making sure all will be able to reach the pot. Bring the simmering broth to the table. To eat pick up an ingredient with chopsticks and immerse it in the bubbling broth. When heated through, dip the piece in 1 or 2 dips and eat.

Near the end of the meal, drain the soaked noodles and slip them into the broth. When heated through, serve with the remaining broth in bowls as a soup. Finish the meal with oranges (see p. 13 for an attractive presentation).

Mustard Dip

¼ cup (50 mL)
5 minutes preparation

Mix mustard and sherry to form a thick paste. Stir in vinegar, soy sauce and honey. Whisk in oil, a little at a time. Let rest for 1 hour to mellow the flavor. Dip will keep up to a week in refrigerator.

1½ tbsp mustard powder (25 mL)
1 tbsp dry sherry (15 mL)
½ tsp cider vinegar (2 mL)
¼ tsp soy sauce (1 mL)
⅛ tsp honey (0.5 mL)
1 tbsp vegetable oil (15 mL)

Sesame Dip

¼ cup (50 mL)
5 minutes preparation

Mix tahini with hot water. Then stir in oil, honey, pepper, vinegar and salt. Dip is ready to use.

2 tbsp tahini (see p. 66) (25 mL)
1 tbsp hot water (15 mL)
2 tsp dark sesame oil (10 mL)
¼ tsp honey (1 mL)
¼ tsp roasted and crushed Szechuan peppercorns (optional) (1 mL)
½ tsp vinegar (2 mL)
pinch salt

Bean-Paste Dip

¼ cup (50 mL)
5 minutes preparation

Add a little extra water, and this dip becomes a delicious sauce for rice.

Stir all ingredients together. Dip is ready to use.

2 tbsp bean paste (miso) (25 mL)
2 tbsp dry sherry (25 mL)
½ tsp grated ginger (2 mL)
⅛ tsp orange zest (0.5 mL)

North Africa

Chakchouka—a stew of fresh tomatoes, eggplant, zucchini and sweet peppers with eggs poached right in with the vegetables—is often available in the bustling markets of North Africa. For each customer, the attendant will break an egg into her steamy cauldron; a few minutes later, she will pull out a poached egg along with a portion of stew. (At home, it's easier to poach the eggs in a casserole in the oven. Serve over rice colored and flavored with saffron.) For dessert, another stall in the market provides a sweet pastry—the ever-popular baklava.

2 cups coarsely chopped
  tomatoes (500 mL)
6-oz can tomato paste
1 bay leaf
6 tbsp olive oil (100 mL)
1 cup diced onion (250 mL)
2 cups ½" (1-cm) cubes
  unpeeled eggplant (500 mL)
2 cups diced zucchini (500 mL)
2 cups diced sweet peppers
  (500 mL)
1–2 hot chilies, minced (wash
  hands afterwards)
2 tbsp ground cumin seeds
  (25 mL)
3 cloves garlic, minced
¼ cup chopped fresh
  coriander OR parsley (50 mL)
2 tbsp fresh basil (25 mL) OR
  2 tsp dried (10 mL)
1 tbsp ground cinnamon
  (15 mL)
8 large fresh eggs

Chakchouka

8 servings
15 minutes preparation
15 minutes cooking

If your eggplant and zucchini are not perfectly fresh they may taste bitter—try a piece of each to check. To draw out any bitterness, sprinkle 2 tbsp (25 mL) salt on the diced pieces and let sit about 30 minutes. Rinse and proceed with the recipe.

In a large shallow pot, bring tomatoes, tomato paste and bay leaf to a gentle simmer. Meanwhile heat oil on medium heat in a heavy frying pan. Add, one at a time, the onion, eggplant, zucchini, sweet peppers, hot chilies and cumin. Cover and let stew 5 minutes.

When tomatoes are hot, stir in fried ingredients, garlic, coriander, basil and cinnamon. Simmer 5 minutes. Stew is now ready for poaching the eggs.

In either the same pot or a shallow casserole, make room for the eggs by pushing aside spoonfuls of the stew. Break the eggs directly into the spaces. Either simmer gently on top of stove at low heat, or bake in a preheated 350°F (180°C) oven until eggs are lightly poached (about 10 minutes). Serve immediately.

Saffron Rice

4 servings
5 minutes preparation
45 minutes cooking

Real saffron may seem expensive, but a little goes an amazingly long way. Leave the stamens whole, so the red flecks show.

While water is coming to a boil, pick over rice and discard any grains with the outer hull still intact. Rinse rice with water to remove any dust.

When water boils, add rice, salt and saffron. When it returns to a rolling boil, reduce heat to low and cover tightly.

Do NOT remove lid or stir for 45 minutes (it won't stick). Remove from heat and let rest until you are ready to serve.

2 cups water, boiling (500 mL)
1 cup long-grain brown rice
  (250 mL)
½ tsp salt (2 mL)
⅛ tsp saffron (0.5 mL)

Baklava

16 baskets
30 minutes preparation
30 minutes baking

This sweet, nutty pastry is less messy to serve and eat when folded into baskets rather than cut in the more common flat diamond shapes. The trick to keeping the pastry crisp, even when swimming in honey syrup, is to have the syrup cold when you pour it over the hot baklava. Do not use a glass baking dish—it may shatter as you pour in the cold syrup.

Preheat oven to 350°F (180°C). Combine chopped nuts and cinnamon. Stir together honey, lemon juice, rose water, zest and cardamom.

Place one sheet of pastry on a flat surface. Generously brush on melted butter and sprinkle on a dusting of ground nuts. Cover with another layer of pastry, butter and ground nuts. Continue with remaining sheets. Cut into 3″ (7.5-cm) squares.

Working quickly so they don't dry out, fold up the corners of each square to form square baskets. Place in an unbuttered 9″ (22.5-cm) square cake pan (to help hold them in shape). Fill baskets with chopped nut mixture. Bake until lightly browned (about 45 minutes).

Remove pan from the oven and let cool just a few minutes. Pour some of the honey syrup into each hot basket. Serve when baskets have cooled to room temperature. Leftovers will keep for several days.

2 cups chopped walnuts,
  hazelnuts, almonds OR
  pistachios (500 mL)
1 tsp ground cinnamon (5 mL)
⅔ cup honey (150 mL)
1 tbsp lemon juice (15 mL)
½ tsp rose OR orange blossom
  water (2 mL)
¼ tsp orange OR lemon zest
  (1 mL)
⅛ tsp freshly ground
  cardamom (0.5 mL)
½ lb phyllo (strudel) pastry
  (250 g)
⅓ lb melted butter (150 g)
2 tbsp ground nuts (25 mL)

North India

Generally dishes from northern India are mildly flavored and substantial, while those from the south tend to be simple and fiery (see p. 70). The essence of all Indian foods is not, as some suppose, their hotness (which comes only from chili peppers, peppercorns and ginger), but the aromatic flavoring that comes from the spice blend known as masala.

The following menu of bean dahl, vegetable curry and chapati bread is typical of north India. Serve it with apple chutney (see p. 91) and a yogurt raita (see p. 71).

Dahl

4 servings
10 minutes preparation
1 hour cooking

1 cup split beans: red lentils, yellow split peas, mung beans (250 mL)
½ recipe Fried Masala
1 tbsp lemon OR lime juice (15 mL)
½ tsp salt (2 mL)

Simmer beans in 4 cups (1 L) water until very soft (about 1 hour). (You can shorten the time by giving the partially cooked beans a spin in the blender.)

When fully softened stir in fried masala, lemon juice and salt. Simmer gently another 15 minutes to amalgamate flavors.

Fried Masala

1 cup (250 mL)
5 minutes preparation
15 minutes frying

2 tsp cumin seeds (10 mL)
2 tsp coriander seeds (10 mL)
2 tsp mustard seeds (10 mL)
2 tsp fennel OR anise seeds (10 mL)
2 tsp fenugreek seeds (10 mL)
2 tsp ground turmeric (10 mL)
1 tsp black peppercorns (5 mL) OR 1 hot chili
¼ tsp cardamom seeds (removed from pods) (1 mL)
4 tbsp clarified butter (ghee) OR ½ unsalted butter and ½ oil (60 mL)
1 cup finely diced onion (250 mL)

In India it's common practice to grind spices freshly for each dish. That way the flavors are never stale, and the cook can create the combination that best suits the specific ingredients.

Put cumin, coriander, mustard, fennel and fenugreek seeds in a small dry frying pan. Toast on medium heat until they begin popping. Transfer to a grinder (a spice grinder, mortar and pestle or coffee mill). Add turmeric, pepper or chili and cardamom. Grind to a powder (substitute it for "curry powder" in Western recipes).

In a small frying pan melt butter, then add onion and masala powder. Fry slowly until onions are very soft and spices aromatic (about 15 minutes)

Vegetable Curry ✴

4 servings
15 minutes preparation
15 minutes cooking

As with any stew, reheating improves the flavor.

Fry vegetables in butter and fried masala. When heated through (about 5 minutes), add liquid and salt. Simmer until vegetables are softened. Serve right away or cool and reheat.

4 cups of 1 or more vegetables:
potato slices, cauliflower
flowerets, eggplant chunks,
green bean pieces, peas, sweet
pepper squares (1 L)
2 tbsp clarified butter OR
oil (25 mL)
½ recipe Fried Masala
1½ cups liquid: tomato juice,
coconut milk (see p. 15), thin
yogurt OR Dahl thinned with
water (375 mL)
¼ tsp salt (1 mL)

ₓChapatis

8 flat breads
15 minutes preparation
45 minutes resting

Mix and knead all ingredients to a moist dough that doesn't stick to your hands (you may have to add more flour). Continue kneading until dough feels elastic (about 5 minutes).

Let dough rest for ½ hour, then form into 2″ (5-cm) balls. Roll balls into 10″ (25-cm) disks. Let rest 10 minutes before cooking.

Preheat dry frying pan. Toss a disk in and "dry" the surface (about 5 seconds each side). The next step depends on your equipment. In India the dried bread is tossed directly onto the coals of the fire. With a gas stove, turn up the flame and set each disk on the pot support. Using tongs, move and turn it frequently until it puffs and the outside is browned. For an electric burner, set a cake rack over the red-hot element to keep the bread ½″ (1 cm) above it.

Serve right away.

3¼ cups unsifted finely ground
hard whole-wheat flour
(800 mL)
1 cup water (250 mL)
1 tbsp butter, softened (15 mL)
¼ tsp salt (1 mL)

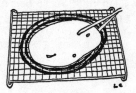

Thailand

Thailand has been strongly influenced by neighboring China and India in many areas, including food. The originality of Thai cuisine lies in its stunning presentation. Here, for example, fried rice flavored with an aromatic curry paste is garnished with golden egg-yolk beads. The cucumbers in the salad may be trimmed in a variety of attractive shapes. Finally, a few simple cuts make plain oranges both visually appealing and easier to eat.

Thai Curry Paste

¼ cup chopped peeled shallots
  OR green onions (50 mL)
3 cloves garlic, peeled
½" (1 cm) fresh ginger, peeled
  and sliced
1–2 hot chilies
2 tbsp chopped fresh coriander
  leaves (25 mL)
2 tbsp sliced lemon grass
  (white inner part) (25 mL) OR
  1 tsp lemon zest (5 mL)
2 tbsp chopped mint (25 mL)
1 tsp honey (5 mL)
¼ cup peanut oil (50 mL)

⅓ cup (75 mL)
10 minutes preparation

Easy to make with a blender or food processor—as long as you don't reduce the quantities. Lemon grass and fresh coriander (available from fancy greengrocers and Chinese food shops) give an authentic Thai flavor, but the dish is still good without them.

Combine all ingredients in a blender or food processor and blend to a paste.

Spiced Cucumbers

4 servings
5 minutes preparation
15 minutes marinating

2 tbsp Thai Curry Paste
  (25 mL)
1 tbsp lime juice (15 mL)
6 small "dill" cucumbers OR
  1 English cucumber, thinly
  sliced

Cut the cucumber slices into attractive shapes with a small cookie cutter, or scratch the skin with the tines of a fork before slicing.

Combine curry paste with lime juice. Brush mixture on cucumber slices. Let marinate at least 15 minutes.

Thai Fried Rice

4 servings
20 minutes preparation

A combination of Chinese and Indian cooking methods with Thai flavors and garnishing.

For the golden beads, bring about 4" (10 cm) water in a small saucepan to a gentle simmer. Lightly beat egg yolks with water until evenly mixed. Strain into a plastic catsup or syrup container.

When water is hot, drizzle ¼ of the egg mixture in a thin stream into the water. Promptly lift the set eggs onto a plate to cool. Repeat with remaining mixture.

For the fried rice, put about 1 cup (250 mL) water in a small saucepan and bring to a simmer. Pour curry paste into a wok or frying pan and cook on low heat until aromatic (about 10 minutes). Turn heat to high. Add beans, mushrooms, then peppers. Periodically splash in a little of the hot water to produce steam (to help cook vegetables more quickly).

When vegetables are nearly softened (about 5 minutes), stir in rice and salt. Sprinkle in more water (the bursts of steam help to break up the rice).

When rice is heated through (about 3 minutes) the dish is ready to serve. Scoop each portion of fried rice mixture into a small round bowl and invert onto plate. Cover each mound with golden beads and accompany with Spiced Cucumbers.

GOLDEN BEADS:
4 egg yolks
2 tbsp water (25 mL)

RICE:
3 tbsp Thai Curry Paste (50 mL)
1 cup sliced green beans (250 mL)
1 cup whole, cleaned button mushrooms (250 mL)
1 cup slivered red sweet peppers (250 mL)
4 cups day-old cooked short-grain rice (see p. 119) (1 L)
½ tsp salt (unless included in rice) (2 mL)

Orange Flowers

4 servings
10 minutes preparation

If your oranges lack flavor, sprinkle on a little Curaçao or Grand Marnier.

Remove stem and cut the skin of each orange into eight wedges nearly all the way to the bottom. Peel back skin and tuck tips in at the base.

Place on pretty small plates to serve. Eat with your fingers, section by section.

4 navel oranges

Indonesia

Roadside stands provide some of the best food in Indonesia. Two dishes that are nearly always on the menu are soto, a soup, and gado gado, a main-course salad with a special peanut dressing. Although Indonesia is an equatorial country, the vegetables in these recipes—cabbage, green beans, corn and potatoes—may not seem very tropical. The reason is that Indonesia's vegetable-growing regions are high in the cool mountains.

Start this meal by preparing the coconut milk, cooking the potato and eggs, pressing the tofu and frying the tempeh. Meanwhile you can prepare the peanut sauce and vegetables for the soup and salad.

Gado Gado

4 large servings
40 minutes preparation

In Indonesia the vegetables are usually lightly blanched—leave them raw if you prefer.

Boil potatoes with bay leaf in a small amount of lightly salted water. Hard cook eggs. Cut tofu block in half and wrap pieces in a clean towel. Carefully balance two dinner plates on top for 20 minutes to press out excess moisture.

Cut tempeh into ½″ (1-cm) strips. Brush with soy sauce. Fry in ¼″ (5 mm) oil until crispy.

Bring a large pot of water to a boil. Blanch cabbage, beans and onion by immersing each for 10 seconds. Promptly refresh in cold water.

When potatoes are cooked, cool in cold water and cut in narrow strips. Shell and cut eggs in wedges or slices. Cut pressed tofu in strips.

To prepare peanut sauce, combine all ingredients in a blender or food processor. Blend until smooth. Add more liquid or peanut butter as necessary to make a consistency that will flow slowly.

Arrange cooked vegetables, pressed tofu, fried tempeh, slivered cucumber and spinach strips attractively on individual salad plates. (Traditionally, they are placed in a mound with the long slender pieces radiating out towards the edge.)

Cover each salad with peanut sauce, then garnish with the hard-cooked eggs.

SALAD:
3 medium red OR new potatoes
1 bay leaf
4 large eggs
½ lb tofu (250 g)
½ lb tempeh (available in the frozen-food section at natural food stores), thawed (250 g)
2 tbsp soy sauce (25 mL)
vegetable oil for frying
2 cups shredded cabbage (500 mL)
1 cup green beans, stems broken off (250 mL)
1 sweet onion, cut in thin strips
1 small English cucumber, cut in slivers 4″ (10 cm) long
4 cups spinach, stems removed and leaves cut in strips (1 L)

PEANUT SAUCE:
1½ cups shelled peanuts (375 mL) OR 1 cup peanut butter (250 mL)
½ cup Coconut Milk (125 mL)
2 tbsp tamarind concentrate OR lemon or lime juice (25 mL)
1 tbsp Barbados molasses OR brown sugar (15 mL)
1 hot chili, minced (wash hands afterwards) OR ⅛ tsp cayenne (0.5 mL)
1 clove garlic, peeled
1 tbsp soy sauce (15 mL)
1 tsp grated ginger (5 mL)

Coconut Milk

3 cups (750 mL)
5 minutes preparation
15 minutes cooling

Contrary to popular belief, this is not the watery liquid found in the center of a fresh coconut. Rather, it is extracted by squeezing juice from the grated flesh.

Combine ingredients in a blender and run at high speed for 5 minutes. Let rest until cool enough to handle (about 15 minutes).

Meanwhile place a colander over a bowl and line it with cheesecloth or nylon sheer material. Pour the slightly cooled coconut pulp and milk into lined colander.

After most of the liquid has drained off, pick up the cloth and wrap around the pulp. Have the strongest hands in the house squeeze the bundle to extract as much liquid as possible. Discard fibrous pulp. Coconut milk is ready to use.

2 cups unsweetened dried coconut (500 mL)
3½ cups boiling water (900 mL)

Soto

4 servings
10 minutes preparation
5 minutes simmering

Heat oil or butter in a frying pan and add shallots. When they begin to turn clear, add cabbage. When nearly softened, add ginger and garlic.

Meanwhile, bring coconut milk to a simmer. Add, one by one, the corn, bean sprouts, fried ingredients, lemon grass, lime juice and salt. Simmer 5 minutes.

Serve soup immediately, garnished with sliced green onion tops.

2 tbsp coconut oil OR butter (25 mL)
½ cup shallots OR white parts of green onions, cut in thin rings (125 mL)
½ cup shredded cabbage (125 mL)
1 tsp grated ginger (5 mL)
1 clove garlic, minced
2½ cups Coconut Milk (625 mL)
½ cup corn kernels (125 mL)
½ cup mung bean sprouts, stringy tails cut off (125 mL)
1 tbsp chopped lemon grass (white inner part) (15 mL) OR ½ tsp lemon zest (2 mL)
1 tbsp lime OR lemon juice (15 mL)
½ tsp salt (2 mL)

Mexico

Some of the most memorable meals I ever had in southern Mexico were provided by a family with a cart outside the ruins buried in the Yucatan jungle. Often the fare consisted of nothing more than a stack of freshly cooked tortillas, a plate of refried beans and a dab of spicy raw tomato sauce, with a piece of fruit to finish off: an avocado cut in half and sprinkled with a little coarse salt, or a juicy mango.

For the best results, you should start with freshly cooked tortillas. But you can freshen factory-made ones by heating them in a warm oven in a moistened paper bag.

Tortillas

20 flat breads
20 minutes preparation
30 minutes resting

2 cups masa harina (500 mL)
1⅓ cups warm water (325 mL)
¼ tsp salt (optional) (1 mL)

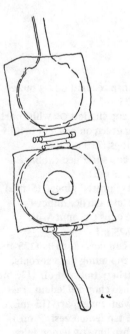

In Mexico, dried corn kernels are soaked in lime (from limestone—not the fruit) to soften the tough skin and add flavor. The swollen kernels are then ground into a dough. For convenience, and nearly as good a flavor, use masa harina ("dough flour"), available at Mexican and natural food stores.

Combine masa harina, water and salt. Knead until thoroughly blended. Add more masa if dough is slippery, or more water if it's crumbly. Let rest 30 minutes.

Preheat an unoiled frying pan on medium-high heat. For easier shaping, put a 1" (2.5-cm) ball of dough between two sheets of plastic and press with a special Mexican tortilla press or a dinner plate. If dough is ragged around the edges, add more water; if it sticks to the plastic, add more flour. Drop each patty directly from plastic into hot pan.

If small bubbles pop up, the pan is too hot. If patties stick, it is too cool. When first side is lightly browned, turn tortilla over and brown other side (about 30 seconds).

Stack tortillas and wrap in a cloth napkin to keep them warm and moist. To eat, roll up and dip into frijoles refritos and salsa cruda. Leftovers can be frozen and used in other Mexican dishes.

Frijoles Refritos ×

4 servings
10 minutes preparation
5 minutes cooking

Affectionately called "nacionales" in Mexico, frijoles refritos find their way into nearly every meal.

Combine beans and their liquid with garlic, mustard, lemon juice, chili and salt. Smash most (but not all) of the beans with a potato masher. Add more bean cooking liquid if mixture is drier than cake batter.

Heat a heavy-bottomed frying pan on medium-high heat. When hot, add butter. Then add bean mixture. Scrape bottom once every minute, turning the browned part into the bean mixture (as for hash browns). Continue frying until mixture is heated through and no longer wet (about 5 minutes), but not excessively dry. Serve right away, garnished with cheese.

2 cups cooked pinto OR black (turtle) beans (see p. 108) (500 mL)
½ cup bean cooking liquid (125 mL)
2 cloves garlic, minced
1 tsp mustard powder (5 mL)
1 tsp lemon OR lime juice (5 mL)
¼ hot chili, minced OR a pinch of cayenne
¼ tsp salt (unless already in beans) (1 mL)
¼ cup clarified butter OR corn oil (50 mL)
4 tbsp grated Parmesan cheese (optional) (60 mL)

Salsa Cruda

¾ cup (175 mL)
5 minutes preparation
30 minutes marinating

Make this "uncooked sauce" as spicy as you want. But make no more than you can use within a day—it begins to ferment quickly. Be sure to start with properly ripened, peeled, seeded and drained tomatoes.

Stir together all ingredients. Do NOT use a blender or food processor, or sauce will lose color and texture. Let rest 30 minutes for flavors to marry.

½ cup finely chopped, peeled, seeded and drained vine-ripened tomatoes (125 mL)
1 tbsp lime OR lemon juice (15 mL)
2 tbsp diced shallot OR sweet onion (25 mL)
1–3 finely minced chilies, preferably red (wash hands afterwards)
1 tbsp chopped fresh coriander leaves (15 mL)
2 tsp vegetable oil (10 mL)
⅛ tsp salt (0.5 mL)

Pizza

Pizza need not be "junk" food, or something just for kids. Homemade pizza may take more time and more work than ordering from a pizza shop, but the results will be memorable—especially when you add a few individual touches. Serve pizza with a tossed salad (see p. 54) and, for dessert, some fresh fruit ice cream (see p. 55).

✗Pizza Dough

3 cups dough (750 mL)
15 minutes preparation
1½ hours rising

1½ cups hot tap water (375 mL)
2 tsp honey (10 mL)
1½ tbsp (1½ packages) dry
  active yeast (20 mL)
4 cups whole-wheat flour (1 L)
½ cup gluten OR unbleached
  white flour (125 mL)
3 tbsp olive oil (50 mL)
¼ tsp finely chopped rosemary
  (optional) (1 mL)
¼ tsp salt (1 mL)

Combine water and honey. When cooled to 100°F (40°C), add yeast. Put 2 cups (500 mL) of the whole-wheat flour in a bowl. When mixture begins to foam, pour into the flour. Stir vigorously until "strings" begin to pull from the sides. If you have time, let dough rest at room temperature for 1 hour; otherwise continue right away.

Add remaining flours, oil, rosemary and salt. Knead for 10 minutes. Dough should be moist, but not sticky; add more water or flour as needed. Put dough in a bowl and cover. Let rise in a warm (90°F/30°C) place. It will have doubled in size and be ready to use in 1 to 1½ hours.

✗ Tomato Sauce

3 tbsp olive oil (50 mL)
½ cup diced onion (125 mL)
¼ cup shredded carrot (50 mL)
3 cups (3 lb) peeled fresh OR
  canned tomatoes
  (750 mL/1.5 kg)
1 bay leaf
¼ tsp salt (1 mL)
· 2 tbsp chopped fresh basil
  leaves (25 mL)
2 tbsp chopped fresh parsley
  (25 mL)
1 tbsp chopped fresh oregano
  OR marjoram (15 mL)
1 tbsp chopped celery leaf
  (15 mL)
3 cloves garlic, minced
¼ tsp ground pepper (1 mL)

1½ cups (375 mL)
15 minutes preparation
35 minutes cooking

If using canned tomatoes, include at least a few fresh ones. Fleshy plum tomatoes give a higher yield and require less cooking than the juicy round kind. And fresh herbs, available at many specialty shops, have a much more satisfying flavor than dried ones (if you must use dried, halve the quantities given).

Heat oil on medium heat in a heavy-bottomed saucepan. Add onions and carrots and fry with occasional stirring. Meanwhile, cut tomatoes in half and remove most of the seeds. When onions turn clear, add tomatoes, bay leaf and salt. Boil gently, uncovered, stirring occasionally

When tomatoes are quite soft and much of the water has evaporated (about 20 minutes), remove from heat. Remove bay leaf. Whisk vigorously to break up remaining flesh. Add the chopped herbs, garlic and pepper. Return to heat and boil gently, uncovered, stirring frequently, until sauce is thick (about 15 more minutes). Cool before spreading over pizza dough.

Pizza ✓

1 14" (35-cm) pizza
15 minutes preparation
25 minutes baking

The brick ovens used in commercial pizzerias give the best results. Use a dark-colored pan in a very hot, steamy oven to approximate the effect.

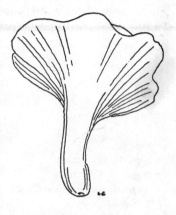

Preheat oven to 450°F (230°C). Place a cake pan containing ½" (1 cm) hot water on the bottom shelf. Spread 1 tsp (5 mL) olive oil on a dark-colored baking sheet and sprinkle with cornmeal.

Roll dough into a circle (or rectangle) and place on prepared sheet. Wipe with 1 tsp (5 mL) oil. If you like a thin crust, use only ⅔ of the dough. (Form the rest into a loaf and let rise while pizza is baking; then bake in a 350°F/180°C oven after pizza is done). If you like a thick crust—dough more than ½" (1 cm) thick— let it rise 20 minutes before proceeding.

Spread dough with tomato sauce nearly to the edges. Sprinkle on the Parmesan. Arrange topping ingredients in an attractive pattern. Vegetables that burn easily (those listed before the tomatoes) will stay moist if you put them under the tomato slices—the others actually taste better slightly charred. Cover with the Mozzarella and sprinkle on remaining olive oil.

Place on middle shelf of the steamy oven. Bake until crust is browned and top bubbly (about 25 minutes). Serve right away, cutting with kitchen scissors—they work well and won't damage your baking sheet.

2 tbsp olive oil (25 mL)
2 tbsp cornmeal (25 mL)
1 recipe risen Pizza Dough
1 recipe thick Tomato Sauce, cooled
¼ cup grated Parmesan OR Romano cheese (optional) (50 mL)
2 cups assorted toppings: sliced mushrooms, broccoli, asparagus, green beans, tomatoes, sweet peppers, hot chilies, onion, eggplant, artichokes, zucchini; bean sprouts, almonds, capers, olives, crumbled Feta, Ricotta or goat cheese, cooked chickpeas, chopped fresh herbs (500 mL)
¼ lb sliced Mozzarella OR Provolone cheese (250 g)

Belgium

This menu highlights some of the trademarks of Belgian cuisine. The appealing bitterness of Belgian endive salad will whet your appetite for a main course of fondue Bruxelloise, accompanied by steamed Brussels sprouts (see p. 122). For dessert, enjoy a rich and crispy waffle with ice cream and fruit.

BASE:
4 eggs, lightly beaten
1 cup milk (250 mL)
½ cup soft whole-wheat flour (125 mL)
⅛ tsp freshly grated nutmeg (0.5 mL)
⅛ tsp ground white pepper (0.5 mL)
2½ cups shredded Swiss cheese (600 mL)

SAUCE:
1 cup finely chopped fresh tomatoes (250 mL)
6-oz can tomato paste
¼ cup freshly grated horseradish (50 mL)
¼ cup cider vinegar OR wine vinegar (50 mL)
½ tsp salt (2 mL)
1 tsp honey (5 mL)
1 clove garlic, minced

COATING:
1 egg, lightly beaten
½ cup bread crumbs (125 mL)
6 tbsp clarified butter OR oil (75 mL)

Fondue Bruxelloise

8 servings
25 minutes preparation
25 minutes baking

This crispy fondue is quite different from the better-known Swiss kind.

Preheat oven to 325°F (160°C). Line a 9″ (22.5-cm) square cake pan with buttered bond paper. For the base, whisk together the eggs, milk, flour, nutmeg and pepper. Stir in cheese and pour into pan. Bake until set (about 25 minutes). Cool. (This base can be kept in the refrigerator for up to 1 week.) Cut into 3″ (7.5-cm) squares, then cut these diagonally in half to form triangles.

For the sauce, stir all ingredients together. Let flavors amalgamate for at least 20 minutes before serving. (Sauce keeps well in refrigerator for up to 2 weeks.)

For the coating, put beaten egg and bread crumbs in separate saucers. Coat the triangles by dipping first in egg, then in crumbs. Heat half the butter in a medium-hot frying pan. Fry half the triangles until coating is crispy and brown. Keep warm in oven while you fry the rest. Serve right away, topped with the spicy tomato-horseradish sauce.

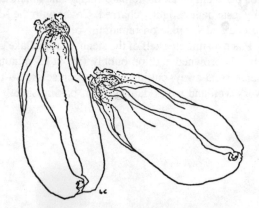

Belgian Endive Salad

4 servings
10 minutes preparation

For maximum flavor and minimum bitterness, choose heads with no green on the leaves.

Cut out the bitter core from each head of endive. Cut each head into ½″ (1-cm) slices. If flavor is too bitter for your taste, soak cut pieces in cool salted water for 15 minutes. Then rinse and drain. Arrange slices on a plate.

Stir capers, green onions and tarragon into mayonnaise. Dab about 2 tbsp (25 mL) of mixture over each serving. Chill and serve.

4 heads Belgian endive
¼ cup capers (50 mL)
¼ cup chopped green onions (50 mL)
2 tsp chopped fresh OR dried tarragon (10 mL)
½ cup mayonnaise (for homemade see p. 38) (125 mL)

Waffles ×

8 waffles
20 minutes preparation
25 minutes cooking

If you don't have a special waffle pan, fry the batter as pancakes.

Whisk together milk, butter, egg yolks and honey. Sift flour, baking powder and salt into this liquid mixture. Stir only until most of the lumps are mixed in. Batter can be used right away, but for lighter and more tender waffles, let it rest at least 2 hours, or up to a day.

Oil and preheat waffle iron. Meanwhile, whisk egg whites until soft peaks form. Fold into batter. Put enough batter in iron to fill it ⅔ full. Close top and cook until steaming stops (about 3 minutes). Lift out waffle. Continue with remaining batter.

Serve waffles, warm or cool, topped with ice cream and crushed fresh or frozen fruit. Leftovers can be frozen and reheated, without thawing, in a toaster.

1½ cups milk (375 mL)
¼ cup melted butter (50 mL)
3 eggs, separated
1 tbsp honey (15 mL)
2 cups sifted soft whole-wheat flour (500 mL)
1 tsp baking powder (5 mL)
pinch salt

Falafels

Fresh parsley is readily available all year round, so there is no need to make do with the papery dried stuff. Parsley comes in three forms. The curly kind looks pretty and is easy to chop. The flat-leaved Italian parsley has more flavor and is most effective in counteracting the negative effects of garlic. Hamburg parsley is grown for its parsnip-shaped root, which is used as a less-sweet parsnip and to flavor soup.

Avoid any bunches that are wilted or yellow, or contain mushy black spots. Wash and drain the parsley as soon as you bring it home, so it won't be wet when you begin to chop it. Store in a plastic bag to keep it moist but not wet.

Parsley is a major ingredient in falafels. A tasty and filling snack, these chickpea patties can also be made into a hearty sandwich in a pita pouch. Keep some on hand for quick light meals.

Falafel Patties ×

about 30 patties
25 minutes preparation

Fresh ingredients provide more flavor than any dried mix could hope for. Bulgar wheat is available in natural food and Middle Eastern shops.

6 cups cooked drained
  chickpeas (garbanzos; see
  p. 108) (1500 mL)
2 cups finely chopped parsley
  (500 mL)
½ cup fine-grade bulgar wheat
  (125 mL)
½ cup hard whole-wheat flour
  (125 mL)
4 cloves garlic, finely minced
1 hot chili pepper, minced
  (wash hands afterwards) OR
  ¼ tsp cayenne (1 mL)
2 tbsp lemon juice (25 mL)
2 tbsp ground cumin seeds
  (25 mL)
½ tsp salt (if not included in
  chickpeas) (2 mL)
½ tsp ground black
  peppercorns (2 mL)

Push cooked chickpeas through an electric shredder attachment or a grinder, or spin briefly in a food processor (they're too thick for a blender). Add remaining ingredients.

Knead mixture until cohesive (about 3 minutes). If dry and crumbly, add some of the chickpea cooking liquid or water; if sticky, add more flour. Let rest for ½ hour. If you're unsure of the proper consistency, form a patty with your hands and fry one—if it falls apart, add more flour to bind.

Form mixture into patties ½" (1 cm) thick. (They can be frozen on a baking sheet and, once solid, packed into plastic bags for up to 6 months.) Mixture will keep in refrigerator for up to 1 week.

Cook patties, fresh or frozen, in 375°F (190°C) deep fat (preferably olive oil); with a little oil in a hot frying pan; or in a 400°F (200°C) oven or toaster oven. Cook until golden brown. Serve as crunchy appetizers or in falafel sandwiches.

Sesame-Yogurt Sauce

2 cups (500 mL)
5 minutes preparation

Combine all ingredients. Spin in a blender or food processor or whisk until smooth. You may wish to thin the consistency with more yogurt or thicken it with more tahini.

Serve right away in a falafel sandwich, over cooked vegetables or pasta, or anywhere you would use a mayonnaise. Keeps well in refrigerator for 1 month.

¾ cup tahini (see p. 66) (175 mL)
1¼ cups plain yogurt (300 mL)
2 cloves garlic, finely minced
¼ tsp salt (1 mL)

Falafel Sandwich

1 sandwich
5 minutes preparation

This is the hamburger of the Middle East.

Slice one edge off the pita, open pocket and insert falafel patties. Fill with cabbage or lettuce, tomato and parsley. Pour in the sesame-yogurt and hot sauces. Serve right away.

1 pita bread
3 cooked falafel patties
½ cup shredded Chinese cabbage (napa) OR romaine lettuce (125 mL)
¼ cup chopped tomato (50 mL)
1 tbsp chopped fresh parsley (15 mL)
¼ cup Sesame-Yogurt Sauce (50 mL)
Hot Sauce to taste

Hot Sauce

1 cup (250 mL)
15 minutes preparation

Roasting over a charcoal fire gives the best flavor. For a green sauce, use green tomatoes and peppers.

Roast peppers and chilies over a charcoal fire or in a preheated 500°F (260°C) oven until charred. Put in a plastic bag for 5 minutes. Remove stems and seeds and pull off skins. Put flesh with tomato, garlic, vinegar, salt and honey through a food mill or blend ingredients briefly in a food processor or blender, leaving some texture.

Fry mixture in oil on medium-high heat until thickened (about 3 minutes). Serve right away. Leftovers keep in refrigerator for at least 1 month.

2 sweet peppers
1–3 hot chilies (wash hands after handling)
½ cup peeled, seeded and chopped tomato (125 mL)
2 cloves garlic, minced
2 tsp wine vinegar (10 mL)
1 tsp salt (5 mL)
½ tsp honey (2 mL)
1 tbsp olive oil (15 mL)

Using a Piping Bag

One of my favorite techniques for making foods look special is piping. An inexpensive plastic-coated bag with a star-shaped nozzle is all you need to get started.

Fill the piping bag with whatever smooth, thick mixture you wish to pipe. Twist the large opening shut and hold it closed as you hold the nozzle end up. Squeeze until all air has been expelled and the mixture begins to exude smoothly. Put the nozzle end down. Use your upper hand to hold the bag closed and squeeze, while your lower hand guides the nozzle.

To draw straight lines hold the nozzle close to the surface. If you raise it slightly, wiggly lines will flow out; a little higher and curlicues will form. Make stars by holding the nozzle in one place as you raise it and release pressure at the same time. Rosettes can be made by lifting and swirling at the same time as the pressure is released.

A simple stew can be a feast fit for guests when the ingredients are chosen for their colors, carefully cut to highlight their shapes, and dramatically encircled with piped duchess potatoes. Serve with crusty bread, a hearty red wine and a light green salad.

Garbure ✗

2 cups stock (see p. 92) OR
  ¼ red wine and ¾ water
  (500 mL)
1 bay leaf
1 cup carrot pieces (250 mL)
1 cup potato pieces (250 mL)
1 cup turnip OR rutabaga
  pieces (250 mL)
1 cup roasted chestnuts
  (see p. 102) (optional)
  (250 mL)
2 cups cooked white (navy)
  beans (see p. 108) (500 mL)
¼ cup butter (50 mL)
1 cup leek (the white part) OR
  onion pieces (250 mL)
2 cups cabbage pieces (500 mL)
1 cup whole or halved
  mushrooms (250 mL)
1 cup sweet pepper (red or
  green) pieces (250 mL)
3 cloves garlic, chopped
1 tbsp lemon juice (15 mL)
1 tbsp thyme (15 mL)
1 tbsp marjoram (15 mL)
½ tsp salt (2 mL)
¼ tsp ground black OR white
  peppercorns (1 mL)

8 servings
30 minutes preparation
1 hour cooling

This stew looks best when the vegetable pieces are the same size. Try to cut each one into bite-sized pieces so it looks like what it is.

In a large pot bring stock and bay leaf to a simmer. Add one by one, in order, carrots, potatoes, turnip, chestnuts and beans.

Meanwhile heat butter on medium heat in a frying pan. Add one by one, in order, leeks, cabbage, mushrooms and peppers. When softened, add to simmering liquid. Stir in remaining seasonings.

Let simmer for 5 minutes, then cover and remove from heat. After 1 hour—or better yet, a day—reheat. This stew is traditionally served over a slice of rye bread in a soup plate. For an attractive alternative, reheat and serve it on ovenproof plates edged with piped duchess potatoes. Keep leftovers in the refrigerator for up to 1 week; they reheat beautifully.

Duchess Potatoes

to decorate 4 dinner plates
15 minutes preparation
15 minutes simmering
6 minutes broiling

This piped version of mashed potatoes is baked to set the eggs and create a light-brown crust.

Simmer potatoes in water to cover with your choice of flavoring. Meanwhile heat milk, butter, salt and pepper.

Preheat broiler. When potatoes have softened (about 15 minutes), dip in cold water just long enough to make peeling painless. Break up and combine peeled potatoes with warmed milk and egg yolks. Mash potatoes until very smooth.

Scoop into piping bag and pipe an attractive pattern around each serving of preheated stew (be sure plates are ovenproof). Put on a rack about 5" (12 cm) under broiler until lightly browned (about 6 minutes). Serve immediately.

1 lb (2 medium) chopped
  starchy (Idaho) baking
  potatoes (500 g)
1 bay leaf, 1 clove garlic OR
  1 stalk celery
½ cup milk OR cream (125 mL)
3 tbsp butter (50 mL)
½ tsp salt (2 mL)
¼ tsp ground white peppercorns (1 mL)
2 egg yolks, lightly beaten

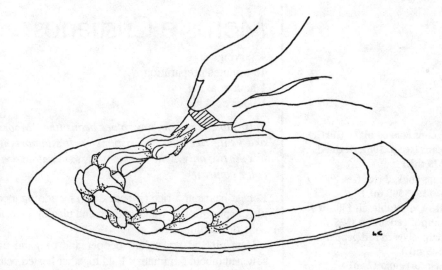

Feeding Baby

It's easy to adapt many family meals to the special requirements of babies. While doing preliminary preparations, simply reserve some of the ingredients before they are combined, spiced and salted. These portions can then be steamed (if additional cooking is needed), puréed for infants, or chopped for toddlers.

Experts tell us the best way to introduce foods to infants is to start with grains, then progress, one at a time, to vegetables and fruits. This procedure allows you to spot allergic reactions and eliminate any offending food promptly from the diet (for the time being).

Avocado Soup

4 cups (1 L)
5 minutes preparation

¾ cup (1 medium) pitted and peeled avocado (175 mL)
3 cups stock (see p. 92) OR ⅔ water and ⅓ white wine (750 mL)
2 tsp lemon juice (10 mL)
¼ tsp salt (1 mL)

This soup needs no cooking. It can be served hot, but should not be cooked more than a few minutes or it will turn bitter. For the richest flavor choose the warty, black-skinned fuerte variety of avocado.

Blend all ingredients. Serve right away, garnished with chopped green onion or crushed tomato pulp.

For infants, simply mash the avocado. For toddlers, cut the flesh into cubes for finger eating.

Moros e Cristianos

4 servings
15 minutes preparation
1 hour soaking
1 hour cooking

1½ cups cooked black (turtle) beans (see p. 108), drained (375 mL)
2 cups cooked rice (see p. 119) (500 mL)
3 tbsp vegetable oil (50 mL)
½ cup diced onion (125 mL)
½ cup slivered red pepper (125 mL)
½ tsp oregano (2 mL)
2 tbsp rum (optional) (25 mL)
4 hard-cooked eggs, sliced

This Cuban dish combines black beans (the "Moors") and white rice (the "Christians"). It's important to mix the two only at the last moment, to maintain a vivid color contrast.

Reheat beans and rice (if necessary) by adding a couple of spoonfuls of water to each and placing in saucepans on medium heat.

Heat oil and fry onion, pepper and oregano until softened (about 5 minutes). Fold together heated beans, rice and fried ingredients. For an authentic flavor, stir in the rum. Garnish with egg slices and serve right away with hot sauce (see p. 23).

For infants, blend some of the cooked rice with a little water to make a gruel. After about 8 months of age, blend a few beans and an egg yolk into the rice. Toddlers will want the rice, beans and egg yolk kept whole and perhaps served separately. After 15 months of age, children will probably want to eat their food just like the "big people".

Vegetable Purée

4 servings
10 minutes preparation

This method highlights the flavor of vegetables, so if you use the best quality, little or no extra flavoring is required.

Steam vegetable until softened. Purée in a blender for the smoothest texture; a food processor or food mill retains some texture. Use a sieve to remove stringy fibers.

Stir in butter, cream, lemon, salt and pepper. If mixture is too thick, add a little water. If too runny, simmer for a few minutes with the lid off.

Can be eaten right away, but flavor is more mellow if first allowed to cool. Reheat to serve. For something more substantial, serve over toast or croutons, and/or top with a poached egg (see p. 169).

The unflavored purée is, of course, a perfect baby food. When your child is learning to wield a spoon, serve the vegetable in chunks rather than puréed.

3 cups coarsely chopped
  trimmed green beans, carrot,
  cauliflower, kohlrabi, leek,
  parsley root, parsnip, peas,
  rutabaga, squash OR sweet
  potato (750 mL)
2 tbsp butter (25 mL)
2 tbsp whipping cream
  (optional) (25 mL)
½ tsp lemon juice (2 mL)
pinch salt
grind white pepper

High Tea

Unlike the regular 4 o'clock tea served with just a few sweets, a late-afternoon high tea includes some savory dishes, making it substantial enough for a light supper. Start with Welsh rarebit and the refreshing pungency of cucumber and cress salad. Then serve the scones accompanied with plenty of butter, jams, jellies, marmalades and, of course, double (Devonshire) cream. Have a large pot of freshly brewed tea available all the while (to keep it hot, use a tea cozy).

Welsh Rarebit

12 servings
15 minutes preparation
5 minutes broiling

The cheese mixture for this open-faced grilled cheese sandwich can be made ahead and used for instant light meals. To prevent curdling or stringiness, be sure to use a fully aged cheese—one that will crumble.

4 cups (¾ lb) shredded
  Cheshire OR fully aged
  Cheddar cheese (1 L/400 g)
2 tbsp butter (25 mL)
1 cup flat beer OR milk
  (250 mL)
1 tbsp arrowroot OR
  cornstarch (15 mL)
1 egg yolk
1 tsp Worcestershire sauce
  (for a version without
  anchovies, see p. 156) (5 mL)
1 tsp mustard powder (5 mL)
12 slices bread OR English
  muffins

Preheat broiler. Put cheese and butter in a heavy-bottomed saucepan on low heat. Stir frequently. Meanwhile whisk together beer, arrowroot, egg yolk, Worcestershire sauce and mustard powder. Toast one side of bread under broiler.

When cheese has melted, slowly stir in the flavored beer mixture. Continue heating, stirring frequently, until mixture begins to plop (it may curdle if cooked too quickly). Can be used right away or stored in refrigerator for up to 2 weeks.

Place bread (toasted side down) on a baking sheet. Spread some cheese mixture over each slice. Put under broiler until cheese is bubbly and lightly browned (about 4 minutes). Lift toasts onto prewarmed serving plates and garnish with olives, walnut halves or apple slices. Serve promptly.

Cucumber and Watercress Salad

8 servings
5 minutes preparation
30 minutes marinating

The bite of watercress complements the cool taste of cucumber.

Cut cucumber in thin, even slices. Arrange attractively on a serving platter. Break off watercress leaves and sprinkle over cucumber.

Sprinkle on salt, vinegar and oil. Let flavors mingle for at least 30 minutes.

1 large English cucumber
1 bunch watercress OR arugula
¼ tsp salt (1 mL)
2 tsp cider vinegar (10 mL)
2 tbsp walnut oil (25 mL)

Scones

1 12" (30-cm) scone OR 12 individual biscuits
15 minutes preparation
25 minutes baking

Richer and sweeter cousins of North American biscuits.

Preheat oven to 375°F (190°C). Sift flour, baking powder, baking soda and salt into a large bowl. Cut butter into flour until mixture looks like rolled oats. Toss in currants.

Whisk together egg, honey and buttermilk. Fluff flour mixture as you slowly splash in liquid mixture. Gently mix only until homogeneous. Place dough on a flat surface dusted with flour. Gently roll out until about ¼" (5 mm) thick. Fold in quarters and coax into a circular shape. Sprinkle on more flour and roll into a disk ½" (1 cm) thick.

Slide disk into an unbuttered pie plate (or, for individual servings, cut circle into triangles and place on a baking sheet). Promptly place in oven. Bake until lightly browned (about 25 minutes, or 15 for individual servings).

2½ cups sifted soft whole-wheat flour (625 mL)
2 tsp baking powder (10 mL)
1 tsp baking soda (5 mL)
⅛ tsp salt (none if butter is salted) (0.5 mL)
⅓ cup butter, room temperature (75 mL)
¼ cup currants (50 mL)
1 egg
¼ cup honey (50 mL)
⅓ cup buttermilk OR sherry OR milk with 1 tsp (5 mL) vinegar (75 mL)

Easter Dinner

April is the time for a celebration of spring. Around the world, eggs and asparagus are symbols of rebirth. Why not make them the centerpiece of an Easter feast?

Surround an asparagus roulade with lightly steamed spinach, baby potatoes and carrots. Follow with a tender leafy green salad, and then finish off with an extra-special chocolate cheesecake, made with fresh Ricotta or cottage cheese.

Asparagus Roulade

8 servings
30 minutes preparation
30 minutes total baking

Unlike most soufflés, this rolled variation can be made several hours before it is to be served.

SOUFFLÉ:
½ cup butter (125 mL)
¼ cup minced shallots OR leeks
  (50 mL)
6 tbsp flour (100 mL)
2 cups milk (500 mL)
1 cup freshly grated
  Parmesan cheese (250 mL)
8 eggs, separated
1 tbsp chopped tarragon, fresh
  OR dried (15 mL)
¼ tsp freshly grated nutmeg
  (1 mL)
¼ tsp ground white
  peppercorns (1 mL)

POTATO SAUCE:
1½ cups diced leeks, white part
  only (375 mL)
1½ cups peeled and chopped
  baking potatoes (375 mL)
1 bay leaf
½ tsp salt (2 mL)
¼ tsp ground white
  peppercorns (1 mL)
½ cup whipping cream
  (125 mL)

Preheat oven to 400°F (200°C). Line a 12" × 15" (25 × 37.5-cm) jelly-roll pan with waxed or bond paper. Butter and dust with flour. Slowly fry shallots in 1 tbsp (15 mL) butter until lightly browned.

On medium heat, melt remaining butter in a saucepan and stir in flour. After about 3 minutes, pour in milk and whisk to break up any lumps. Bring to a simmer with periodic whisking. When thickened, remove from heat and whisk in fried shallots, cheese, egg yolks, tarragon, nutmeg and pepper.

Beat egg whites until firm peaks form. Fold half the whites into the thickened mixture, then fold in the rest. Promptly spread mixture onto prepared sheet. Bake on a lower shelf only until set (about 15 minutes) (overcooking makes it difficult to roll).

Remove from oven and let cool for several minutes. (The mixture will collapse, but remain light.) Invert over a clean dish towel and remove pan and liner. Trim off any crisp edges.

To prepare potato sauce, put leeks, ¼ cup (50 mL) water, potatoes, bay leaf, salt and pepper in a saucepan. Cover and simmer until potatoes have softened (about 15 minutes).

Remove bay leaf. Push mixture through a food mill, then stir in cream. To use a food processor, add the cream first, and be sure to process only with quick bursts (otherwise the results will be gummy). A blender is not suitable.

Prepare asparagus by cutting off tough bottoms (reserve for soup stock). Peel and steam until bright green (about 4 minutes).

Spread potato sauce over the cooked soufflé, leaving a 2" (5-cm) strip along one long side uncovered. Arrange asparagus lengthwise over the sauce. From the long side coated with sauce, roll up the sheet with the aid of the towel. Slide roulade onto a baking sheet. It can now rest for up to 2 hours.

Preheat oven to 350°F (180°C). Reheat roulade until top is golden brown (about 15 minutes). Transfer to a serving platter and garnish with lightly cooked spring vegetables. At the table cut into 1" (2.5-cm) slices on the diagonal and serve with the emerald-studded spiral facing up.

Chocolate Cheesecake

1 10" (25-cm) cake
20 minutes preparation
1 hour baking
2 hours chilling

Preheat oven to 325°F (160°C). Very slowly melt chocolate and butter in a heavy-bottomed saucepan.

Combine Ricotta, honey, eggs, vanilla, cinnamon, orange zest, salt and melted chocolate mixture in a blender or food processor. Blend until light and smooth. Pour into prepared crust. Tap pan to release any air bubbles. Arrange nuts attractively over the top. Bake on a lower shelf until set nearly to the center (about 1 hour).

Turn off oven and leave door ajar. Cake can be served when it reaches room temperature, but its flavor improves after an overnight room-temperature rest.

½ lb asparagus spears (250 g)

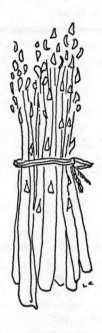

1 10" (25-cm) prebaked crumb OR pastry crust (see p. 146)
4 oz unsweetened chocolate (125 g)
¼ cup butter (50 mL)
2¼ lb (5 cups) fresh Ricotta (see p. 50) OR pressed cottage cheese (1 kg/1250 mL)
1 cup honey (250 mL)
8 eggs
3 tsp vanilla extract (15 mL)
1 tsp ground cinnamon (5 mL)
¼ tsp orange zest (1 mL)
pinch salt
½ cup shelled pistachio nuts (125 mL)

Signs of Spring

One sunny day during a March thaw when my family and I were cooking down some sap from our maple trees, we went out to survey parts of our garden not still covered by snow. The plants were already anticipating spring—rhubarb sprouts had already pushed to the surface, new green leaves were sprouting from the strawberries, and the chives and mint leaves had grown enough for us to have a nibble.

A few weeks later, we enjoyed cream of chives, fresh mint frittata, and rhubarb shortcake sweetened with another sign of spring—maple syrup.

Rhubarb Shortcake

6 servings
20 minutes preparation
30 minutes baking

With a rhubarb topping, you don't have to wait for strawberry season to enjoy shortcake.

SHORTCAKE:
2½ cups sifted soft whole-wheat flour (625 mL)
3 tsp baking powder (15 mL)
1 tsp baking soda (5 mL)
¼ tsp salt (none if butter is salted) (1 mL)
⅓ cup butter, room temperature (75 mL)
⅓ cup liquid honey (75 mL)
2 eggs, lightly beaten
2 tbsp buttermilk OR yogurt (25 mL)

RHUBARB SAUCE:
2 tbsp water (25 mL)
8 cups (2 lb) rhubarb stalks cut in 1" (2.5-cm) pieces (1 kg)
¾ cup maple syrup OR honey (175 mL)
pinch salt

Preheat oven to 375°F (190°C). To prepare shortcake, sift together flour, baking powder, baking soda and salt. Cut butter into flour mixture until chunks are the size of split peas. Whisk together honey, eggs and buttermilk. Fluff butter-flour mixture while you sprinkle in honey-egg mixture. Toss only until evenly mixed. Squeeze together in a ball.

Dust a flat surface with flour. On it gently roll the dough into a rectangle about ¼" (5 mm) thick. Fold into quarters and roll out again. Fold into quarters again, trim the sides and cut into six pieces.

Put cakes about 1" (2.5 cm) apart in a 9" (22.5-cm) square cake pan. Bake until lightly browned (about 30 minutes). Let cool.

To prepare rhubarb sauce, combine all ingredients in a saucepan. Slowly bring to a simmer. When rhubarb pieces begin to break up (about 10 minutes), remove from heat and let slowly cool (uncovered).

When cakes have cooled, split in half and put rhubarb sauce in the middle and over the top. Garnish with whipped cream (see p. 47).

Mint Frittata

4 servings
15 minutes preparation
10 minutes cooking

This Italian omelette should be firm but moist—don't overcook it.

Preheat broiler. Slowly fry onions, mushrooms and pine nuts in oil in a 10″ (25-cm) seasoned frying pan with a non-flammable handle. Meanwhile whisk together eggs, water, cheese, pepper and mint. When onion mixture has softened, stir into egg mixture.

Reheat frying pan and pour in vegetable-egg mixture. Cook slowly until nearly set. Then put pan under broiler until top is browned.

To serve, cut frittata into wedges and accompany with steamed spring greens—spinach, chard or dandelion (see p. 40). Any leftovers are best cold.

2 tbsp olive oil OR butter (25 mL)
¾ cup finely diced onions (175 mL)
½ cup chopped mushrooms (125 mL)
¼ cup pine nuts (optional) (50 mL)
6 eggs
¼ cup water (50 mL)
¼ cup freshly grated Parmesan cheese (50 mL)
⅛ tsp freshly ground white pepper (0.5 mL)
½ cup chopped fresh mint OR parsley with 1 tbsp (15 mL) dried mint (125 mL)

Cream of Chives

8 bowls
15 minutes preparation
30 minutes cooking

Melt butter in a large soup pot and slowly fry parsnip and celery. When softened, add potato, flour and chives. When heated through, add stock, mace and salt. Gently simmer until potatoes have softened (about 15 minutes). Remove mace.

For a velvety smooth soup, spin in a blender. For a coarser texture, spin in a food processor or put through a food mill. Stir in cream and lemon juice.

Can be served right away, but flavor is more mellow if soup is first cooled, then gently reheated. Garnish with a few snips of fresh chives.

3 tbsp butter (50 mL)
½ cup shredded parsnip (125 mL)
½ cup thinly sliced celery (125 mL)
1 cup peeled and chopped baking potato (250 mL)
2 tbsp white flour (25 mL)
3 cups chopped fresh chives (reserve a few for garnishing) (750 mL)
2 cups stock OR ¾ water and ¼ white wine (500 mL)
1 blade mace OR ½ nut nutmeg
½ tsp salt (2 mL)
2 cups cereal cream (500 mL)
1 tsp lemon juice (5 mL)

Mother's Day Breakfast

Treat your mother to breakfast in bed on Mother's Day morning—bran muffins dabbed with fresh homemade butter, a delicate baked egg, and freshly squeezed orange juice. Fresh juice is by far the best, but you can bring the frozen kind to life by giving it a brief spin in a blender or food processor just before serving.

On Saturday evening, soak the bran and raisins and add buttermilk to the cream. On Sunday morning, make the butter, then mix and bake the muffins. While they're baking, get the eggs ready to cook, clean up and set the tray. As soon as the muffins are done, bake the eggs and prepare the orange juice, then carry it all in to Mom.

×Buttermilk Bran Muffins

12 muffins
15 minutes preparation
12 hours soaking (optional)
25 minutes baking

To avoid a coarse texture, soak the bran overnight. If you skip the soaking, reduce the amount of buttermilk to ¾ cup (175 mL).

1 cup wheat bran (250 mL)
1 cup buttermilk (250 mL) OR
   use fresh milk and replace
   4 tsp (20 mL) of it with
   vinegar or lemon juice
½ cup raisins (125 mL)
½ cup honey (125 mL)
⅓ cup melted butter OR
   vegetable oil (75 mL)
¼ cup Barbados molasses
   (50 mL)
2 large eggs
1 tsp vanilla extract (5 mL)
2 cups sifted soft whole-wheat
   flour (500 mL)
1 tsp baking powder (5 mL)
1 tsp baking soda (5 mL)
¼ tsp ground cinnamon (1 mL)
pinch salt

Combine the bran, buttermilk and raisins. Let soak for 12 hours (or while you prepare the other ingredients).

Preheat oven to 400°F (200°C). Butter the bottoms and sides of 12 muffin cups. Whisk honey, butter, molasses, eggs and vanilla until frothy. Sift and measure the flour, then sift it again with baking powder, baking soda, cinnamon and salt into the liquid ingredients.

Add the soaked bran mixture. Gently fold the dry ingredients into the liquid ones. Try to use as little motion as possible—working the batter too much will make tough muffins.

Fill each muffin cup ¾ full with the batter. Clean up any spills. Promptly put the muffins in the oven. Bake until they have a dark crust and a toothpick stuck into the center comes out clean (about 25 minutes).

Remove from oven and let sit in cups for about 5 minutes. Remove and place in a basket lined with a napkin. Serve with homemade sweet butter.

Homemade Sweet Butter

¾ lb (375 g) butter plus 4 cups real buttermilk (1 L)
10 minutes preparation
24 hours culturing (optional)

If you have time for it, stir the optional buttermilk into the cream and let sit at room temperature for up to 36 hours. This step gives a nuttier flavor, but it can be skipped.

Adjust temperature of cream to about 55°F (12°C)—it should feel cold but not frigid—by adding either warm water or ice. Pour half the cream into a blender or a food processor with a plastic blade. Run machine at slowest speed until mixture turns yellow (about 4 minutes).

Pour off buttermilk and chill it for a delicious beverage. Place butter in a bowl to drain. Repeat process with remaining cream.

Press out excess buttermilk from butter with a spatula. When butter is firm and smooth, scoop it into a serving dish. For the freshest flavor, serve promptly.

2 tbsp cultured buttermilk, sour cream OR yogurt (optional) (25 mL)
1 quart whipping cream (available by special order from most milk stores) (1 L)
1 cup warm water OR crushed ice (250 mL)

Baked Eggs

4 servings
5 minutes preparation
15 minutes baking

Cook in custard dishes or ramekins that hold either 1 or 2 eggs each.

Preheat oven to 325°F (160°C). Butter 4 custard dishes. Whisk together the cream, herbs, salt and pepper. Divide mixture among prepared dishes. Carefully break 1 or 2 eggs into each one.

Place dishes in a tray of hot water deep enough to come half-way up the sides. Bake until eggs are set (about 12 minutes for single eggs or 17 minutes for 2) Serve immediately, while still warm and soft

4 tbsp whipping cream (60 mL)
2 tsp chopped fresh tarragon, chives or parsley (10 mL) OR
1 tsp crushed dried tarragon (5 mL)
pinch salt
grind white or black peppercorns
4 OR 8 large eggs

Children's Cooking

Children of all ages will enjoy preparing (and eating) this simple meal of spaghetti, Greek salad, and rich, chewy brownies. So that everything comes out at the right time, start with the brownies, then make the tomato sauce. While you make the salad, bring the water for the noodles to a boil. Then dress the salad while the noodles are cooking. The first time you make this dinner, allow 1½ hours to do everything.

Spaghetti

4 servings
20 minutes preparation
20 minutes cooking tomato sauce
3 to 8 minutes cooking pasta

Whole-wheat pasta frequently becomes gummy or gritty. Experiment to find a brand that remains firm and smooth.

TOMATO SAUCE:
16-oz can tomatoes,
  chopped
½ green pepper
½ medium onion
1 stalk celery
¾ cup mushrooms (175 mL)
1 tbsp butter (15 mL)
2 tbsp olive oil (25 mL)
2 tsp oregano (10 mL)
½ tsp salt (2 mL)
¼ tsp pepper (1 mL)

SPAGHETTI:
3 quarts water (3 L)
1 tbsp salt (15 mL)
1 lb dried spaghetti (500 g)
1 tbsp olive oil (15 mL)
1 cup freshly grated Parmesan
  cheese (250 mL)

To make the sauce, slowly heat tomatoes in a large saucepan. Meanwhile, cut the pepper in half and remove the pith and seeds. Cut the onion lengthwise in half and pull off brown skin. Clean the celery and discard the leaves. Clean the mushrooms. Chop all these vegetables into small pieces.

In a frying pan, melt the butter and oil and fry the chopped vegetables until lightly browned. Stir them into the tomatoes. Then add the oregano, salt and pepper. Let the sauce simmer gently with the lid off while you prepare the rest of the dinner.

For the spaghetti, 10 minutes before serving put water and salt in a large (4-quart/4-L) pot and bring to a rolling boil. Add the spaghetti. Stir frequently so the strands don't stick to the pot or to each other.

After about 3 minutes, test for doneness by biting through a strand to see if there is still a tiny white "nerve" in the center. When this "nerve" is nearly gone (this may take up to 8 minutes), drain the spaghetti through a colander in the sink. Toss in olive oil to keep the sauce from soaking into the pasta.

Rinse a large bowl with hot water, dry it, and put in the drained spaghetti. Toss in the tomato sauce, then sprinkle the Parmesan cheese over the top. Serve right away with extra Parmesan.

Greek Salad

4 servings
10 minutes preparation

Fill the sink with cold water and gently wash the lettuce leaves. Tear them into bite-sized pieces. Put in a lettuce drier and spin, or pat them dry with a towel.

Clean the celery and slice. Remove the seeds and pith from the pepper and dice. Peel any waxed skin from the cucumber and slice. Put these vegetables, the lettuce and Feta cheese in a large salad bowl. Keep in the refrigerator until just before dinner.

The oil, vinegar and salt for the dressing must be added in the right order, or the lettuce will turn soggy. Sprinkle on the oil and toss. Sprinkle on the vinegar and toss again. Sprinkle on the salt and pepper and give it one final toss, bringing any small pieces to the top of the bowl.

1 small head romaine lettuce
1 stalk celery
1 red pepper
½ cucumber
½ cup crumbled Feta cheese
 (125 mL)
4 tbsp olive oil (50 mL)
1½ tbsp wine vinegar (20 mL)
¼ tsp salt (1 mL)
generous grind of black pepper

Brownies

24 squares
20 minutes preparation
25 minutes baking

Preheat oven to 350°F (180°C). Butter a 9″ x 13″ (22.5 x 32.5-cm) cake pan.

Slowly heat the butter and chocolate in the top half of a double boiler, over hot water, only until melted. Meanwhile beat the eggs and salt in a medium-sized bowl with an electric beater until thick and foamy (about 5 minutes). While continuing to beat, slowly add honey and vanilla.

With a wooden spoon, gently stir the warm chocolate into the beaten egg mixture. Before it is fully mixed in, sift in the flour (discard any bran that doesn't go through the sifter). Gently stir in the flour, lifting up the liquid from the bottom. Before the batter is fully mixed, stir in the walnuts.

Scrape batter into the prepared cake pan, spreading it in a smooth layer. Bake right away until it puffs up (about 25 minutes). Cool in the pan for at least 5 minutes. Cut into 2″ (5-cm) squares.

½ cup unsalted butter (125 mL)
4 oz unsweetened chocolate
 (120 g)
4 eggs, at room temperature
¼ tsp salt (1 mL)
1 cup honey (250 mL)
2 tsp vanilla extract (10 mL)
1 cup soft whole-wheat flour
 (250 mL)
½ cup chopped walnuts
 (125 mL)

Spring Brunch

We have a tradition in our family: on the first warm day in May, we have a special brunch in the garden. The centerpiece is always a huge stack of fresh asparagus, with a bowl of homemade mayonnaise on the side. A warm ginger loaf served with homemade sweet butter takes off any morning chill.

Homemade Mayonnaise

1⅓ cups (325 mL)
5 minutes preparation

With a blender or food processor, homemade mayonnaise is virtually foolproof. If you still prefer to use commercial mayonnaise, give it some life by stirring in the juice and grated rind of 1 small lemon.

2 large eggs
1 small lemon, grated zest and
   juice
¼ tsp powdered OR Dijon
   mustard (1 mL)
1 clove garlic (optional)
pinch salt
pinch cayenne
1¼ cups vegetable OR olive oil
   (300 mL)

Put eggs, lemon zest and juice, mustard, garlic, salt and cayenne in food processor or blender. Blend until well mixed (10 seconds).

With machine running at slow speed, slowly pour in oil. By the time you have added 1 cup (250 mL), the mixture will have transformed itself into a creamy sauce. Continue until you have added all the oil. If machine begins to bog down, increase speed; if mayonnaise begins to thin, immediately stop adding oil. Scoop or pour mayonnaise into an attractive serving container.

Steamed Asparagus

4 servings
10 minutes preparation
3 minutes steaming

At the peak of the season, asparagus needs no dressing at all.

2 lb asparagus (1 kg)

Rinse any sand from asparagus and cut off the tough ends (save for soups and stock). If skin seems stringy, peel the lower half of each spear with a vegetable peeler.

Stand spears in a tall narrow pot (a camp coffee pot is ideal), or put some crumpled foil along one side of a large squat pot, lay the asparagus tips on it, and cover the bottoms with water.

Cook on high heat only until asparagus turns a brilliant green (about 3 minutes). Serve hot or quickly immerse in cold water to halt any further cooking.

To serve, stack the asparagus on an attractive platter.

Ginger Loaf

1 loaf
20 minutes preparation
45 minutes baking

For a light texture, avoid over-mixing.

Preheat oven to 350°F (180°C). Butter the bottom of a 9″ × 4″ (22.5 × 10-cm) loaf pan. In a bowl combine honey, butter, lemon juice and zest, ginger, eggs and vanilla. Whisk until foamy (about 3 minutes).

Sift flour with baking soda, nutmeg and salt. Then sift again into liquid ingredients. Add chopped nuts.

Fold everything together gently—a few splotches of flour are acceptable. Quickly scoop mixture into pan and place in oven. Bake until top is golden and a toothpick stuck in the center comes out clean (about 45 minutes). Remove loaf from oven and cool. Tip out of pan, slice and serve with homemade sweet butter (see p. 35).

½ cup honey (125 mL)
¼ cup butter, melted (50 mL)
1 tbsp lemon juice (15 mL)
½ tsp lemon zest (2 mL)
3 tsp freshly grated ginger (15 mL)
2 large eggs
1 tsp vanilla extract (5 mL)
2¼ cups sifted soft whole-wheat flour (550 mL)
1 tsp baking soda (5 mL)
¼ tsp nutmeg (1 mL)
pinch salt
½ cup coarsely chopped walnuts OR pecans (125 mL)

Garden-Fresh Greens

Before our gardens start producing fruits and vegetables, they provide a bounty of fresh greens and herbs. Take advantage of leafy greens in late spring and early summer, when they're at their tender best. Greens are an excellent source of practically all the vitamins and minerals we require. They also provide fiber and protein (especially when combined with a grain).

The Iranians combine greens with herbs and eggs for an omelette-like dish called kuku. Accompany it with rice cooked in the Iranian manner—with potatoes.

2 tbsp butter (25 mL)
2 tsp lemon juice (10 mL)
⅛ tsp salt (0.5 mL)
⅛ tsp ground black
  peppercorns (0.5 mL)

Cooked Greens

4 servings
5 minutes preparation
1 to 7 minutes cooking

Choose greens with a bright green color, avoiding any that are wilted or have yellow splotches or black decaying spots. Here is a list of suggestions, with recommended quantities (chopped) and cooking times.

BEET TOPS (2 cups/500 mL; 4 minutes): high in oxalic acid; use in moderation.

CABBAGE (3 cups/750 mL; 6 minutes): savoy, Chinese (*napa*), red, or green are all delicious.

CHARD (4 cups/1 L; 3 minutes): a spinach-like vegetable; cook stems separately.

COLLARDS (2 cups/500 mL; 7 minutes): very nutritious; remove tough stems.

DANDELION (2 cups/500 mL; 5 minutes): bitter unless very young or a large cultivated variety.

ESCAROLE (2 cups/500 mL; 4 minutes): a delicate bitter flavor.

KALE (3 cups/750 mL; 6 minutes): beautiful curly leaves; remove tough stems.

LETTUCE (4 cups/1 L; 3 minutes): small heads of leaf lettuce hold together best.

RAPINI (3 cups/750 mL; 4 minutes): a delightful broccoli-like taste, especially after the first frost.

SPINACH (8 cups/2 L; 1 minutes): wash carefully to remove all sand; moderately high in oxalates.

TURNIP (3 cups/750 mL; 5 minutes): use a variety grown specifically for greens.

Cut leaves to whatever size you wish, in the quantity suggested. If they taste bitter, put in a potful of boiling water; if mild, use just ¼" (5 mm) water. Simmer for the suggested number of minutes. If, after cooking, the taste is still too strong, pour out the water, add fresh boiling water and simmer for a few more minutes. Add butter, lemon juice, salt and pepper.

Kuku

4 servings
15 minutes preparation
30 minutes baking

This thick, green, aromatic omelette is traditionally served for good luck on the Iranian New Year (celebrated in early spring). Baking turns the zucchini slices into an intricate filigree.

Preheat oven to 325°F (160°C). Slowly fry onion, cumin and cinnamon in butter. Stir cooked greens, fried onion mixture, herbs, walnuts, salt and pepper into the eggs. Pour into a hot, buttered 9" (22.5-cm) frying pan. Arrange zucchini slices on top.

Bake until set (about 30 minutes). Serve in wedges directly from pan. Leftovers make a delicious sandwich filling.

3 tbsp butter (50 mL)
2 cups diced onion OR leek (500 mL)
½ tsp ground cumin (2 mL)
½ tsp ground cinnamon (2 mL)
1 recipe seasoned Cooked Greens, chopped
6 eggs, lightly beaten
½ cup mixed chopped fresh herbs: parsley, dill, coriander OR mint (125 mL)
¼ cup chopped walnuts (optional) (50 mL)
¼ tsp salt (1 mL)
⅛ tsp ground black peppercorns (0.5 mL)
¼ cup zucchini slices, ¼" (5 mm) thick (50 mL)

Polo Rice

4 servings
10 minutes preparation
40 minutes cooking

Any long-grain variety will do, but for a heavenly scent use basmati rice. When cooked, most of the rice will be fluffy. But don't forget the crust that sticks to the pan—it's considered a delicacy.

Bring water and salt to a boil (most of the salt will be discarded). Add rice and boil only until no longer hard (about 10 minutes—30 minutes for brown rice). Drain.

Heat oil in a large, shallow, heavy-bottomed pot on low heat. Add potatoes and cover with partially cooked rice. Place a towel on top and steam for about 30 minutes.

Serve the fluffy rice garnished with the crispy potatoes and rice scraped from the bottom of the pot.

4 quarts water (4 L)
1 tbsp salt (15 mL)
2 cups basmati OR long-grain rice (500 mL)
3 tbsp olive oil (50 mL)
2 medium white potatoes, sliced ½" (1 cm) thick

Early Summer Dinner

Early summer asparagus, peas and strawberries are some of the most succulent delicacies of the year. To celebrate their arrival, here's an international menu of asparagus à la Grècque, Italian risi e bisi, and English gooseberry fool.

Asparagus à la Grècque

12 servings
15 minutes preparation
24 hours marinating

Marinating is a tasty way of extending the season for many summer vegetables.

VINAIGRETTE:
⅔ cup olive oil (150 mL)
⅓ cup freshly squeezed lemon
 juice (75 mL)
2 cloves garlic, minced
¼ tsp lemon zest (1 mL)
¼ tsp salt (1 mL)
¼ tsp ground black
 peppercorns (1 mL)

2 lb asparagus (1 kg)

To prepare vinaigrette shake all ingredients well.

Rinse any sand off the asparagus. Trim by breaking off tough bottoms where they snap easily (usually the bottom quarter), and peeling any stringy parts from lower stalks (usually about two-thirds of the way up).

Place spears in a large pot with ¼" (5 mm) water and the tips propped up with some crumpled aluminum foil. Steam until they turn a brilliant green (about 3 minutes). To dry, toss in a towel, spin in a salad drier or, best of all, blow with a hair drier. Put the still-warm asparagus in a dish.

Pour vinaigrette over asparagus and marinate in the refrigerator for at least 24 hours, periodically shaking vinaigrette over asparagus. Flavor will continue to improve for several days.

Serve as an appetizer, salad, side dish or separate vegetable course. Leftovers will keep well in refrigerator for at least 3 weeks. Use any extra vinaigrette for salads and marinating other vegetables (see p. 86).

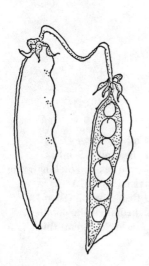

Risi e Bisi

4 servings
25 minutes preparation

The Venetian version of risotto. Be sure to use a good stock. For the requisite creamy, nutty texture, choose Italian arborio rice.

Bring stock to a simmer and keep hot. Meanwhile, fry onions in butter in a saucepan on medium heat. When clear, stir in rice, then add 1 cup (250 mL) stock. When mixture begins to thicken (about 3 minutes for arborio or 10 for brown rice), stir in another cup of hot stock. Stir frequently and add more stock as mixture thickens.

Arborio rice should be nearly al dente—perfectly cooked—in about 15 minutes (50 minutes for brown). Just before it's done, stir in peas, mint and 1 cup (250 mL) Parmesan. Continue cooking for 2 or 3 minutes.

Like a soufflé, this dish waits for no one. Serve promptly with remaining grated Parmesan at the table. The consistency should be runny enough to require a soup bowl but it should soon turn thick enough to be eaten with a fork.

5–6 cups stock (see p. 92)
  (1250–1500 mL)
3 tbsp butter (50 mL)
1 cup diced onions (250 mL)
2 cups arborio OR short-grain
  brown rice (500 mL)
2 cups peas, fresh OR frozen
  (500 mL)
2 sprigs mint OR 2 leaves
  lettuce
1¼ cups freshly grated
  Parmesan cheese (300 mL)

Gooseberry Fool

4 servings
10 minutes preparation
10 minutes cooking
20 minutes chilling

Try making this delectable froth with other fruits too. Strawberries and raspberries should not be cooked— just blend and sweeten them before adding the whipped cream.

Put berries and ¼ cup (50 mL) water in a heavy-bottomed saucepan. Cover and slowly bring to a simmer. When softened (about 10 minutes), push through a strainer into a bowl. Discard seeds, skins and stems. Stir honey into the pulp. Cool to room temperature.

Meanwhile whisk whipping cream until soft peaks form. Fold into the sweetened pulp. Serve right away in stemmed glasses, perhaps with honey-lemon cookies (see p. 136).

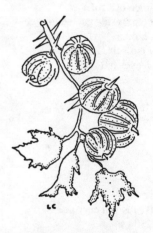

3 cups (12 oz) gooseberries OR
  other fruit: red or black
  currants, cranberries, strawberries, raspberries (750 mL/
  375 g)
½ cup honey (125 mL)
¾ cup ice-cold whipping cream
  (175 mL)

Strawberry Social

In earlier times, the strawberry social was an unmistakable sign that summer had arrived. To make sure your berries have been picked at their peak (they don't ripen afterwards), go to a pick-your-own farm. If you pick more than you can use within a couple of days, freeze them on baking sheets and, when frozen, slide into freezer bags for storage.

Cucumber and Strawberry Salad

½ English cucumber, unpeeled
1 pint strawberries, rinsed and hulled (500 mL)
2 tbsp freshly squeezed lemon juice (25 mL)
½ tsp freshly grated ginger (2 mL)
¼ tsp salt (1 mL)
4 leaves lettuce

4 servings
10 minutes preparation

Cut cucumber lengthwise in quarters. Cut cucumber sections and strawberries in thin slices. Whisk together lemon juice, ginger and salt. Gently toss cucumbers and strawberries in mixture. Arrange a portion over each lettuce leaf. Serve immediately.

Red Currant Jelly

10 cups red currants (2500 mL)
5 cups mild honey (1250 mL)
¼ cup lemon juice (50 mL)

about 5 cups (1250 mL)
1 hour preparation
1 hour setting

Use as a glaze for strawberry custard.

Preheat oven to 225°F (160°C). Put all ingredients in a 4-quart (4-L) or larger heavy-bottomed pot. Quickly bring to a gentle boil with lid off. Meanwhile sterilize small canning jars and lids in oven for at least 10 minutes. Put a saucer in the freezer to chill.

When fruit has softened (about 15 minutes), pour with liquid into a jelly bag or a piece of muslin draped over a colander. Tie up and drain into a bowl. When cool enough to handle, squeeze gently, but take care not to release any cloudy juice.

Bring strained juice back to a boil, uncovered. When temperature reaches 221°F (105°C) or syrup "sheets" when dripped from a spoon (about 20 minutes), put ¼ tsp (1 mL) of it onto the chilled saucer. If ready, it will quickly set enough to wrinkle as you push the surface.

Pour syrup into sterilized containers. Cover and seal. Do not disturb until jelly has cooled to room temperature and set (1 to 3 hours). If for some reason it does not set, serve as a syrup or cook it down some more.

Strawberry Soup

4 servings
10 minutes preparation
1 hour chilling

Serve this cold soup as a first course (with some crusty bread) or a dessert (with cookies).

Save a few strawberries for garnishing. Put remaining berries, wine and water through a food mill. (A blender or food processor can be used but both incorporate air and turn the soup pink.) Pour into a jar and stir in orange zest, allspice and buttermilk. Chill in refrigerator for several hours, or in freezer no more than 1 hour. Serve in bowls, garnished with slices of reserved berries.

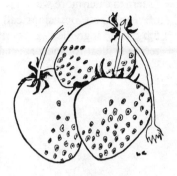

1 quart strawberries, rinsed
  and hulled (1 L)
½ cup white OR rosé wine
  (125 mL)
½ cup water (125 mL)
⅛ tsp orange zest (0.5 mL) OR
  1 tbsp orange liqueur (15 mL)
⅛ tsp ground allspice (0.5 mL)
1 cup buttermilk OR cereal
  cream (250 mL)

Strawberry Custard

8 servings
15 minutes preparation
1 hour baking
1 hour cooling

Preheat oven to 325°F (160°C). Stir together cream, eggs, honey and vanilla.

Strain mixture into a shallow baking dish. Place in a tray of hot water and bake on a lower shelf until custard has set nearly to center (about 1 hour). Cool on a cake rack.

Melt jelly with sherry in a small saucepan on low heat. Take off heat. Cut strawberries in half and arrange, cut side down, over custard. When jelly reaches consistency of raw egg whites, carefully brush it over berries.

Chill and serve when jelly has set. Any leftovers will keep in refrigerator for up to 1 day.

2 cups cereal OR whipping
  cream (500 mL)
6 eggs, lightly beaten
1 tbsp honey (15 mL)
1 tsp vanilla extract (5 mL)
⅓ cup Red Currant Jelly
  (75 mL)
1 tbsp sherry OR water (15 mL)
1 pint large strawberries,
  rinsed and hulled (500 mL)

Special Occasion Cake

I seem to cater more weddings and birthday parties in early summer than at any other time of year. These occasions call for a special cake. To make your own, all you need are top-quality ingredients, accurate measurements, careful technique, and a little time. This recipe is ideal for most special occasions—and not just in summer.

Lemon Sponge Cake

2 9″ (22.5-cm) layers
20 minutes preparation
20 minutes baking
1 hour cooling

To double the quantity, make the recipe twice rather than double the ingredients.

6 eggs
½ cup honey (125 mL)
¼ cup butter (50 mL)
1½ cups (7 oz) sifted soft
  whole-wheat flour
  (300 mL/200 g)
pinch salt
3 tbsp lemon juice (45 mL)
½ tsp lemon zest (2 mL)
2 tbsp water (25 mL)

Preheat oven to 325°F (160°C). Warm eggs by immersing in hot tap water in a mixing bowl. In a heavy-bottomed pot, slowly melt honey and butter and bring to a simmer. Sift together flour and salt. Combine lemon juice, zest and water. Line two 9″ (22.5-cm) springform pans with waxed paper, then butter and dust them with flour. Rinse a clean copper or glass bowl with ¼ tsp (1 mL) lemon juice (discard juice).

Separate eggs, putting whites in the lemon-rinsed bowl. Put yolks in the (dried) warming bowl. Mix yolks at high speed until thick enough to leave a trail (about 4 minutes). While still mixing, slowly pour in hot honey-butter mixture. Finally, beat in lemon juice mixture. (For the most delicate results, the mixture should remain thick and homogeneous, but if it separates don't worry.)

With clean beaters, beat egg whites until soft peaks form. Fold sifted flour into yolk mixture. Then fold in beaten whites. Immediately spread batter into prepared pans. Tap pans on counter to release any air bubbles. Promptly set on lower oven shelf.

Bake until lightly browned (about 20 minutes). Let cool on a cake rack (cakes will collapse somewhat). Before completely cool, turn out cakes and peel off paper. Leave on rack to cool and dry (ideally, overnight).

Whipped Cream

4 cups (1 L)
10 minutes preparation

For the most volume, start with very cold cream and add any sweetener only near the end of beating. For the best flavor, avoid using ultra-pasteurized whipping cream.

Put chilled cream in a cold mixing bowl. Beat with a hand balloon whisk or electric beater. When mixture begins to get fluffy, add honey and vanilla extract. Continue to beat until soft peaks form. Do not overbeat, or cream will separate into butter—in which case see p. 35.

If not using whipped cream right away, put it in a colander over a bowl and keep in refrigerator for up to 4 hours.

2 cups ice-cold whipping (35%) cream (500 mL)
3 tbsp honey (45 mL)
1 tsp vanilla extract (5 mL)

Layer Cake

1 9" (22.5-cm) 4-layer cake
20 minutes assembling

For a naturally colorful garnish, use edible flowers.

For easier decorating, place cake plate on a lazy susan. Center one cake layer on plate. Slip strips of waxed paper under cake on all sides. Spread ¾ cup (175 mL) butter cream over cake. Repeat with two more layers of cake. Top with final layer.

Brush off any loose crumbs. Spread half the whipped cream over the sides of the cake, starting from the bottom. Cover top with half the remaining cream.

Then put remaining whipped cream into a piping bag with a large star nozzle and pipe (see p. 24) messages, pictures or flowers on cake. Garnish with a few fresh flowers. Pull out strips of waxed paper. Serve within 1 hour after adding whipped cream.

2 recipes Lemon Sponge Cake
1 recipe Butter Cream
(see p. 135)
1 recipe Whipped Cream
flowers for garnishing: roses, tiger lilies, geraniums, hollyhocks OR violets

Raspberries

Raspberries are so special, I don't think it excessive to incorporate a taste of them in every course of a summer meal—cold borscht with slabs of buttered dark bread, summer slaw, vinegar cooler and for dessert, elegantly plain berries with nothing more than a dollop of whipped cream.

Raspberry Vinegar

1 quart (1 L)
20 minutes preparation
2 days resting

Preserve the essence of tender summer fruit for winter days when you need a quick shot of summertime. To avoid off-flavors, use non-metallic containers (or stainless or enamelled steel).

3 cups crushed fresh raspberries OR other fruit: strawberries, blueberries, peaches, cranberries (750 mL)
2 cups mild vinegar: cider, rice OR white wine (500 mL)

Combine fruit and vinegar in a saucepan. Cover and let stand in a cool place for 1 day. Slowly heat to a simmer, then let cool and rest for 1 more day.

Strain out juice through cheesecloth. Then squeeze until juice begins to run cloudy. Boil 5 minutes. Pour the hot liquid into clean bottles and seal tightly.

Fruit vinegar will keep in refrigerator for up to a year.

Beet Borscht

8 bowls
15 minutes preparation
2 hours chilling

4 cups stock (see p. 92) OR ½ water and ½ wine or beer (1 L)
4 cups peeled and chopped beets (1 L)
1½ cups diced onion (375 mL)
2 whole garlic, minced
4 cloves
1 bay leaf
½ cup Raspberry Vinegar (125 mL)
2 tbsp vegetable oil (25 mL)

Bring stock to a boil. Add beets, onion, garlic, cloves and bay leaf. Simmer until beets and onions soften (about 15 minutes). Remove any scum that floats to the top. Remove from heat and allow soup to cool (in the freezer if you're in a hurry).

Once cool, remove cloves and bay leaf. Add vinegar and oil and purée in a blender (for velvety smoothness), or in a food processor or food mill (for a coarser texture).

Borscht can be reheated, but in the summer it's best ice-cold. Garnish each serving with a dollop of sour cream or yogurt, a sprig of fresh dill, and an ice cube.

Summer Slaw

4 servings
15 minutes preparation

Crinkly savoy cabbage makes the best slaw.

If the cabbage tastes strong, soak in ice water for ½ hour before using. Toss with shredded vegetables, texture ingredients and dill.

For dressing, whisk together mayonnaise, vinegar and mustard. Mix into salad.

Summer slaw can be served right away, but improves with an hour of chilling. It begins to turn soggy after 8 hours.

2 cups (½ small head) shredded savoy cabbage (500 mL)
1 cup of 1 or 2 shredded ingredients: carrot, celery, green onion, sweet pepper, turnip, zucchini, apple (250 mL)
¼ cup of 1 or 2 other ingredients for texture and color: chopped hard-cooked egg, chopped nuts, shelled peanuts, sunflower seeds, corn kernels, crumbled blue cheese, currants, crushed pineapple (50 mL)
¼ cup chopped fresh dill leaves (50 mL)

DRESSING:
½ cup mayonnaise (see p. 38) (125 mL)
2 tbsp Raspberry Vinegar (25 mL)
½ tsp prepared mustard OR horseradish (2 mL)

Raspberry Cooler

1 quart (1 L)
5 minutes preparation

Keep a supply of this thirst-quenching drink on hand in the refrigerator.

Combine all ingredients and taste. If it bites the back of your throat, add a little more water; if it's too watery, add more vinegar or honey.

Can be served right away, but flavor mellows if it's chilled. Will keep in refrigerator for up to 1 week.

4 cups water OR soda water, mixed with crushed ice (1 L)
3 tbsp Raspberry Vinegar (50 mL)
3 tbsp honey OR other sweetener (50 mL)
pinch salt (omit if using soda water)

Homemade Cheese

Milk seems to have a cleaner and richer flavor in early summer—perhaps because many cows have been let out of their barns to receive the benefit of fresh air, sunshine and green grass. This special flavor is most evident in freshly made cheeses such as Ricotta.

Fresh Ricotta is surprisingly easy to make. Try it in cannelloni topped with pesto and accompanied by steamed sugar snap peas or green beans (see p. 100). For dessert serve a bowl of strawberries with more fresh Ricotta.

Ricotta

¾ lb (1 ½ cups) (375 g/375 mL)
5 minutes preparation
30 minutes heating and draining

For an old-country flavor, try goat's milk. If you plan to drink the refreshing and highly nutritious whey, use lemon juice as the souring agent, for extra vitamins.

2 quarts homogenized cow's
  OR goat's milk (2 L)
2½ tbsp lemon juice OR
  light-colored 5% vinegar
  (40 mL)

Rinse a heavy-bottomed saucepan with water and add milk and lemon juice. Heat on low heat, with periodic stirring, until a scum forms. If the white curds have not separated from the yellow whey, add 1 tsp (5 mL) more lemon juice.

Remove from heat and let rest while you line a colander with cheesecloth or nylon sheer material. Set in a larger bowl (to catch the whey). Ladle in hot curds and whey. Drain. After about 5 minutes, cheese will be ready to use. Save whey for drinking or using in bread or soup.

Pesto

1 cup (250 mL)
10 minutes preparation

Basil is the traditional (and I think the best) flavor for pesto, but marjoram, mint and parsley are good too.

1 cup (packed) chopped fresh
  basil, marjoram, mint OR
  parsley leaves (250 mL)
⅓ cup olive oil (75 mL)
3 tbsp freshly grated Sardo OR
  Parmesan cheese (50 mL)
2 tbsp pine nuts OR cashews
  (25 mL)
1 clove garlic
½ tsp lemon juice (2 mL)
¼ tsp salt (1 mL)

Put all ingredients in a blender or food processor. Blend until smooth (about 3 minutes). Serve right away over cooked pasta. Leftovers will keep in refrigerator for 2 weeks, or in freezer for a year.

Cannelloni con Ricotta

4 servings
20 minutes preparation
40 minutes baking

*These "pipes" are best made from fresh pasta sheets—
either homemade or store-bought—cut to the standard
4" × 5" (10 × 12.5 cm). Since dried cannelloni tubes
often shatter in the box, it's less wasteful to cook lasa-
gna strips and then cut them in 5" (12.5-cm) lengths.*

Preheat oven to 350°F (180°C). Bring 4 quarts (4 L)
lightly salted water to a boil. Drop in pasta, one piece
at a time. Cook for 30 seconds after water returns to a
boil (7 minutes for dried pasta). Drain and rinse in
cold water.

Wipe a shallow 9" × 14" (22.5 × 35-cm) baking dish
with olive oil. Combine Ricotta, onion, nutmeg, salt
and pepper. Put 3 to 4 tbsp (50 mL) filling along one
of the shorter sides of each piece of pasta. Roll and
place in baking dish (for easier serving, leave all flaps
hanging from the same side). When all rolls are done,
brush tops and sides with oil.

Cover dish and bake until heated through (about 40
minutes). Serve right away with tomato sauce (see
p. 18) or pesto.

1 lb fresh pasta (500 g) OR ¾ lb
  dried (375 g)
1 recipe Ricotta
½ cup diced sweet onion
  (125 mL)
⅛ tsp freshly grated nutmeg
  (0.5 mL)
⅛ tsp salt (0.5 mL)
⅛ tsp ground white
  peppercorns (0.5 mL)

Cold Soba Plate

Summer months in Japan are hot and muggy, but relief is around nearly every corner in any town. In a gazebo-like hut you can sit in the shade and enjoy a plateful of ice-cold soba—buckwheat noodles garnished with an assortment of colorful condiments. The Japanese have long known that an artful presentation can be as satisfying as a full belly, and an attractively arranged soba plate makes an ideal snack if you don't want to over-indulge. Served with a sunomono salad and some fresh summer fruit, it becomes a full meal.

Sunomono

4 servings
15 minutes preparation
30 minutes marinating

Combine all ingredients for marinade. Let flavors amalgamate while you prepare an appropriate combination of 3 or 4 of the following:

BROCCOLI: blanch flowerets until bright green, then refresh in cold water.

CARROT: peel and cut in thin curled strips with a vegetable peeler.

CUCUMBER (preferably "dill" type): cut in very thin diagonal slices.

DULSE (*wakame*)—(available at Japanese and some natural food stores): presoak for 30 minutes and cut in slivers.

GREEN ONION: cut off rootlets and most of the green part; slit remaining green part to make fans.

LOTUS ROOT (available in Oriental food stores): peel and cut in thin slices to highlight the internal pattern, then blanch for 5 minutes to soften.

GREEN BEANS: remove stems and blanch until bright green, then refresh in cold water.

Cover salad ingredients with marinade and stir periodically. Remove from marinade before they lose their crispness (about 30 minutes). Arrange on serving plates.

MARINADE:
¼ cup rice vinegar (50 mL)
1 tbsp sake OR mirin (15 mL)
½ tsp dark sesame oil (2 mL)
½ tsp honey OR other sweetener (2 mL)
¼" (5 mm) fresh ginger, peeled and thinly sliced
¼ tsp salt (1 mL)
¼ tsp orange zest (optional) (1 mL)

SALAD:
2 cups assorted ingredients (see recipe) (500 mL)

Soba

4 servings
15 minutes preparation
5 minutes cooking

Since the cooking times for various brands of buckwheat noodles vary, watch carefully the first time you use a particular brand (there's nothing refreshing about soggy noodles). Generally the Japanese imports take longer to cook and are less likely to lose their texture.

Combine all sauce ingredients. Sauce is ready to use right away, but flavor will be more mellow if given an hour to ripen.

To prepare noodles, bring 4 quarts (4 L) water to a rolling boil and drop in noodles. Cook only until softened—they should still retain some bite (generally 1 to 4 minutes). Strain and rinse with cold water, then store in ice water until ready to use (leave no more than 1 hour).

Drain noodles well and place on chilled plates. Garnish each serving with a colorful assortment of 3 or 4 of the following:

TOFU: press until firm (place on towel and weight down with a dinner plate—about 30 minutes), then cut in cubes, or slivers—acts as a bland foil, and provides a protein complement.

EGG: whisk with 1 equal part water and slowly fry a thin omelette, then cut in slivers—for color and nutrition.

SEAWEED (*nori*—available in sheets at Japanese and some natural food stores): cut in 1″ × 3″ (25 × 75-mm) pieces—for color and nutrition.

GREEN ONIONS: cut green parts in fine rings—for color and taste.

SESAME SEEDS: toast in a dry frying pan until aromatic— for aroma and a protein complement.

ICE CUBE: cooling and attractive.

Pour sauce onto a small plate and around the rim put a small mound of 1 or 2 of the following spicy condiments:

WHITE RADISH (*daikon*): grate finely.

GINGER: grate finely.

WASABI (Japanese horseradish, available in powder form at Japanese food stores): mix with enough water to make a paste.

HORSERADISH: grate finely (or use prepared horse radish).

SAUCE:
3 tbsp soy sauce OR tamari (50 mL)
1 tbsp rice vinegar OR white wine vinegar (15 mL)
½″ (1 cm) fresh ginger, peeled and grated

NOODLES:
½ lb dried buckwheat noodles (250 g)

Keep the Kitchen Cool

A simple tossed salad with lemonade and a slice of crusty bread is so satisfying on a hot summer day that you may want little else. But everyone always has room for homemade ice cream.

Freshly made ice cream needs no emulsifiers or stabilizers to keep it smooth. And although commercial ice creams contain a legal minimum of 10% cream, if you make your own it need not contain any cream at all. Ice cream can be "still" frozen in the freezer of a two-door refrigerator (the freezer in a one-door model doesn't get cold enough). But it will be smoother if made with the continuous action of a special ice-cream machine.

Tossed Salad

4 servings
15 minutes preparation

6 cups torn or cut lettuce:
  Boston, butter OR Bibb
  (delicate); oak leaf OR red leaf
  (tender); romaine OR chinese
  lettuce (crunchy); endive OR
  escarole (bitter) (1.5 L)
½ cup shredded ingredients:
  watercress OR arugola
  (peppery); chives OR green
  onion (aromatic); sorrel OR
  grape leaves (tart); mint, dill
  OR celery (refreshing);
  red cabbage OR radicchio
  (colorful) (125 mL)
1 tbsp minced fresh herbs:
  tarragon, chervil OR dill;
  savory OR basil; parsley,
  thyme OR marjoram (15 mL)
¼ cup olive oil (50 mL)
2 tbsp lemon juice OR vinegar
  (25 mL)
¼ cup garnish: shredded raw
  beets, carrots, turnip; diced
  cheese; croutons; whole corn
  niblets, cherry tomatoes,
  asparagus tips, olives, capers;
  sliced cucumber, mushroom,
  avocado, hard-cooked egg
  (50 mL)

Lettuce can be either cut or torn. If cut, the edges begin to turn brown in about half an hour (though this is no problem if the salad will be eaten promptly).

Rinse and dry the leafy greens well by dabbing each leaf with a towel or spinning in a salad drier. (If you leave any water on the leaves, the dressing will slip to the bottom of the salad bowl.)

Cut or tear lettuce into bite-sized pieces. Put in a large salad bowl with shredded ingredients and herbs. Toss with the oil. Finally, toss with the lemon juice. Arrange garnish either over the whole salad or over individual servings.

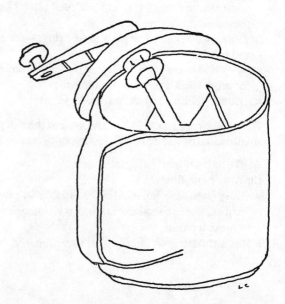

Lemonade

1 quart (1 L)
5 minutes preparation

If you use soda water, be sure to add it just before serving.

Whisk all ingredients together and serve in a pitcher, perhaps garnished with mint. For a fresher flavor, leave the whole lemon rinds in the pitcher for an hour or two. To avoid diluting the flavor, use lemonade ice cubes.

¼ cup lemon juice (50 mL)
up to ¼ cup honey OR other sweetener (50 mL)
pinch salt (unless using soda water)
4 cups ice water (1 L)
1 egg white, lightly beaten (optional)
1 cup brewed tea OR soda water (reduce ice water by 1 cup) (250 mL)

Fruit Ice Cream

about 2 quarts (2 L)
30 minutes preparation
2 hours chilling

A base of scalded milk thickened with egg custard gives a rich taste without the extra calories of cream.

Bring milk to a simmer in a heavy-bottomed saucepan on medium heat. Meanwhile in another bowl whisk together honey, egg yolks and arrowroot. Add half the hot milk, then pour mixture back into saucepan. Return to heat and stir constantly on medium heat until thick enough to coat the back of a spoon.

Set mixture in a basin of cold water. Stir in vanilla, salt and puréed fruit. Chill in refrigerator, preferably overnight.

To use an ice cream maker, follow the manufacturer's directions. Pour in the fruit custard and churn until quite thick.

For "still" freezing, beat the egg whites to soft peaks and fold into mixture. Pour into a shallow metal pan and place on the floor of the freezer. As slush forms, whisk it. When quite thick, break up any ice crystals by spinning in a blender or food processor.

This soft ice cream can be served now. For firm ice cream, place in freezer until solid (about 4 hours). Ice crystals will develop, so enjoy it within a week.

2 cups milk OR cream (500 mL)
⅔ cup honey (150 mL)
5 egg yolks
2 tsp arrowroot OR other starch (10 mL)
1 tsp vanilla extract (5 mL)
pinch salt
2 cups puréed tender fruit: apricots, avocado, blueberries, kiwis, mangoes, plums, raspberries, strawberries, peaches, nectarines (500 mL)

FOR STILL-FREEZING:
3 egg whites

Planned Leftovers

To make the most of summer—and keep the kitchen cool—I often cook double portions of dishes that are especially good served chilled. Freshly made onion and potato soup is delightful both hot and, with the addition of puréed cucumber, cold—like a lighter and more refreshing vichyssoise.

Tian resembles quiche, but without a crust it requires less work and less baking. Although, as with most egg dishes, leftovers do not take well to reheating, they are delicious served cold. Cooked rice goes well with hot tian; convert it into a rice salad to serve with tian the second time around.

Tian

8 servings
20 minutes preparation
25 minutes baking

Tian gets its name from the shallow dish in which it is traditionally baked, but any shallow ovenproof dish—such as a pie plate or au gratin dish—will do. Baking time can be shortened if the vegetables are still hot when the eggs are added.

6 cups (1 large bunch) chopped and packed leafy greens: spinach, Swiss chard, lettuce, turnip greens OR collards (1500 mL)
3 tbsp olive oil OR butter (50 mL)
2 cups diced onion (500 mL)
1 cup finely diced carrot, turnip, kohlrabi OR radish (250 mL)
2 tbsp white wine, Pernod OR water (25 mL)
1 cup peas, diced green or wax beans, zucchini OR mushrooms (250 mL)
3 eggs, lightly beaten
3 tbsp freshly grated Parmesan (50 mL)
¼ cup bread crumbs OR cooked rice (50 mL)
½ cup Swiss cheese (125 mL)

Preheat oven to 350°F (180°C). Butter a shallow baking dish. Rinse leafy greens well and put in a pot with ¼″ (5 mm) water. Gently steam until bright green and tender (about 5 minutes). Drain.

Heat oil in a large frying pan on medium-high heat. Add onion and fry until lightly browned. Add first (firm) vegetable and fry until heated through. Add wine and second (tender) vegetable. When all have softened, stir in cooked greens.

Let mixture cool a few minutes, then stir in eggs and Parmesan. Turn into baking dish. Sprinkle bread crumbs and cheese on top. Bake until set (about 25 minutes).

Serve right away with cooked rice or pasta, or a loaf of crusty bread. Leftovers keep for 1 week in refrigerator. Warm to room temperature before serving.

Onion and Potato Soup

8 bowls
20 minutes preparation
40 minutes cooking

In a heavy-bottomed saucepan on medium heat, melt butter and slowly fry onions. When clear, turn up heat and add potatoes, stock, salt, bay leaf and nutmeg. When mixture reaches a simmer, reduce heat to low. Simmer until potatoes have softened (about 15 minutes).

Remove bay leaf and nutmeg. Purée soup by pushing through a food mill. (A food processor will work if you use many quick pulses. Or you can use a blender— but the soup will have a gummy consistency.) Stir in buttermilk and pepper. To serve hot, garnish with chopped herbs.

Leftovers will keep in refrigerator up to 1 week. To serve cold, freshen the flavor by adding puréed cucumber. Garnish with chives—purple flowers or freshly snipped leaves.

3 tbsp butter (50 mL)
3 cups diced fresh onions (the white part) (750 mL)
3 cups chopped potatoes (small ones need not be peeled) (750 mL)
3 cups stock (see p. 92) OR water (750 mL)
½ tsp salt (2 mL)
1 bay leaf
¼ nut nutmeg OR 1 blade mace
½ cup buttermilk (125 mL)
¼ tsp ground white peppercorns (1 mL)
freshly chopped mint, thyme OR parsley

1 cup (1 medium) peeled, seeded and puréed cucumber (250 mL)

Rice Salad

8 servings
15 minutes preparation

Short-grain rice is best for keeping the grains firm and separate.

Gently toss rice and oil with a fork (a spoon tends to mash). Toss in diced ingredients, lemon juice, herb(s), salt and pepper.

Rice salad can be served right away, but it tastes better after the flavors have blended (about 2 hours). Serve on a lettuce leaf or in a hollowed-out tomato or pepper, or press into a lightly oiled mold and turn·out after refrigerating for several hours.

3 cups cooked rice (see p. 119), cooled (750 mL)
⅓ cup olive oil (75 mL)
4 cups of 3 or 4 diced ingredients: blanched asparagus or peas; raw avocado, sweet pepper, carrot, celery, cucumber, fennel, green onion, mushroom, nuts OR olives (1 L)
3 tbsp lemon juice (50 mL)
2 tbsp chopped fresh herb(s): parsley, basil, mint, lemon balm (25 mL)
¼ tsp salt (unless cooked with rice) (1 mL)
⅛ tsp ground peppercorns (0.5 mL)

Mid-Summer Feast

Many people look forward to mid-summer as the season for produce that isn't usually available any other time. But even such common vegetables as peas, potatoes and lettuce have a very special flavor at the height of summer. Try this meal of fresh pea soup, new potato rösti and braised lettuce.

Cream of Fresh Peas

8 servings
15 minutes preparation
15 minutes cooking

If you have the new sugar snap variety, you can use the tender pods as well as the peas.

3 tbsp butter (50 mL)
½ cup chopped green onion, white part only (125 mL)
1 cup peeled and chopped potato (250 mL)
2½ cups (2 lb/1 kg) freshly shelled peas OR (1 lb/500 g) destringed sugar snap peas (600 mL)
2 tbsp flour (25 mL)
2 cups stock (see p. 92) OR ¾ water and ¼ white wine (500 mL)
¼ cup whipping (35%) cream (50 mL)
1 tsp lemon juice (5 mL)
½ tsp salt (2 mL)
8 sprigs fresh mint

In a soup pot on medium heat slowly heat butter, then fry onion until clear. Stir in potato, peas and flour. When heated through, add stock. Simmer until potatoes have softened (about 15 minutes).

Purée mixture in a blender, food processor, or food mill. Stir in cream, lemon juice and salt. Serve hot or cold, garnished with sprigs of mint.

Braised Lettuce

4 servings
5 minutes preparation
10 minutes cooking

When you have more lettuce than you can use, remember this recipe.

1 tbsp olive oil (15 mL)
4 small heads leaf lettuce (inner leaves if only large heads are available)
2 cloves garlic, minced
1 tbsp tarragon vinegar OR wine vinegar (15 mL)
½ cup stock (see p. 92) OR water (125 mL)
2 tsp flour (10 mL)

Heat oil in a frying pan on medium heat. Add lettuce heads and garlic. Gently fry until all sides of lettuce have wilted (about 3 minutes). Combine vinegar, stock and flour and pour into pan. Turn heat to low and simmer (uncovered) for 10 minutes. Serve immediately with some of the broth.

Rösti

4 servings
15 minutes preparation
10 minutes cooking

This potato dish is a popular evening meal in the German parts of Switzerland. With new potatoes the cheese is unnecessary. When they aren't available, use red potatoes with the cheese to give the flavor a boost. If your grater doesn't produce long shreds at least ⅛" (3 mm) thick, cut julienne pieces with a sharp knife.

Heat a well seasoned frying pan on medium-high heat. Add butter and, when hot, onions. When onions turn clear, add potatoes. Wait a couple of minutes, then turn them. To avoid mashing, first scrape the bottom, then turn very carefully with a spatula. Repeat no more than once every couple of minutes.

Precooked potatoes need to fry only about 5 minutes. To speed cooking of raw potatoes, sprinkle periodically with a spoonful of hot water. They should be softened in about 10 minutes. When done sprinkle on vinegar, then fold in cream, cheese, dill, salt and pepper. Turn heat to low and fry 5 more minutes without stirring. Cover with an upside-down serving platter. Remove from heat and let rest 5 minutes.

Place your palm firmly on platter and invert pan. The rösti should turn out onto the platter in one piece. Garnish with sprigs of fresh dill. Serve in wedges as you would a pie, with sour cream or applesauce (see p. 155).

4 tbsp clarified butter OR ½ butter and ½ oil (50 mL)
1 cup diced onion (250 mL)
4 cups shredded potatoes, raw OR precooked and cooled (1 L)
1 tbsp cider vinegar OR white wine vinegar (15 mL)
¼ cup whipping (35%) cream (50 mL)
1 cup shredded Swiss cheese (optional) (250 mL)
2 tbsp chopped fresh dill (25 mL)
½ tsp salt (¼ tsp if using cheese; none if potatoes were precooked in salted water) (2 mL/1 mL)
¼ tsp ground white peppercorns (1 mL)

Food for Camping

Campers usually put in long hours of physical work—work that builds substantial appetites. But a number of considerations—the need to travel lightly, to have something that can be ready to eat in short order, to use foods that keep well without refrigeration—impose some unusual constraints on menu-planning.

A meal of miso soup, polenta served with sesame sauce, and dried fruit compote fits the bill admirably (and is suitable for home cooking as well). For a cooking fat that will neither burn nor leak from containers, prepare clarified butter before you leave.

Miso Soup

4 bowls
5 minutes preparation

The world's quickest, tastiest and most nutritious instant soup. The ingredients are available in Japanese and some natural food stores.

3 cups water (750 mL)
2 tbsp sliced dried mushroom,
  wakame OR tofu (25 mL)
2 tbsp miso paste (25 mL)
¼ cup (additional) water
  (50 mL)

Bring water and dry ingredient(s) to a simmer. Meanwhile mix miso paste and additional water. When water reaches a simmer, remove from heat. Stir in miso mixture and serve.

Clarified Butter

1¾ lb (850 g)
5 minutes preparation
10 minutes melting
2 hours cooling

Clarified butter does not burn when fried, and will stay fresh without refrigeration for more than a week.

2 lb butter (1 kg)

Put butter in a saucepan on medium heat. As soon as it begins to bubble, remove from heat and refrigerate until solid (about 2 hours).

Scrape off any foam from the top. Lift out the block of butter, leaving the buttermilk behind. Rinse with cold water. Clean the pan and remelt butter. Gently simmer until all moisture has bubbled and spurted away. Cool and pour into a suitable container to solidify

Polenta

8 servings
10 minutes preparation
1 hour cooling

Save time by preparing the cornmeal porridge in the morning and letting what's left set for the evening meal. Serve it with sesame sauce (see p. 67) to provide a protein complement for the corn.

Bring water and salt to a simmer. Remove from fire and whisk in cornmeal. Return to fire and stir frequently until mixture is thick enough to hold a spoon upright (about 5 minutes).

Serve hot cornmeal as a breakfast porridge with milk and a sweetener or topped with fruit compote. Before the rest cools, pour it into a loaf pan (or over a flat rock, or even onto the bottom of a canoe).

When cool (about 1 hour), the cornmeal will have set into a firm cake. Cut into portions and pack in a sturdy container. It will keep for 2 days unrefrigerated.

To reheat polenta, either fry in a little clarified butter or place on a grill directly over the fire. When the outside is crispy and the inside hot, it's ready to serve with sesame sauce or garlic butter and grated Parmesan. If any is left for the morning, fry and top with maple syrup or dried fruit compote.

4 cups water (1 L)
¾ tsp salt (4 mL)
1 cup medium-grind cornmeal
(250 mL)

Dried Fruit Compote

8 servings
10 minutes preparation
8 hours soaking

To avoid spilling, take along a sturdy plastic container.

Bring dried fruit, water, honey and cardamom to a simmer. Simmer 5 minutes, then remove from fire. Let fruit rehydrate in water overnight (or for the day). In a dry frying pan toast almonds until fragrant.

When fruit has plumped (about 8 hours), add toasted almonds. Serve for breakfast with polenta or pancakes; as a day-time snack; or for dessert in the evening. Rehydrated fruit will keep for 2 days unrefrigerated.

1 cup dried apricots (250 mL)
1 cup dried black mission figs
(250 mL)
2½ cups water (625 mL)
¼ cup honey (optional)
(50 mL)
3 pods green OR white
cardamom, cracked open
½ cup unblanched almonds
(optional) (125 mL)

61

Backyard Barbeque

Choosing not to eat meat doesn't mean forgoing the pleasures of food cooked over an open fire. If you're invited to a backyard barbeque, take along your own food—just be sure to take plenty, because curious friends will all want to try some.

Lentil burgers have an added dimension when they're barbequed. They can go into the usual bun with catsup and mustard, but I like them served on a plate topped with a garlicky skordalia sauce and accompanied by grilled vegetables and crusty bread toasted over the open fire. Start the meal with a lettuce salad and end it with your favorite summer fruit, or—if the grill converts into an oven—perhaps a clafouti (see p. 65).

Lentil Burgers

16 burgers
20 minutes preparation
30 minutes soaking
45 minutes cooking

5 cups tomato juice OR stock
   (see p. 92) (1250 mL)
2 cups brown lentils, cleaned
   (500 mL)
4 tbsp oil (50 mL)
½ cup finely diced onion
   (125 mL)
½ cup chopped mushrooms
   (125 mL)
¼ cup finely diced celery
   (50 mL)
3 cloves garlic, minced
2 tsp oregano (10 mL)
2 tsp thyme (10 mL)
2 tsp ground cumin (10 mL)
1 tsp sage (5 mL)
⅛ tsp cayenne (0.5 mL)
½ cup quick-cooking oats OR
   bread crumbs (125 mL)
½ cup flour (125 mL)
¼ cup tahini (see p. 66)
   OR peanut butter (50 mL)
2 tsp prepared mustard
   (10 mL)
½ tsp salt (5 mL)

These nutritious patties can be made up ahead and frozen for quick meals.

Bring tomato juice to a boil, add lentils and remove from heat. After 30 minutes of soaking, return to heat and simmer until lentils have softened (about 45 minutes).

Meanwhile, heat oil on medium heat and add onion, mushrooms and celery. Fry until softened (about 10 minutes). Then add garlic, oregano, thyme, cumin, sage and cayenne and remove from heat.

Stir together the cooked lentils, fried ingredients, oats, flour, tahini, mustard and salt. Add more liquid if mixture is dry and crumbly, or more flour if wet and sticky.

Shape into patties. Cook both sides over a grill, on a baking sheet under a broiler, or in a lightly oiled frying pan until surface is crisped (about 5 minutes).

The mixture will keep in refrigerator for up to 1 week. Or you can freeze patties on a cookie sheet and, when solid, store in a freezer bag. Cook without thawing.

Grilled Vegetables

8 servings
5 minutes preparation
10 minutes grilling

Choose vegetables from the following list:

SWEET PEPPERS: grill whole until charred on all sides. Put in a plastic bag until cool enough to slip off skins and remove seeds. Slice and serve as is, or coarsely chop and toss with a little chopped garlic and olive oil.

EGGPLANT: cut into ½" (1.5-cm) steaks. Embed a few slivers of garlic and place on grill. Brush occasionally with olive oil. Serve when lightly charred on both sides.

ZUCCHINI: cut lengthwise in half, slicing again along the side to remove some of the remaining skin. Place slabs on the grill and brush with olive oil until charred and tender.

ONIONS: to keep them from falling apart, cut into ¼" (5-mm) vertical slices and grill only the pieces attached to the root (trimmings can be used for other purposes). Grill until golden—when cooked slowly they become incredibly sweet.

CORN ON THE COB: fold back husk, remove silk and return husk before grilling. Grill until husk is singed. Remove husk and rub with butter and sprinkle kernels with salt and pepper, or simply fresh lemon juice.

SMALL NEW POTATOES: grill until skin is splitting open. Serve with butter and chopped fresh mint.

Alternatively, you could place vegetables on skewers. For extra flavor, drop a few moistened bay or rosemary leaves onto the coals as you grill the vegetables.

8 cups (2 lb) trimmed assorted vegetables (see recipe) (2 L/ 1 kg)

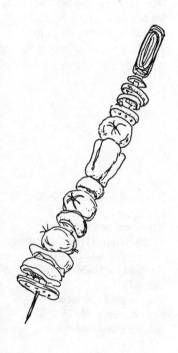

Skordalia

1 cup (250 mL)
5 minutes preparation
15 minutes cooking

This Greek sauce can be made in a food processor or blender, but the results tend to be gummy.

Boil potato until tender (about 15 minutes). Drain. Mash in a small bowl. Add garlic, lemon juice and salt. Whisk until smooth. Slowly drizzle in olive oil, whisking constantly, until mixture is thick. Use as mayonnaise.

½ cup peeled and chopped potato (125 mL)
3 cloves garlic, finely minced
2 tbsp lemon juice (30 mL)
½ tsp salt (if not cooked with potatoes) (2 mL)
¼ cup olive oil (50 mL)

Leftover Barbeque Coals

Why not take advantage of leftover barbeque coals to pre-roast tomorrow's dinner? Long, slow roasting over a charcoal fire is the best way to prepare eggplant. It not only tenderizes the flesh, but also reduces the water content, eliminates any bitter juices, and adds a delicious smoky flavor. Eggplant roasted this way can be kept in the refrigerator for up to three days for use in many recipes. (While you're at it, you might also roast some peppers for hot sauce—see p. 23.)

A kind of crustless quiche, Egyptian eggah highlights the subtle flavor of roasted eggplant. Accompany it with steamed greens (see p. 40), hot sauce (p. 23), yogurt and a tomato salad, and follow with a clafouti for dessert.

Eggah

8 servings
20 minutes preparation
30 minutes pre-roasting
45 minutes baking

2 lb (2 medium) eggplants
 (1 kg)
3 medium onions
3 tbsp chopped fresh coriander
 leaves (50 mL) OR 1 tsp
 ground coriander seeds
 (5 mL)
1 clove garlic, minced
1 tsp cumin seeds (5 mL)
¼ tsp ground cinnamon
 (1 mL)
⅛ tsp ground black
 peppercorns (0.5 mL)
8 eggs
¼ tsp salt (1 mL)
1 medium zucchini, sliced ⅛"
 (3 mm) thick

Pierce eggplants and onions with a knife. Roast over hot coals or in a 500°F (260°C) oven. Turn periodically until all sides have charred (about 30 minutes). Remove from heat and let cool. Scrape flesh from the eggplant and onion skins and cut into 1" (2.5-cm) pieces. Stir in coriander, garlic, cumin, cinnamon and pepper.

Preheat oven to 325°F (160°C). Whisk together eggs, 1½ cups (375 mL) water and salt. Stir into vegetable mixture. Pour into an 8" x 10" (20 x 25-cm) shallow casserole. Arrange zucchini slices over the top. Bake, uncovered, only until mixture begins to puff up (about 40 minutes).

Let cool 5 minutes before serving. Leftovers are best served cold.

Tomato-Oregano Salad

4 servings
5 minutes preparation
30 minutes draining

Tomato skins add nothing to this salad—please remove them as directed. If you don't have fresh oregano (or its flavor is too strong) substitute any other fresh herb.

Dip tomatoes in boiling water for 30 seconds. Refresh in cold water, then cut out core and pull off skins. Cut tomatoes in ⅜" (5-mm) vertical slices. Place on a platter. Sprinkle with oil, oregano, salt and pepper. Let tomatoes drain on platter. Just before serving, tip up one side of platter and drain off juice.

3 large tomatoes
1 tbsp olive oil (15 mL)
1 tbsp chopped fresh oregano (15 mL)
¼ tsp salt (1 mL)
⅛ tsp ground black peppercorns (0.5 mL)

Clafouti

8 servings
15 minutes preparation
30 minutes baking

This French fruit "pie" is traditionally made with unpitted cherries, but it's a quick and delicious way to serve any summer fruit. If your grill has a cover that converts it into a backyard oven, use it to bake your clafouti as the coals die down.

Preheat oven to 350°F (180°C). Butter a 10" to 12" (25 to 30-cm) pie plate. Beat eggs and honey until foamy (about 4 minutes). Whip cream and vanilla. Fold whipped cream, flour and nutmeg into beaten eggs.

Pour half the batter into prepared pie plate. Sprinkle on the fruit. Cover with remaining batter. Bake until golden brown (about 30 minutes).

Clafouti is at its best served warm, with whipped cream (see p. 47).

3 eggs
½ cup honey (125 mL)
¼ cup whipping cream (50 mL)
1 tsp vanilla extract (5 mL)
1½ cups sifted soft whole-wheat flour (375 mL)
⅛ tsp freshly grated nutmeg (0.5 mL)
2 cups fresh fruit cut in cherry-sized pieces: sweet or sour cherries, gooseberries, apricots (fresh or rehydrated dried), blueberries, peaches, Italian plums (others are too juicy), pears, OR apples (500 mL)

Processing Zucchini

Zucchini patties are a handy way to use up one of summer's most abundant crops. A food processor or kitchen machine will quickly shred the zucchini to the proper size for quick cooking, good texture, and an attractive lacy appearance. You can also use it to grind your own oat flour and sesame seeds for tahini. Serve the patties with sesame sauce and whatever steamed in-season vegetables strike your fancy, then finish off with a tofu cake topped with fresh berries.

Zucchini Patties

12 patties
25 minutes preparation

To avoid bland, soggy patties, choose zucchini no more than 6" (15 cm) long. Onions are sweeter and less bitter when diced by hand, but if you want to use a processor, follow the technique described below.

½ cup rolled oats (125 mL)
1" (2.5 cm) fresh ginger, peeled and sliced
2 tsp chopped fresh thyme OR sage (10 mL)
1 medium onion, peeled and finely diced, either by hand or in a food processor (see recipe)
4 small (1 lb) zucchini (500 g)
3 eggs, lightly beaten
1 tsp soy sauce (5 mL)
butter and oil for frying

With the steel blade in a dry bowl, process oats to a fine flour. Pour out and reserve. With steel blade turning, drop in ginger and herbs. Stop the machine and, if you have not chopped them by hand, add onion slices. Process with quick on-off pulses until coarsely chopped. Remove and set aside.

Wrap in a clean towel and wring out excess water. In a medium-sized bowl, stir together eggs, oat flour and soy sauce. Add chopped and shredded ingredients and mix well.

Heat 1 tbsp (15 mL) each of butter and oil in a heavy frying pan on medium heat. When hot, drop in spoonfuls of batter and fry until browned on both sides (about 4 minutes). Add more butter and oil as needed to fry the rest.

Serve while still crispy and hot. If necessary they can be kept hot between layers of towelling in a 350°F (180°C) oven for up to 30 minutes.

Tahini

2 cups/1 lb (500 mL/500 g)
5 minutes preparation

This sesame seed butter is exceedingly nutritious and not as oily as some commercial versions. Chew a few seeds to make sure they are fresh—stale ones will have a bitter after-taste, but fresh ones will be sweet. Use tahini as you would peanut butter or to enrich your favorite sauces.

Put seeds into a food processor or blender. Process until all are crushed. With machine still running, dribble in oil and process until a smooth butter has formed. Keep in refrigerator and use within 1 month.

2 cups white or unhulled sesame seeds (500 mL)
⅓ cup light sesame OR olive oil (75 mL)

Sesame Sauce

2 cups (500 mL)
5 minutes preparation

Make this quick sauce after preparing tahini, to clean out the food processor or blender.

Combine all ingredients. Blend in food processor or blender, or just stir with a fork until well mixed. Thin with more water, or thicken with more tahini.

Sesame sauce can be served right away, warmed if desired. Leftovers will keep in refrigerator for up to 1 week.

¾ cup Tahini (175 mL)
¾ cup hot stock (see p. 92) OR water (175 mL)
3 tbsp lemon juice (50 mL)
2 tbsp olive oil (25 mL)
1 clove garlic, pressed
½ hot chili OR ⅛ tsp cayenne (0.5 mL)
¼ tsp salt (1 mL)

Tofu Cake

1 10″ (25-cm) cake
15 minutes preparation
1 hour cooling

If you are unfamiliar with agar, see the note on p. 171.

Soak agar (whatever its form) in cider for 10 minutes. Slowly bring to a simmer. Meanwhile, blend tofu, honey, oil, lemon juice and zest, vanilla and salt in food processor or blender.

When agar has dissolved, stir tofu mixture as you strain cider into it. Promptly—before it begins to set—pour onto prepared crust. Put in refrigerator to chill and set for about 1 hour.

Serve chilled or at room temperature, attractively garnished with fruit.

1 pre-baked and cooled (½ recipe) Lemon Sponge Cake (see p. 46), Whole-Wheat Pie Crust (see p. 146) OR crumb crust in a 10″ (25-cm) springform pan
1 tbsp powdered agar (15 mL) OR ¼ oz (8 g) stick OR ¼ cup flakes (60 mL)
1½ cups unfiltered apple cider (375 mL)
2 lb tofu (preferably solidified with calcium sulfate) (1 kg)
½ cup honey (125 mL)
2 tbsp vegetable oil (25 mL)
1 tbsp lemon juice (15 mL)
½ tsp lemon zest (2 mL)
1 tsp vanilla extract (5 mL)
¼ tsp salt

Late Summer Dinner

Freshly picked vine-ripened tomatoes combine very well with the other edible members of the *Solanum* family—eggplants and potatoes. Fortunately, these too are at their best in late summer. One of my favorite methods for preparing eggplant and tomato is a spicy Turkish concoction called imam bayildi (literally, "the priest fainted"). Start with a cold potato gazpacho and serve the main course with steamed green beans, nutty bulgar wheat and plain yogurt. A wedge of fresh melon would make a refreshing conclusion.

Potato Gazpacho

4 bowls
15 minutes preparation
1 hour chilling

Don't limit yourself to red tomato gazpacho—try this "potato salad" in a bowl.

**2 cups diced new potatoes
 (500 mL)
1 bay leaf
2 cups cool stock (see p. 92)
 OR ¼ white wine and ¾ water
 (500 mL)
½ cup mayonnaise (see p. 38)
 (125 mL)
1 clove garlic, pressed
1 tbsp lemon juice (15 mL)
¼ tsp salt (1 mL)
chopped parsley**

Bring potatoes, bay leaf and ½ cup (125 mL) water to a boil. Simmer until tender (about 15 minutes). Meanwhile, slowly whisk stock into mayonnaise. (If you add it too quickly, the mayonnaise may curdle.) Stir in garlic, lemon juice and salt. Add drained hot potatoes. Chill 1 hour in freezer or overnight in refrigerator.

Stir and serve with a garnish of chopped parsley.

Bulgar Wheat

4 servings
5 minutes preparation
20 minutes cooking

If you like brown rice but want a grain that cooks more quickly, try bulgar—whole-grain wheat that has been soaked and baked, then cracked. It can be purchased in several sizes—fine, medium and coarse—in Middle Eastern and natural food stores.

**¼ tsp salt (1 mL)
1 cup bulgar wheat, medium
 or coarse grade (250 mL)**

Add salt to 2 cups (500 mL) water and bring to a boil. Stir in bulgar. Reduce heat to a simmer and cover pot. Do not stir again. Grain will be tender and fluffy in 20 minutes.

Imam Bayildi

8 servings
30 minutes preparation
30 minutes draining
1 hour baking

Place each eggplant on a plate and cut ¾″ (2-cm) crosswise slices nearly through to the bottom. Remove green caps. Sprinkle salt in slits (to draw out any bitter juices and reduce the amount of oil eggplant will absorb). After ½ hour rinse and drain well.

Meanwhile boil tomatoes, uncovered, stirring frequently. Continue until no longer watery (about 40 minutes for fresh tomatoes, or 10 minutes with paste).

Fry onions in the oil. When tomatoes have thickened, add fried onions, garlic, currants, pine nuts, basil, cinnamon and pepper.

Preheat oven to 325°F (160°C). Place drained eggplant in a small casserole with slits up. Pour sauce over, helping it into slits. Bake, basting periodically with sauce, until eggplant begins to sag (about 1 hour).

Imam bayildi can be served right away, but the flavor improves after a day in the refrigerator. Serve hot, cold or at room temperature (as in Turkey).

Leftovers keep well in refrigerator for up to 1 week. Because of the high water content, this dish does not freeze well.

2 lb (3 medium) eggplants (1 kg)
2 tbsp salt (25 mL)
7 cups peeled and chopped fresh tomatoes (1750 mL) OR 2 cups fresh tomatoes (500 mL) with 6-oz can tomato paste
¼ cup olive oil (50 mL)
1 cup finely diced onion (250 mL)
8 cloves garlic, minced
¼ cup dried currants (optional) (50 mL)
¼ cup pine nuts (optional) (50 mL)
2 tbsp chopped fresh basil (25 mL) OR 2 tsp dried (10 mL)
2 tsp cinnamon (10 mL)
¼ tsp ground black peppercorns (1 mL)

South India

One reason the food of southern India is different from that of northern India is that for much of the year, the climate of the south is hotter. So eating less substantial foods with spices like chilies and ginger, which induce sweating, is a practical way to keep cool.

The nutritious bean and rice pancakes called dosa play an important role in the cuisine of southern India. Here they accompany sambar, a simple stew flavored with masala paste, coconut milk and tamarind concentrate. Serve with a spicy chutney and a fresh mango for dessert.

Sambar

2 cups (500 mL)
20 minutes preparation
30 minutes cooling
1 hour cooking

This aromatic stew goes well with any starchy food. For an authentic flavor use asafetida (a resin with a taste of garlic) and tamarind (a tart brown fruit)—both available from Indian food shops.

COCONUT MILK:
1½ cups dried unsweetened OR
   freshly grated coconut
   (375 mL)
2½ cups boiling water
   (625 mL)

COOKED PEAS:
½ cup yellow split peas
   (125 mL)
½ tsp turmeric powder (2 mL)

MASALA PASTE:
1 tbsp mustard seeds (15 mL)
1 tbsp cumin seeds (15 mL)
2 tsp coriander seeds (10 mL)
4 tbsp clarified butter (see
   p. 60) OR oil (50 mL)
1" (2.5 cm) fresh ginger, peeled
   and thinly sliced
1–2 hot chili peppers
½ tsp asafetida (2 mL) OR 2
   cloves garlic

OTHER INGREDIENTS:
1 cup sliced okra OR green
   beans (250 mL)
2 tsp tamarind concentrate OR
   lime juice (10 mL)
½ tsp salt (2 mL)
2 tbsp chopped fresh coriander
   OR mint leaves (25 mL)

For coconut milk, combine coconut and boiling water in a blender or food processor. Run at high speed for 5 minutes. Let rest until cool enough to handle (about 20 minutes).

Line a colander with cheesecloth or nylon sheer material. Pour cooled coconut mixture into cloth and drain. Squeeze out as much liquid as possible. Discard fibrous pulp.

For cooked peas, bring split peas, turmeric and coconut milk to a simmer. Stir at first to prevent sticking. Simmer until peas have softened (about 45 minutes).

For masala paste, toast mustard, cumin and coriander seeds in a dry frying pan until popping. Put in a blender or food processor with butter, ginger, chili and asafetida. Blend until smooth, scraping down sides as necessary. Fry masala paste on low heat until aromatic (about 10 minutes).

To assemble stew, stir the fried masala mixture, okra, tamarind and salt into cooked peas. Simmer until okra has softened (about 5 minutes). Serve immediately, or let cool and reheat. Serve over dosa and garnish with freshly chopped coriander leaves.

Dosa

8 pancakes
20 minutes preparation
1 day soaking

Prepared dosa batter can be the base for a delicious fast meal.

Soak rice and lentils in 3 cups (750 mL) water for 8 to 24 hours. Pulverize mixture in a blender or food processor. The consistency should be about that of pancake batter. Stir in yeast and soak another 8 to 24 hours. (This mixture can be kept in the refrigerator for up to 2 weeks.)

Stir in onion and salt. Wipe a well-seasoned frying pan with a dab of oil and heat on medium heat. Pour in enough batter to form a thin patty. Cook both sides until lightly browned.

Serve dosa with sambar spooned over the first cooked side.

1 cup brown rice (250 mL)
½ cup lentils OR black-eyed
  peas (125 mL)
1 tsp dry active yeast (5 mL)
½ cup finely diced onion
  (125 mL)
¼ tsp salt (1 mL)

Raita

4 servings
10 minutes preparation

Nothing cools the heat of a fiery curry better than yogurt.

Mix together yogurt and additional ingredient(s). Toast seeds in a dry frying pan until they pop. Sprinkle over top.

1 cup yogurt (250 mL)
⅓ cup of 1 or 2 additional
  ingredients: grated cucumber,
  chunks of boiled potato, diced
  banana, minced sweet onion,
  chopped fresh mint or
  coriander leaves OR grated
  coconut (75 mL)
1 tbsp mustard, cumin OR
  coriander seeds (optional)
  (15 mL)

Holland

In the Netherlands the government assists in the development of produce with superior flavor and nutrition—unlike so many of our vegetable varieties that have been bred for looks, ease of harvesting and long shelf life.

The locally grown produce available to us in summer gives us a hint of the freshness and superb flavor the Dutch enjoy year round. Huzarensla, or soldier's salad, relies on the nutty flavor of freshly dug potatoes. Served over melba toast and accompanied by slices of Gouda or Edam cheese, it can be the centerpiece of a fine Dutch meal. Start with a refreshing tomato soup. Finish with the low fat hang-op topped with fresh fruit. If you have not planned ahead, use sour cream or yogurt.

Huzarensla

4 servings
20 minutes preparation
15 minutes cooking

For extra color and flavor use yellow potatoes (available in some specialty markets).

10 small (2 lb) uniformly sized
   new potatoes (1 kg)
1 tsp salt (5 mL)
2 cups green beans (preferably
   the wide European style pole
   beans), cut in 2" (5-cm)
   lengths (500 mL)
2 eggs, lightly beaten
3 tbsp cider vinegar (50 mL)
¼ tsp ground peppercorns
   (1 mL)
½ cup chopped sweet red onion
   (125 mL)
1 head Boston lettuce
¼ cup shredded cooked beets
   (optional) (50 mL)

Put potatoes and salt in a small pot and add ½" (1 cm) water. Bring to a boil and simmer just until tender (about 15 minutes). Steam green beans until bright green (about 4 minutes). Refresh in cold water.

Briefly rinse potatoes in cold water and, if you like, peel off their skins. Cut in bite-sized pieces. Toss warm potatoes with eggs, then gently toss in vinegar, pepper, and onion. Finally, mix in beans.

Line a serving bowl with 2 or more layers of lettuce leaves. For color, garnish with beets.

Because raw eggs and chopped onions can turn sour within a few hours, this salad should be served right away, or at least the same day it's made. Let your guests help themselves, putting salad and lettuce on pieces of melba toast and garnishing with the beets.

Fresh Tomato Soup

4 servings
15 minutes preparation

Blanching and seeding the tomatoes takes only a moment, and greatly improves this soup's texture.

Blanch tomatoes in boiling water for 30 seconds. Dip in cold water and slip off skins. Cut in half and scoop out seeds with your little finger. Coarsely chop flesh.

On medium heat in a medium-sized pot, slowly bring tomatoes, water, thyme and bay leaf to a simmer. Meanwhile melt butter and gently fry onion and pepper. Add fried ingredients to simmering tomato mixture, with salt and pepper. Serve hot.

8 medium (2 lb) fresh
  vine-ripened tomatoes (1 kg)
1 cup water OR stock (see p.
  92) (250 mL)
4 sprigs fresh thyme OR ½ tsp
  dried (2 mL)
1 bay leaf
2 tbsp butter (25 mL)
1 cup diced onion (250 mL)
½ cup seeded and diced green
  sweet pepper (125 mL)
¼ tsp salt (1 mL)
¼ tsp ground black
  peppercorns (1 mL)

Hang-Op

4 servings plus 2½ cups whey (600 mL)
5 minutes preparation
48 hours thickening
6 hours draining

When you "hang up" the buttermilk to drain, you get two products: delicate curd and yellow whey, which contains most of the milk's water-soluble vitamins and minerals, and makes a refreshing beverage.

Let buttermilk thicken by leaving it at room temperature for 48 hours. Pour into a colander with 4 layers of moist cheesecloth or a single layer of nylon sheer material. If the liquid flowing through is milky, recycle this through the cloth until it is a clear yellow whey. Tie up the corners and hang it from the knob of a kitchen cabinet with a bowl underneath to catch the whey.

In about 6 hours the curd should be thick and creamy. Scrape into a bowl and serve with tender fresh fruit.

1 quart commercial buttermilk
  (1 L)

Peaches

Fine flavor, fragrance, abundance, nutrition and low cost have made peaches second only to apples in world production. You can use them in place of apples in your favorite pie, strudel, cobbler (see p. 79), betty and crisp recipes; or for a special touch serve them with sparkling wine, whipped cream (see p. 47), stirred custard, zabaglione (see p. 83) or shortcake (see p. 32).

But don't stop with dessert. Peaches are so delicious and the season so short that you should enjoy them in every course of a meal. The Iranians are experts at using fruits in savory as well as sweet courses. This menu features peaches in koresh (an aromatic stew served over basmati rice), with yogurt in borani salad, and in a fruit compote for dessert.

½ cup split peas (125 mL)
3 cups stock (see p. 92) OR
  water (750 mL)
1 large eggplant
4 tbsp olive oil (50 mL)
1 cup diced onion (250 mL)
½ cup coarsely chopped
  almonds (125 mL)
1 hot chili pepper, minced
  (wash hands afterwards) OR
  ¼ tsp cayenne (1 mL)
4 cups bite-sized chunks of
  mixed vegetables: green or
  wax beans, zucchini, new
  potatoes OR okra (1 L)
1½ cups peeled and sliced
  peaches (375 mL)
2 tbsp chopped parsley
  (25 mL)
1 tsp marjoram (5 mL)
2 cloves garlic, minced
½ tsp ground turmeric (2 mL)
¼ tsp orange zest (1 mL)
¼ tsp grated nutmeg (1 mL)
¼ tsp rose water (optional)
  (1 mL)

Khoresh

8 servings
30 minutes preparation
45 minutes cooking

The peas used for thickening this stew also provide a protein complement for the rice with which it is served. Almonds (related to peaches) add a compatible flavor and contrasting texture.

Bring peas and stock to a simmer, stirring at first to prevent sticking. Cut eggplant into bite-sized chunks, leaving some skin on each one. Put in a bowl and dust with 2 tbsp salt (25 mL).

After 30 minutes drain eggplant, then rinse and pat dry. Heat oil in a frying pan and add eggplant. Add onion, almonds and chili, and fry until everything browns. When peas begin to thicken (about 45 minutes), add mixed vegetables. Simmer until they soften (about 5 to 10 minutes).

Add fried ingredients, peaches and remaining flavorings. Simmer 5 minutes. Serve right away with rice. Leftovers keep and reheat well.

Basmati Rice

4 servings
5 minutes preparation
20 minutes cooking

Basmati is a naturally white and aromatic rice available at Middle Eastern and Indian shops and some natural food stores

Bring 2 cups (500 mL) water and salt to a boil. Meanwhile rinse rice. Add to boiling water, then cover and reduce heat to medium-low. Do not stir. Rice will be ready to eat in 20 minutes.

¼ tsp salt (1 mL)
1 cup basmati rice (250 mL)

Borani

4 servings
10 minutes preparation

If your yogurt is runny, let it sit in a colander lined with cheesecloth to drain for a couple of hours.

Steam spinach in water that clings to leaves only until it wilts (about 1 minute). Immerse in cold water to stop the cooking, then drain well. Gently whisk together yogurt, lemon juice, oil, mint, cumin and salt. Stir in blanched spinach and peaches.

Serve immediately, garnished with toasted sesame seeds.

4 cups (10 oz) spinach OR chard, washed and coarsely chopped (1 L)
2 cups thick yogurt (500 mL)
1 tbsp lemon juice (15 mL)
1 tbsp olive oil (15 mL)
1 tbsp chopped fresh mint (15 mL) OR ½ tsp dried (2 mL)
½ tsp ground cumin (2 mL)
¼ tsp salt (1 mL)
1 cup peeled, pitted and sliced peaches (250 mL)
1 tbsp toasted sesame seeds (15 mL)

Peach Compote

8 servings
20 minutes preparation
1 hour cooling

If your peaches are ripening more quickly than you can use them, this is a good way to keep them for an additional week.

Combine honey, water, salt, allspice and pepper. Bring to a simmer. Meanwhile bring a large pot of water to a boil. Immerse peaches for 30 seconds, then rinse in cold water and slip off skins.

Add peaches to marinade, reduce heat and poach for 4 minutes. Remove from heat and cool, uncovered. When mixture is lukewarm stir in rose water. Compote can be eaten now, but flavor continues to improve for a day. For crunch serve with almond macaroons (see p. 5).

½ cup honey (125 mL)
1½ cups water OR white wine (375 mL)
pinch salt
12 corns allspice
12 corns black pepper
8 peaches
¼ tsp rose water (available in drug stores and Middle Eastern food stores) (1 mL)

Sweet Red Peppers

Usually red peppers are less common and more expensive than green ones. But since the opposite is the case in late summer, I take advantage of the low prices then to buy a bushel of them.

When it comes to cooking peppers I think of Hungary, where paprika (literally "pepper") plays such an important role. For an end-of-summer Hungarian meal, a plate of lesco and boiled potatoes is a perfect main course. Clear the palate with black radish salad and finish with Hungarian sweet noodles—they make dessert a good source of protein.

Lesco

4 tbsp vegetable oil (50 mL)
3 cups onion crescents (750 mL)
6 cups (2 lb) sweet peppers, cut in 2″ (5-cm) strips (1500 mL/ 1 kg)
3 cups peeled and coarsely chopped tomatoes (750 mL)
½ hot pepper, minced OR ⅛ tsp cayenne (0.5 mL)
¼ cup red wine vinegar (50 mL)
3 tbsp chopped fresh dill (optional) (50 mL)
¼ tsp salt (1 mL)

8 servings
15 minutes preparation

Especially attractive with a colorful mixture of peppers. Any leftovers are exceptionally good cold.

Heat oil in frying pan on medium heat and add, in this order, onion, sweet peppers, tomatoes and hot peppers. Stir-fry until softened (about 5 minutes). Stir in vinegar, dill and salt. Let sit uncovered until ready to serve. Reheat or serve cold with flavored boiled potatoes, spätzle (see p. 117) or cornmeal polenta (see p. 61). Top each serving with a dollop of sour cream.

Flavored Potatoes

4 servings
5 minutes preparation
20 minutes cooking

New potatoes need little or no embellishment, but for a change you can flavor the cooking water with your choice of flavoring.

1 tsp salt (5 mL)
1 or more flavorings: 2 crushed garlic cloves, 1 bay leaf, 1 sprig or tea-bag of mint, 1 tbsp (15 mL) caraway seeds
1½ lb small new potatoes, cleaned (750 mL)

Bring 2 cups (500 mL) water to a simmer with salt and desired flavoring(s). Before water boils add potatoes. Cook until softened (15 to 20 minutes). Don't prick them any more than necessary, or they'll become waterlogged.

Drain and serve promptly with butter and pepper

Radish Salad

4 servings
10 minutes preparation
30 minutes marinating

Black radishes—milder than red and at their best in the fall—are slowly becoming more widely available.

Stir together vinegar, oil, honey, mint and salt. Toss with radishes. Let them sit for ½ hour, stirring periodically. Drain and serve in mounds on lettuce leaves.

3 tbsp cider vinegar (50 mL)
2 tbsp vegetable oil (30 mL)
1 tsp honey (5 mL)
1 tsp chopped mint (5 mL)
¼ tsp salt (1 mL)
1½ cups peeled and thinly
  sliced black radishes OR sliced
  (unpeeled) mild red ones
  (375 mL)

Sweet Noodles

4 servings
10 minutes preparation

Bring a large pot of water to a boil. Meanwhile melt honey, butter and cinnamon. When water boils add noodles. Cook only until al dente (about 2 minutes for fresh noodles, 5 minutes for dried). Drain and place on prewarmed plates. Drizzle with warm honey-butter mixture, then sprinkle on cottage cheese and nuts. Serve immediately.

If you don't want do all the cooking in the middle of dinner, use a trick from my restaurant days. Cook the noodles before dinner, then refresh them in cold water for up to 1 hour. Put a pot of warm water on the stove and adjust heat so it reaches a boil by the end of the meal. When ready to serve, put noodles in a strainer and dip in the boiling water just long enough to reheat (about 30 seconds). Finish as above.

⅓ cup honey (75 mL)
¼ cup butter (60 mL)
½ tsp ground cinnamon
  (2 mL)
⅔ lb fresh egg noodles or
  fettucine OR ½ lb dried
  (250 g)
1 cup crumbled cottage cheese
  OR Ricotta (see p. 50)
  (250 mL)
¼ cup chopped walnuts
  (50 mL) OR 2 tbsp poppyseeds
  (25 mL)

End of Summer

When the evenings become a little cooler, you may not be so averse to turning on the oven. One of my favorite end-of-summer meals consists of souffléed potatoes, with fresh corn succotash and a sliced tomato salad (see p. 65) dusted with chopped fresh basil leaves and drizzled with olive oil. For dessert, make a peach cobbler—it can bake at the same time as the potatoes.

Souffléed Potatoes

4 large potatoes
15 minutes preparation
1 hour baking

4 medium Idaho-type potatoes
3 tbsp butter (50 mL)
½ cup finely diced onion
  (125 mL)
2 egg whites
¼ cup milk (50 mL)
1 tsp prepared horseradish OR
  mustard (5 mL)
¼ tsp salt (1 mL)

Preheat oven to 400°F (200°C). Clean, pierce and bake potatoes until softened (about 45 minutes). Meanwhile, slowly fry onions in butter. Beat egg whites to soft peaks.

Remove potatoes from oven and cut ovals from the tops. Scoop out most of the flesh and put in a bowl. Beat in fried onions, milk, horseradish and salt. Fold in beaten egg whites.

Scoop mixture into potato jackets, or pipe in with a large star-shaped nozzle (see p. 24). Return potatoes to hot oven and bake again until lightly browned (about 10 minutes). Serve right away as a main course.

⋏Succotash

4 servings
15 minutes preparation
5 minutes cooking

4 tbsp butter (50 mL)
½ cup diced onion (125 mL)
1½ cups assorted vegetables:
  freshly shelled Romano
  beans; fresh green beans;
  diced new potatoes, white
  turnip, sweet peppers (preferably red); fresh or frozen
  lima beans (500 mL)
2 cups corn kernels (freshly cut
  from about 4 ears) (500 mL)
2 tbsp whipping cream
  (optional) (25 mL)
pinch salt
grind pepper

To cut the kernels from corn cobs, slide a sharp knife from the tip to the stem.

Heat butter and fry the onion and vegetable(s). When softened, add the corn and 2 tbsp (25 mL) water. Cook briefly, then add cream, salt and pepper. Serve right away.

Peach Cobbler

8 servings
20 minutes preparation
30 minutes baking

Preheat oven to 400°F (200°C). To prepare filling, whisk together flour, honey, butter, egg yolks, lemon juice, mace and salt in a 2-quart (2-L) casserole. Stir in prepared peaches. Wipe edges clean.

To prepare topping, sift together flour, baking powder and salt. Cut in butter until pieces are the size of barley corns. Whisk together the buttermilk and honey. Fluff the flour while slowly dribbling in the buttermilk and stir until mixed.

Drop about 8 mounds of topping on the peaches. Put in oven and bake until golden brown (about 30 minutes). Serve with whipped cream or ice cream.

FILLING:
⅓ cup flour OR arrowroot
  (75 mL)
¼ cup honey (50 mL)
1 tbsp butter (15 mL)
2 egg yolks, lightly beaten
1 tbsp lemon juice (15 mL)
¼ tsp ground mace OR nutmeg
  (1 mL)
pinch salt
6 cups blanched, peeled and
  sliced peaches (1500 mL)

TOPPING:
1 cup sifted soft whole-wheat
  flour (250 mL)
1½ tsp baking powder (7 mL)
⅛ tsp salt (0.5 mL)
¼ cup butter, softened
  (50 mL)
½ cup buttermilk OR fresh
  milk with 1 tsp (5 mL)
  lemon juice (125 mL)
2 tbsp honey (25 mL)

First Frost

The first fall frost usually encourages a quick harvest of many garden vegetables. But you don't have to be a gardener to enjoy this menu of garlic soup—at its best with lots of freshly dug garlic—and cheese pie in a potato crust, served with fried green tomatoes and candied carrot sticks.

Garlic Soup

4 bowls
15 minutes preparation
15 minutes simmering

¼ cup olive oil (50 mL)
3 cups whole-wheat bread
 (preferably stale), cut into
 ½" (1-cm) cubes (750 mL)
2 heads (yes) garlic, peeled and
 minced
4 cups stock OR ¼ white wine
 and ¾ water with ½ tsp
 (2 mL) salt (1 L)
¼ cup chopped parsley
 (50 mL)
½ tsp chopped fresh rosemary
 OR sage (2 mL)
½ cup chopped tomato
 (optional) (125 mL)

Don't be intimidated by all the garlic—the flavor is actually quite tame. To simplify peeling, first crush the buds with the side of a cleaver or cook's knife. The skin then slips off easily.

Heat oil in a large frying pan on medium heat, add bread cubes and fry until golden brown. Add garlic and fry until it starts to turn brown. Add stock and simmer 10 minutes. Then add parsley, rosemary and tomato. Simmer another 5 minutes.

Can be served right away, but flavor will be more mellow if cooled then reheated.

Candied Carrot Sticks

4 servings
5 minutes preparation
12 minutes cooking

4 large carrots, peeled
¼ cup orange juice (50 mL)
2 tbsp butter (25 mL)

Cut carrots lengthwise in half. Cut halves into 2" to 3" (5 to 7.5-cm) lengths. Slice pieces in halves, thirds or quarters (depending on thickness). Pieces should be about the same size.

Put orange juice and carrots in a wide saucepan and steam, covered, over medium heat until carrots are nearly tender (about 8 minutes). Remove lid and turn up heat to high. If there is still some liquid in the pan, let it boil away. Add butter and fry carrots, tossing frequently, until they have a golden glaze. Serve immediately (no salt or pepper is needed).

Cheese Pie

8 servings
20 minutes (total) preparation
80 minutes (total) baking

The potato crust can be used for sweet fillings too.

Preheat oven to 400°F (200°C). Squeeze shredded potato through a cloth to extract most of the water. Whisk together flour, egg, oil and salt. Toss into potatoes.

Scoop mixture into a lightly oiled pie plate and press evenly across bottom and up sides. Even out the top edge. Bake until lightly browned (about 40 minutes). Shell need not be cooled before filling, but will keep for up to 1 week unrefrigerated.

To assemble, preheat oven to 325°F (160°C). Put cheeses, eggs, herb, coriander, pepper and half the milk in a blender or food processor. Blend until smooth. Add more milk until mixture is just liquid enough to flow.

Pour mixture into prepared crust. Bake until set (about 40 minutes; 50 minutes if crust has cooled). If cheese begins to puff or crack, immediately remove from oven. Let cool and set for 5 minutes before serving. Leftovers are best served at room temperature.

POTATO CRUST:
2 cups peeled, finely shredded
  potato (not new) (500 mL)
¼ cup soft whole-wheat flour
  (50 mL)
1 egg
1 tbsp vegetable oil (15 mL)
½ tsp salt (2 mL)

FILLING:
2 cups (1 lb) Ricotta, cottage
  OR cream cheese (500 mL/
  500 g)
1 cup (¼ lb) crumbled Feta OR
  blue cheese (125 g)
3 eggs
1 tsp chopped fresh sage,
  rosemary OR thyme (5 mL)
1 tsp ground coriander seeds
  (5 mL)
¼ tsp ground white peppercorns (1 mL)
½ cup milk (approx.)
  (125 mL)

Fried Green Tomatoes

4 servings
5 minutes preparation
5 minutes frying

Heat a heavy-bottomed frying pan on medium heat. Cut out tomato stems. Slice tomatoes vertically ¼" (5 mm) thick. When pan is hot, add oil, tomato slices and garlic.

Slowly fry until each side is lightly browned (about 5 minutes). Sprinkle with salt and pepper and serve.

3 medium tomatoes
2 tbsp olive oil (25 mL)
3 cloves garlic, minced
salt and pepper to taste

Fennel

Florence fennel (sometimes called anise) is at its best in fall. The bulb is the part of most interest. The feathery leaves can be chopped for use as an herb and the stringy stalk—not usually eaten—used to flavor stock (see p. 92).

Try this licorice-flavored vegetable in a salad. And since fennel is known to tame the side effects of beans, you might like to serve it with a main course of Italian baked beans. A light but rich-tasting zabaglione completes the Italian theme.

Fagioli al Forno

8 servings
15 minutes preparation
45 minutes cooking

6 cups cooked white beans (see p. 108) (1500 mL)
2 cups coarsely chopped tomatoes (500 mL)
1 cup diced onion (250 mL)
½ cup pitted olives, green or black (125 mL)
½ cup grated Parmesan cheese (125 mL)
¼ cup butter OR olive oil (50 mL)
4 cloves garlic, minced
1 tbsp mustard powder (15 mL)
½ tsp salt (unless cooked with beans) (2 mL)
6 oz Mozzarella cheese, sliced (200 g)

These baked beans from the Piedmont region are simply flavored with tomatoes and thickened with Parmesan cheese. To speed up the cooking, first heat ingredients on top of the stove before placing in a bean pot in the oven.

Combine everything except the Mozzarella and quickly heat in a saucepan until simmering. Reduce heat and simmer, uncovered, until mixture begins to thicken (about 30 minutes).

Preheat oven to 350°F (180°C). Transfer the thickening beans to an ovenproof casserole. Cover with Mozzarella and bake until cheese is browned (about 15 minutes). Serve right away or cool and reheat.

Fennel and Cucumber Salad

4 servings
5 minutes preparation
15 minutes marinating

MINT DRESSING:
⅓ cup olive oil (75 mL)
2 tbsp lemon juice (25 mL)
2 tbsp chopped fresh mint (25 mL) OR 2 tsp dried (10 mL)
1 clove garlic, minced
¼ tsp salt (1 mL)
⅛ tsp ground white peppercorns (0.5 mL)

Try to find either small "dill" cucumbers or the seedless English kind. To use regular cucumbers, peel off the waxed skin and scoop out the watery seeds. If the new crop of walnuts has arrived where you shop, by all means use them—last year's are likely to be rancid. Otherwise use olives or Feta cheese.

Combine all dressing ingredients and whisk with a fork until creamy.

Mix salad ingredients with dressing and let marinate for 15 minutes to 1 hour, tossing periodically.

SALAD:
1½ cups bite-sized pieces fennel (375 mL)
3 cups bite-sized pieces cucumber (750 mL)
½ cup walnut halves (optional) (125 mL)
½ cup pitted black olives (optional) (125 mL)
½ cup diced Feta cheese (optional) (125 mL)

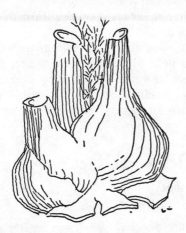

Zabaglione

4 servings
10 minutes preparation

Because steady whisking is required, you may be tempted to use an electric beater. Don't—the speed will make the foam so light it may collapse. Though you may prefer to use the top of a double boiler, it's quicker to cook in a heavy-bottomed pan set on medium heat.

6 oz Marsala OR other sweet wine (175 mL)
3 tbsp honey (50 mL)
6 large egg yolks
pinch salt

Fill a large bowl with cold water. Pour all ingredients into a heavy-bottomed saucepan. With slow but steady whisking, heat on low heat. As mixture warms it will become foamy. Whisk a little faster, making an effort to scrape the bottom and all the corners.

As soon as mixture is thick enough to leave a trail when whisk is lifted, remove pot from heat. Dip in the waiting cold water and continue to whisk until mixture has cooled slightly (about 2 minutes).

Serve right away in stemmed wine glasses, or as a sauce over fresh fruit or cake.

Celeriac

Available during the fall and early winter months, celeriac (celery root or knob celery) has a richer flavor than ordinary celery—and no strings. Most often it is sold with the dark green stalks removed, leaving a root that looks like a tangled ball of brown twine, about the size of a softball. Choose one that is heavy for its size and avoid any that feel soft. Celeriac will keep for several weeks in a cool damp place.

To use the white interior flesh, rinse off as much dirt as possible, then slice off the knobby skin with a knife. Brush the exposed flesh with lemon juice to keep it white. Trimmed celeriac is delicious raw in salad, but for a fine main dish, try it in an Italian sfromato. To prepare this dinner menu, start by poaching the pears for dessert. Then make the sfromato and, while it is cooking, prepare the bagna cauda appetizer and a side vegetable.

Bagna Cauda

4 to 8 servings
10 minutes preparation

This convivial "hot bath" for dipping vegetables comes from northern Italy.

HOT BATH:
½ cup butter (125 mL)
½ cup olive oil (125 mL)
5 cloves garlic, minced
1 tsp vinegar OR lemon juice (5 mL)
½ tsp salt (2 mL)
¼ tsp ground white peppercorns (1 mL)

VEGETABLES:
8 cups assorted vegetables (see recipe), cut in finger-sized pieces (2 L)

Combine all ingredients for the hot bath in a small, heavy pot. Place on low heat until butter melts, then remove from heat and let rest 5 minutes. Serve sauce in pot, keeping it warm over a candle flame.

Have ready an attractively arranged platter of vegetables: carrot, celeriac, kohlrabi and celery sticks; sweet pepper and fennel slices; parsley leaves; trimmed green onions; broccoli and cauliflower flowerets; and whole small green beans and mushrooms. Dip the vegetables into the hot bath and enjoy.

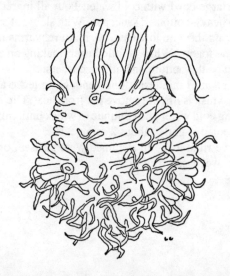

Celeriac Sfromato

4 servings
15 minutes preparation
30 minutes baking

A cross between a quiche and a soufflé. There is no crust (as with a quiche) and the eggs are not separated (as for a soufflé).

Preheat oven to 350°F (180°C). Immerse eggs in a bowl of hot tap water. Heat oil in a frying pan. When hot, add celeriac and onion. When softened (about 5 minutes) stir in flour, then add milk, cheese and pepper. Bring to a simmer and remove from heat after mixture thickens.

Beat warm eggs until creamy and lemon-colored (about 3 minutes). Fold into vegetable mixture. Pour into a buttered 2-quart (2-L) casserole. Bake, uncovered, until set (about 30 minutes).

Serve right away with steamed greens (see p. 40) and tomato slices for color.

4 large eggs
3 tbsp olive oil OR clarified butter (50 mL)
2 cups peeled and diced celeriac (500 mL)
1 cup diced onion (250 mL)
3 tbsp soft whole-wheat flour (50 mL)
1½ cups milk (375 mL)
½ cup freshly grated Parmesan cheese (125 mL)
½ tsp ground white peppercorns (2 mL)

Poached Pears

12 servings
15 minutes preparation
3 hours baking

The trick to preparing this elegant yet simple dessert is long, slow cooking, preferably well ahead of time— the flavor improves for several days after cooking.

Preheat oven to 275°F (140°C). Core pears from the blossom ends, leaving stems intact. Combine nuts and half the honey with cinnamon and nutmeg. Stuff mixture into pears. Place snugly in a deep casserole.

Combine wine, remaining honey and cardamom. Pour over pears. Cover dish and place in oven. Bake until pears are tender and skins chocolate brown (about 3 hours). Turn off heat and let slowly cool in oven.

The pears are ready to serve right away, but they'll taste even better if they marinate for a day (save the wine marinade for another use). Serve stem up in an attractive dish, perhaps garnished with whipped cream.

12 large pears, any firm winter variety
1 cup finely chopped walnuts OR almonds (250 mL)
⅔ cup honey (150 mL)
½ tsp ground cinnamon (2 mL)
¼ tsp freshly grated nutmeg (1 mL)
2½ cups red wine (625 mL)
3 pods cardamom, white or green, broken open

Extending the Harvest

A great way to prolong the life of fresh summer vegetables for several extra weeks is to preserve them in a marinade. Serve à la Grècque vegetables either as a salad or as a side dish with burek, another Greek dish—its crust will provide the crunch the vegetables have lost. In keeping with the Greek theme, serve figs stuffed with cheese for dessert. (They can be made well ahead of time and served on a moment's notice.)

⚑ Vegetables à la Grècque

12 servings
30 minutes preparation
1 day marinating

The vegetables will absorb the marinade better if they start out dry and warm—a hair drier works very well. Fresh coriander adds a special Greek flavor.

⅔ cup olive oil (150 mL)
⅓ cup lemon juice (75 mL)
2 tbsp chopped fresh coriander (25 mL) OR 2 tsp chopped oregano (10 mL)
2 cloves garlic, minced
¼ tsp salt (1 mL)
⅛ tsp ground peppercorns (1 mL)
6 cups of 3 or 4 vegetables (figures are suggested cooking minutes): carrot sticks (10), celery sticks (8), white part of green onions (7), fennel sticks cut from bulb (6), cauliflower flowerets (6), broccoli flowerets (5), green or wax bean segments (5), eggplant chunks with skin attached (4), zucchini sticks (4), red or green sweet pepper strips (4)

Whisk together olive oil, lemon juice, coriander, garlic, salt and pepper. Let rest while you prepare vegetables.

Choose a colorful combination of three or four vegetables. Blanch each kind in at least 4 quarts (4 L) boiling water only until it is just beginning to soften (see list for recommended cooking minutes). Remove from water and drain on a cake rack. Promptly blow with a hair drier set on high heat. When warm and dry, toss with vinaigrette.

Keep at room temperature and toss every few hours for 1 day. Serve as an appetizer, a salad over lettuce leaves, a side vegetable, or over cooked pasta as a main course. Leftovers keep in refrigerator for up to 3 weeks.

Burek

8 servings
20 minutes preparation
35 minutes baking

Carve this large cheese-stuffed pastry at the table.

Combine cheeses, cumin and oregano. (This can be done a day ahead.)

Preheat oven to 375°F (190°C). Place two sheets of phyllo on a clean dry towel to form a base about 12″ ×30″ (30 ×75 cm). Brush lightly with olive oil and sprinkle with sesame seeds. Lay down two more sheets, overlapping them in different places so there will be no bulges or weak spots. Again spread with olive oil and sesame seeds and follow with more sheets of pastry. Brush top layer generously with oil.

Spread cheese mixture along one long side, keeping it 2″ (5 cm) from edges. Lifting with towel, roll very loosely into a long "snake" (you may need some helping hands). Gently bend pastry into a coil, then slide onto a shiny baking sheet. Promptly place on an upper oven shelf and bake until golden (about 35 minutes).

Slide onto a prewarmed platter and serve with cooked greens (see p. 40).

1 cup Ricotta cheese (250 mL)
1 cup crumbled Feta cheese (250 mL)
1 tsp ground cumin seeds (5 mL)
2 tsp fresh OR dried oregano (10 mL)
10 sheets (½ lb) phyllo (strudel) pastry (250 g)
¼ cup sesame OR anise seeds (50 mL)
½ cup olive oil (125 mL)

Stuffed Figs

8 servings
15 minutes preparation
1 day soaking

Put figs and lemon slices in water and let sit overnight.

For the stuffing, put almonds in an unoiled frying pan and toast on low heat until aromatic (about 10 minutes). Cut a small hole in the bottom of each fig and insert a toasted almond.

Mash together cream cheese and Kasseri. Insert a dab into each fig—most easily done with the nozzle of a piping bag. Serve on a platter, stem ends up.

FIGS:
2 cups dried black mission figs (500 mL)
2 slices fresh lemon
2 cups water (500 mL)

STUFFING:
¼ cup whole unblanched almonds (50 mL)
¼ cup cream cheese (50 mL)
2 tbsp finely grated Kasseri OR aged Provolone cheese (25 mL)

Indian Summer

Fall weather is fickle—one day may be almost summery, and the next a foretaste of winter. So if you need to cook a meal ahead of time, you will probably want at least one dish that can be served either cold or hot, depending on the weather.

Fassoulada—a Greek bean soup that is equally good chilled or piping hot—makes an adaptable starter before a main dish of moussaka made with potatoes instead of eggplant. While the moussaka is baking, you can also have dessert in the oven. Served with a scoop of ice cream, Indian pudding is both refreshing enough for a warm day, and substantial enough for a chilly one. Add crunch to the meal with a salad either before or after the moussaka.

Fassoulada

4 cups cooked white beans (see
 p. 108) with their cooking
 liquid (1 L)
2 cups stock (see p. 92) OR
 water (500 mL)
¼ cup freshly squeezed lemon
 juice (50 mL)
½ tsp lemon zest (2 mL)
3 tbsp olive oil (50 mL)
6 cloves garlic, chopped
¼ tsp salt (unless cooked with
 beans) (1 mL)

8 servings
15 minutes preparation

A variation of navy bean soup with a refreshing lemon-garlic flavor. It's best made a day ahead.

Blend all ingredients in a blender or food processor. Bring to a simmer in a saucepan. Turn off heat and cool.

Serve either cool (it may need to be thinned) or reheated. Garnish with chopped mint, parsley or celery leaves.

Indian Pudding

8 servings
15 minutes preparation
2 hours baking

If you are in a hurry, the basic hot pudding mixture is delicious served unbaked.

6 cups milk (1500 mL)
2" (5 cm) cinnamon stick
½ nut nutmeg
½" (1 cm) fresh ginger, peeled
 and sliced
1 cup cornmeal (250 mL)
½ cup maple syrup (125 mL)
½ cup raisins (optional)
 (125 mL)
2 tbsp butter (25 mL)
⅛ tsp salt (0.5 mL)

Preheat oven to 350°F (180°C). Slowly heat 4 cups (1 L) of the milk with cinnamon, nutmeg and ginger on medium heat in a heavy-bottomed pot. When it reaches a simmer, remove from heat and pull out cinnamon, nutmeg and ginger. Whisk in cornmeal. Return to heat and simmer, stirring, until thick. Stir in syrup, raisins, butter and salt.

Pour mixture into a shallow casserole and cover with remaining milk (do not stir it in). Bake uncovered until top is crusted (about 2 hours). Serve with ice cream or whipped cream (see p. 47).

Potato Moussaka

8 servings
30 minutes preparation
45 minutes baking

Preheat oven to 350°F (180°C). Heat oil on high heat in a large frying pan. Add onions and potatoes and fry, scraping the bottom frequently. When lightly browned (about 10 minutes), reduce heat to medium and add flour. Stir well and add chickpeas, tomatoes, chickpea liquid, parsley, garlic, oregano, cinnamon, salt and pepper. Simmer for 5 minutes. Turn into a shallow 9" × 14" (22 × 35-cm) casserole.

To prepare topping, whisk together yogurt, egg yolks, cheese and flour. Pour evenly over vegetable mixture. Bake on a lower oven shelf until top is lightly browned (about 45 minutes).

Let cool 15 minutes before serving or, better yet, let cool completely, then reheat in a 325°F (160°C) oven for 20 minutes.

⅓ cup olive oil (75 mL)
2 cups onion crescents (500 mL)
6 cups (2 lb) new or red potato slices ¼" (5 mm) thick (1500 mL/1 kg)
5 tbsp flour (75 mL)
2 cups drained cooked chickpeas (see p. 108) (500 mL)
2 cups chopped tomatoes (500 mL)
1 cup chickpea cooking liquid (250 mL)
3 tbsp chopped parsley (50 mL)
4 cloves garlic, minced
1 tbsp chopped OR rubbed oregano (15 mL)
2 tsp ground cinnamon (10 mL)
salt and pepper to taste

TOPPING:
3 cups yogurt (750 mL)
3 egg yolks
½ cup grated Kasseri (available in Greek and some cheese shops) OR Romano cheese (125 mL)
1 tbsp flour (15 mL)

Raclette Picnic

Fall may seem an unusual time of year for a picnic, but raclette cooked over a campfire makes a welcome pause on a hike through the autumn woods. And if you'd rather stay home, it's just as good cooked in the fireplace or over a hibachi on the balcony.

Since the cheese tends to twist loose from a barbeque fork, try bending a coat hanger as illustrated. This works well until the cheese is nearly finished. Then put the remaining cheese bits on a piece of foil bent in the shape of a saucer, and set it over the coals until hot and bubbly. (Be sure to eat the rind—it's the best part.)

About 45 minutes before you want to eat, light a fire and start boiling the potatoes. Have on hand some coleslaw and an assortment of condiments.

Raclette

8 servings
15 minutes preparation

Raclette is a rich Swiss cheese with a thick brown rind. You can substitute a well aged Fontina, Provolone or Gruyère, but a cheap "Swiss" cheese will not give satisfactory results. Use whole, unpeeled red potatoes— they are attractive and hold together best.

4 lb boiled potatoes (2 kg)
3-lb (1.5-kg) wedge Raclette
cheese

Spear the wedge of cheese through the crust with a long-handled fork or a coat hanger bent as illustrated. Hold over hot coals until cheese begins to bubble. (If it runs before it browns, it's too close to the heat.) With a large knife scrape the melted cheese onto a plate.

Eat right away with potatoes and condiments—tiny onions and gherkins are traditional, but you might also consider dills, chilies, olives, freshly grated horseradish, prepared mustard and fresh apple chutney. Raclette goes best with a dry white wine.

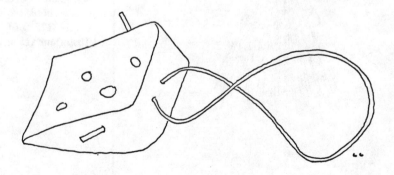

Coleslaw

8 servings
20 minutes preparation
15 minutes marinating

Chinese and Savoy cabbage make the tenderest and mildest salads. Ordinary green and white cabbage are crunchier and more dominating in flavor. Red cabbage adds sweetness and color.

If the cabbage tastes strong, soak in ice water for ½ hour. Combine oil, vinegar, honey and mustard powder. Drain and toss cabbage with prepared apples, peppers, celery, sunflower seeds and dill. Toss in dressing. You can eat this coleslaw right away, but it tastes better if you wait 15 minutes. If kept cool, it will remain in good condition for several hours. You might like to serve it in a bowl made from an outer cabbage leaf.

4 cups finely shredded cabbage (1 L)
¼ cup vegetable oil (50 mL)
¼ cup cider vinegar (50 mL)
1 tbsp honey (15 mL)
½ tsp mustard powder (2 mL)
½ cup diced apples, dipped in lemon juice (125 mL)
½ cup diced red or green sweet peppers, pith and seeds removed (125 mL)
½ cup diced celery stalks (125 mL)
¼ cup sunflower seeds (50 mL)
¼ cup chopped fresh dill leaves (50 mL)

Fresh Apple Chutney

1½ cups (400 mL)
10 minutes preparation

Be sure the spices are fresh, otherwise the chutney may be bitter.

Toss all ingredients together and serve immediately. Will keep for several days in refrigerator.

1½ cups peeled, cored and shredded apples (200 mL)
1 tbsp freshly grated ginger (15 mL)
2 tsp lemon juice (10 mL)
2 tsp vegetable oil (10 mL)
1 tsp ground coriander seeds (5 mL)
½ tsp ground fennel OR anise seeds (2 mL)
½ tsp ground cinnamon (1 mL)
pinch salt

Making Stock

Homemade stock not only makes soups, sauces, stews, grains and beans taste better—it's also a practical way to extract the nutrition and flavor from many vegetable trimmings that otherwise would be thrown away. Although it takes a few hours, most of the time is unattended simmering and cooling.

There is no set formula for making stock. Just follow the general guidelines below. Then, with a good supply on hand, see how easy it is to make a hearty cabbage soup. Served with a bowl of kasha, it makes a fine Russian meal.

4 cups peeled and sliced onions (1 L)

2 cups peeled and sliced carrots (500 mL)

2 cups sliced celery stalks (500 mL)

4 cups assorted vegetables: artichoke stems and leaf-tips, asparagus bottoms, cauliflower cores and leaves, presoaked chickpeas, fennel stalks, green bean tips and stems, green leek stems, tomato cores (1 L)

2 tbsp salt (25 mL)

1 bay leaf

1 tbsp rubbed basil (15 mL)

1 tbsp rubbed thyme (15 mL)

1 tsp rubbed sage (5 mL)

½ head garlic, cut crosswise in half

12 whole black peppercorns

1 hot chili, slit in half

½ nut nutmeg

Vegetable Stock

4 quarts (4 L)
15 minutes preparation
1½ hours heating and simmering
1 hour cooling

You should have a tall narrow pot that will hold 2 gallons (8 L). There's no need to measure ingredients exactly. Just make sure you heat everything very slowly, to extract the most flavor.

You may also include beets, apple cores, potato skins and winter squash, but they will discolor or make the stock cloudy. DON'T include cabbage, zucchini, radish, cucumber, eggplant or leafy greens—they will either leave a bitter taste or absorb more flavor than they contribute.

Put all ingredients in stock pot (it should be half to two-thirds full). Cover with cold water and put on the lid. Set pot on low heat. It should take about 1 hour to reach a simmer. Simmer gently for about 30 minutes. (Don't stir, or stock will turn cloudy; don't cook any longer, or it will lose flavor.) Turn off heat and slowly cool to room temperature (about 1 hour).

When cooled, pour through a colander lined with cheesecloth into a bowl. Discard vegetables—there's little flavor or nutrition left in them—and let any particles left in the stock settle in bowl. Pour stock into a storage container. It will keep for 2 weeks in the refrigerator; for longer storage, put in small containers and keep in freezer for up to 4 months.

Cabbage Soup

8 servings
20 minutes preparation
5 minutes simmering

To avoid a strong cabbagey taste, fry the cabbage before adding it to the hot stock, then cook for only a short time.

Heat the stock. When it reaches a simmer add, one at a time, carrots, potatoes, celeriac and parsnip. While these soften, heat butter in a large frying pan. Add, one at a time, onions, mushrooms, cabbage and caraway. Fry on high heat, stirring constantly, until everything is softened. Then stir fried ingredients into broth. Add dill and vinegar or sauerkraut. Let simmer 5 minutes.

Top each serving with a dollop of sour cream. Accompany with a plate of kasha or thickly sliced dark bread, pickles, prepared mustard and grated horseradish.

5 cups Vegetable Stock
 (1250 mL)
½ cup diced carrots (125 mL)
1 cup diced potatoes (250 mL)
½ cup diced celeriac OR celery
 (125 mL)
½ cup diced parsnip (125 mL)
4 tbsp clarified butter OR ½
 butter and ½ oil (50 mL)
1 cup onion slivers (250 mL)
½ cup sliced mushrooms
 (125 mL)
4 cups chopped green and/or
 red cabbage (1 L)
¼ tsp caraway seeds (1 mL)
¼ cup coarsely chopped fresh
 dill (50 mL)
¼ cup cider vinegar (50 mL)
 OR 1 cup sauerkraut
 (250 mL)

Kasha

4 servings
5 minutes preparation
20 minutes cooking

In Russia, the name kasha signifies any cooked grain. But for us it usually means the most common Russian grain—buckwheat (see p. 154 for more information). For exceptionally fluffy kasha, cook it first with the egg. If you prefer to skip this step simply add the grain to boiling water.

Bring water and salt to a boil in a saucepan. Meanwhile heat a frying pan on medium heat while tossing buckwheat and egg until each grain is coated and dry. Stir into boiling water, cover pot and turn heat to low. Simmer until water has been absorbed (about 20 minutes). Serve right away.

4 cups water (1 L)
½ tsp salt (2 mL)
2 cups raw OR toasted
 buckwheat (500 mL)
1 large egg, lightly beaten

Home-Baked Breads

The quick-rise method below makes it possible to have a fragrant freshly baked loaf on the table in less than two hours. Essene bread takes more time but the results are worth it. Even when it contains nothing more than sprouted wheat, it tastes almost like cake.

Quick-Rise Bread

1 medium loaf
15 minutes preparation
30 minutes rising
45 minutes baking

If using a food processor for kneading, don't try to increase the quantities in this recipe—your machine probably won't be able to handle any more. It is not necessary to sift the flour before measuring it. The vitamin C helps speed the growth of the yeast.

½ cup warm water (125 mL)
1 tbsp honey (15 mL)
1 tbsp dry active (baking) yeast (15 mL)
25 mg pulverized vitamin C OR ascorbic acid
2 cups hard whole-wheat flour (500 mL)
2 cups soft whole-wheat flour (500 mL)
¼ cup 40% gluten flour OR white flour (50 mL)
¼ tsp salt (1 mL)
1 cup milk, buttermilk OR water (250 mL)
1 tbsp butter OR oil (15 mL)

Preheat oven to 175°F (80°C). Combine water, honey, yeast and vitamin C in a small bowl.

If using a food processor, put the flours and salt in the bowl. When yeast begins to bubble, give it a stir and pour into the spinning machine. Follow with milk and butter. Without turning machine off, process until a ball of dough has formed and bounced on the blades for at least 4 minutes. (If your processor overheats or stalls, divide dough and process half at a time.) Remove dough and knead briefly with lightly oiled hands.

To make by hand, combine all liquid ingredients with half the flour. Stir until well mixed, then knead in remaining flour. A little more flour may be required. Knead for at least 8 minutes.

Shape (machine-or hand-) kneaded dough into a loaf. Put in a bread pan and place in the warm oven. Then turn off heat. When dough has nearly doubled in size (about 30 minutes) remove it from oven.

To bake, preheat oven to 350°F (180°C). When heated, put in the risen dough. Bake until crust is lightly browned (about 40 minutes). Let bread cool on a rack for 15 minutes before slicing.

Essene Bread

1 1-lb loaf (500 g)
20 minutes preparation
3 days sprouting
4 hours rising
1¼ hours baking

A modern method for making an ancient bread.

Put wheat in a 1-quart (1-L) jar and fill it with water. Cover with cheesecloth, secure with a rubber band, and let sit 8 hours. Drain. Invert jar on a plate (to drain away excess water) with one edge against the rim (to let fresh air in). Store at room temperature in a dark place. Rinse wheat with fresh water at least once a day.

When sprouts are about ¼" (5 mm) long (about 3 days), grind drained berries in a food processor or food mill until they take on a doughy consistency. (If using a blender, do it in small batches.)

Mix in sunflower seeds. With oiled hands, shape the sticky dough into a round loaf and place on an oiled baking sheet. Let rise in a warm place until slightly risen (about 4 hours).

Preheat oven to 350°F (180°C). Bake bread until crust is crispy (about 1¼ hours). Let cool completely before slicing, or it will be exceedingly sticky. This moist bread does not stale, so it will keep in refrigerator for more than 1 week.

1½ cups soft wheat berries (375 mL)
¼ cup sunflower seeds, raisins OR chopped nuts (optional) (50 mL)

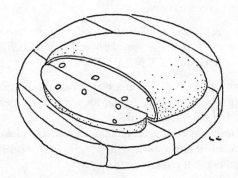

Sandwich Fillings

In most families back-to-school also means back-to-sandwich-making. But don't limit yourself to ordinary sliced bread. Quick-rise bread (see p. 94), hard rolls, burger buns, crusty stick bread, pitas, bagels, English muffins, pumpernickel bread and biscuits all make fine sandwiches.

Instead of butter and mayonnaise, consider mashed avocado, liptauer spread or tofu mayonnaise. For crispy coolness, use cucumbers and sweet peppers as well as tomatoes and lettuce; for crunch, try sun pickles or cheese crisps. As a special treat you might also include crunchy granola bars (see p. 159), brownies (see p. 37) or honey-lemon cookies (see p. 136).

Sun Pickles

1 quart (1 L)
10 minutes preparation
3 days marinating

These sun-ripened pickles are quicker and easier than the ordinary kind.

1½ cups water (400 mL)
½ cup cider vinegar (125 mL)
2 tbsp pickling salt (30 mL)
4 cups of 1 or more prepared
  vegetables: whole "dill"
  cucumbers or small zucchini
  with blossoms removed;
  cauliflowerets; carrot sticks;
  sweet pepper strips; turnip or
  rutabaga sticks
3 large flowers of dill OR sprigs
  of oregano

Bring water, vinegar and salt to a simmer. Arrange vegetables and dill attractively in a large, clean jar. Pour hot marinade over, making sure vegetables are completely covered. Jiggle the jar to release any air bubbles. Loosely cover the top.

Let jar sit at room temperature for at least 3 days, preferably in a sunny window. You can start using the pickles after 3 days. After 1 week put them in the refrigerator, where they will remain fresh and crispy for 1 month.

Tofu Mayonnaise

1 cup (250 mL)
5 minutes preparation

For the best flavor, use very fresh tofu; for the smoothest texture, look for a brand solidified with calcium sulfate (noted on the label).

½ lb tofu (250 g)
¼ cup vegetable oil (125 mL)
2 tbsp lemon juice OR vinegar
  (25 mL)
¼ tsp mustard powder (1 mL)
¼ tsp honey (1 mL)
¼ tsp salt (1 mL)
1 clove garlic (optional)

Combine all ingredients in a blender or food processor. Blend until smooth. Let sit for several minutes to permit flavors to amalgamate.

Use tofu mayonnaise as regular mayonnaise. Just be sure to finish it soon—it will remain fresh no more than 5 days in the refrigerator.

Liptauer Spread

½ lb (250 g)
10 minutes preparation

My version of a traditional Eastern European recipe. The butter and Feta not only improve the flavor and texture, but help to keep the spread fresh.

Blend all ingredients in a food processor or blender. Spread can be used right away, but flavor mellows after a few hours. Store in a covered container in refrigerator; it should remain fresh for 2 weeks.

1 cup (½ lb) cottage cheese OR
  Quark (250 mL/250 g)
¼ cup (2 oz) crumbled Feta
  cheese (50 mL/50 g)
3 tbsp yogurt OR sour cream
  (50 mL)
2 tbsp butter, softened
  (25 mL)
1 tbsp minced shallot OR onion
  (15 mL)
1 tsp sweet paprika (preferably
  Hungarian) (5 mL)
⅛ tsp ground caraway
  (0.5 mL)
⅛ tsp mustard powder
  (0.5 mL)
⅛ tsp hot paprika OR a pinch
  of cayenne (0.5 mL)

Cheese Crisps

8 crisps
5 minutes preparation

A crunchy, salty bite is often a welcome addition to a sandwich. Provolone works best, but feel free to experiment with other cheeses.

Place cheese in a seasoned or Teflon frying pan on low heat. The first time you do this you may have to adjust the heat, depending on your stove, pan and cheese. It should be warm enough that the cheese bubbles and sizzles, but not so hot that it burns before bubbling.

When bubbles are brown around the edges (about 5 minutes), turn slices over. Fry until lightly browned throughout. Cool and drain on paper.

Kept dry, cheese crisps will remain fresh for a month. Enjoy them in sandwiches or crumble them over salads, scrambled eggs and omelettes, steamed vegetables, grains or pasta.

8 slices firm, well aged cheese,
⅛"–¼" (3–5 mm) thick

Sprouts

You can easily convert a few square inches of kitchen space into an indoor garden by growing sprouts. Your produce will be inexpensive, you'll have none of the bug, fungus and weather hazards you can expect outdoors, and you'll be assured of both freshness and the absence of unwanted chemicals. All you need is a wide-mouthed glass bottle with gauze over the top.

Many varieties of sprouts can be grown at home, but the easiest and most reliable are alfalfa and red clover. Use them in salads (they're more nutritious than lettuce) or try an open-faced sprout melt with a bowl of squash soup for a fine light meal.

Easy Sprouting

1 quart (1 L)
15 minutes preparation
3 to 5 days sprouting

The key to high yield is to choose viable seeds—this year's crop. So look for a supplier with a rapid turnover of inventory. And remember that you don't want treated agricultural seeds.

2 tbsp alfalfa OR red clover seeds (25 mL)

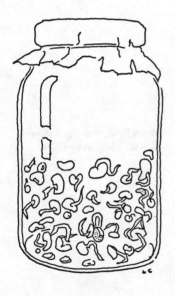

Put seeds in a wide-mouthed 1-quart (1-L) jar and add 1″ (2.5 cm) water. Cover jar with cheesecloth or some other porous material and secure with an elastic band. Let seeds soak for about 12 hours (after 24 hours they may start to mold).

Pour off the excess water. (Drink this nutritious liquid or, if it tastes bitter, give it to your plants.) Let seeds drain by inverting the jar on a plate and leaving one edge against the rim so fresh air can reach them. For the sweetest flavor, keep jar in the dark. Sprouts will begin to grow within a day or two.

Once a day, rinse and shake the seeds with 2 cups (500 mL) fresh water. Pour off water and again invert jar at an angle. The rinsing provides water and washes away any mold.

When sprouts are about 1″ to 1¼″ (2.5 to 3 cm) long, put jar in a sunny window to increase the chlorophyll and turn the leaves green. After a day of sunshine (two if it's cloudy), the sprouts will be ready to eat. They may then be stored in the refrigerator for up to 5 days.

Sprout Melt

1 serving
10 minutes preparation
5 minutes broiling

Though sprouts are too tender to stand up to much cooking, the cheese topping here protects them from the heat of the broiler.

Preheat broiler. Place bread under it and brown one side. Remove from oven. Place toasted side down and cover with mustard, sprouts, condiments, yogurt and cheese. Compress lightly.

Place under broiler again just until cheese has melted and lightly browned (about 5 minutes). Serve right away.

1 thick slice whole-grain bread
1 tsp prepared mustard (5 mL)
**½ cup alfalfa sprouts
   (125 mL)**
**½ cup sliced condiments:
   pickles, olives, nuts, mushrooms, raisins (125 mL)**
2 tbsp yogurt (25 mL)
1 thin slice Mozzarella cheese

Squash Soup

8 servings
20 minutes preparation

When I served "squash soup" at my restaurant, guests would hesitate to order it. But if the menu listed the same soup under the Spanish name "sopa de calabeza", they loved it. When told what it was, many said they never knew squash could be so good.

Bring squash, stock, ginger and nutmeg to a simmer. Meanwhile, slowly fry onion in butter until soft and lightly browned.

When squash has softened (about 15 minutes), remove nutmeg (and bay leaf). Add fried onion and lemon juice. Blend or, for more texture, spin in a food processor or push through a food mill.

Serve with a dusting of paprika or finely chopped fresh parsley, or a swirl of whipping cream.

**4 cups peeled, seeded and diced
   winter squash (1 L)**
**4 cups stock (see p. 92) OR
   water (1 L) with 1 bay leaf and
   ½ tsp (2 mL) salt**
**1" (2.5 cm) fresh ginger, peeled
   and thinly sliced**
½ nut nutmeg
¼ cup unsalted butter (50 mL)
1 medium cooking onion, diced
1 tsp lemon juice (5 mL)

Cooking with Steam

Steaming is one of the best cooking methods for retaining nutrients and minimizing consumption of both saturated fats and unsaturated oils. And steam can be used to cook many things besides vegetables—bread and eggs, for instance. Serve steamed vegetables with lemon butter sauce, Boston brown bread and a poached egg (see p. 169) for a low-fat meal.

Steamed Vegetables

4 servings
5 minutes preparation
5 minutes cooking

Here is a list of vegetables that you might consider steaming, with the amount to start with for four servings and the cooking time:

ASPARAGUS (2 cups/500 mL; 4 minutes): rinse sand from tips, cut off tough ends and peel lower stalks; cook with tips elevated above bottoms (place on crumpled foil or use a tall pot).

GREEN BEANS (2 cups/500 mL; 5 minutes): snap off stem end and leave whole or break into shorter lengths.

BROCCOLI (3 cups/750 mL; 5 minutes): break into flowerets, slice part way up the stem of larger stalks and cook with stem ends down.

BRUSSELS SPROUTS (2 cups/500 mL; 5 minutes): trim off dried stems and pull off wilted leaves; for even cooking cut an "X" in stems of larger ones.

CABBAGE (3 cups/750 mL; 4 minutes): cut in strips or bite-sized pieces.

CAULIFLOWER (3 cups/750 mL; 4 minutes): break into flowerets; slice part way up the stem of larger ones for more even cooking.

KOHLRABI (2 cups/500 mL; 4 minutes): peel if fingernail will not easily pierce skin; slice, sliver or dice.

OKRA (2 cups/500 mL; 4 minutes): must be fresh or it may be stringy; best left whole, but can be sliced.

PEAS (1½ cups/375 mL; 4 minutes): if not fresh, may be bitter (skins should squeak when two are rubbed together); shell just before cooking.

RUTABAGA (2 cups/500 mL; 8 minutes): slice off thick (paraffined) skin and slice, sliver or dice; use within a day after cutting or it may turn bitter

TURNIP (2 cups/500 mL; 8 minutes): small white cousin of the rutabaga; peel skin if tough; slice, sliver or dice. ZUCCHINI (3 cups/500 mL; 2 minutes): leave skin on so flesh does not disintegrate.

Put vegetable in a heavy-bottomed pot (avoid new aluminum and old cast-iron pots, as these sometimes give off-flavors). Add about 2 tbsp (25 mL) water for each minute of cooking.

A few minutes before you are ready to serve, turn heat to high. When steam begins to emerge reduce heat. Steam for the time indicated. Every minute or so, remove the lid to check progress and release some of the acid gasses that turn vegetables prematurely gray.

As soon as the vegetable begins to soften and while color is still brilliant, toss with the sauce ingredients. Serve immediately.

Boston Brown Bread

5 small loaves baked in 14-oz (398-mL) cans
15 minutes preparation
2 hours steaming

Tin cans are the traditional baking containers for this bread. Be sure there are no ribs around the sides— they make it nearly impossible to remove the loaves.

Butter the bottoms and sides of 5 14-oz (398-mL) cans. Put 1" (2.5 cm) water in a pot large enough to hold them and bring to a simmer.

Sift flours with cornmeal, soda and salt. Whisk together buttermilk, molasses and ginger. Then fold liquid ingredients into dry ones. Stir in raisins. Promptly fill prepared cans two-thirds full of batter. Cover each can with foil.

Place in the pot of hot water. When water returns to a simmer, reduce heat to low. Steam about 2 hours, adding more water if necessary.

Loaves can be removed from the cans after 15 minutes' cooling. Turn each can upside down, open the other end and push the bread out. Slice and serve plain or with butter.

SAUCE:
2 tbsp butter (25 mL)
2 tsp lemon juice (10 mL)
pinch salt
grind pepper

1 cup sifted soft whole-wheat flour (250 mL)
1 cup rye OR buckwheat flour (250 mL)
1 cup cornmeal (250 mL)
2 tsp baking soda (10 mL)
½ tsp salt (2 mL)
2 cups buttermilk OR fresh milk with 2 tbsp (25 mL) vinegar (500 mL)
¾ cup molasses OR maple syrup (175 mL)
1 tbsp freshly grated ginger (optional) (15 mL)
1 cup raisins (250 mL)

Thanksgiving Dinner I

Holiday celebrations are so steeped in tradition that it's not easy to change them. And since food is so central to Thanksgiving, many find this a particularly difficult time to maintain a vegetarian diet.

    For most families carving the main course at the table is an important holiday ceremony. To keep up the tradition, serve a large, whole stuffed squash as the centerpiece. It goes well with all the traditional trimmings.

Chestnut-Stuffed Squash

8 servings
45 minutes preparation
1 hour precooking
2 to 3 hours baking

RICE AND CHESTNUTS:
4 cups water (1 L)
½ tsp salt (2 mL)
1 cup (7 oz) wild rice
  (250 mL/200 g)
2 cups (½ lb) chestnuts
  (500 mL/250 g)

FILLING:
1 cup small silver onions
  (250 mL)
1 cup small mushrooms
  (250 mL)
1 cup small Brussels sprouts
  (250 mL)
½ cup butter, divided
  (150 mL)
½ cup diced onion (125 mL)
½ cup diced celery (125 mL)
3 cloves garlic, minced
½ hot chili pepper, minced
1 tbsp thyme (15 mL)
1 tbsp sage (15 mL)
½ tsp freshly grated nutmeg
  (2 mL)
8 lb hubbard squash (4 kg) OR
  4 medium pepper or acorn
  squashes
1 tbsp freshly grated ginger
  (15 mL)

Pumpkins have a beautiful shape and color, but they tend to be stringy and watery; a large squash generally has better taste and texture. Just keep in mind that most home ovens can only accommodate a 15-lb (7-kg) squash. If you're in a hurry, you can precook the squash while preparing the filling, but it's better to bake the two together, so the flavors can intermingle.

To prepare the rice, bring water and salt to a rolling boil. Add rice, cover and turn heat to medium low. Do not stir at any time during cooking, or you'll end up with mush.

    After 30 minutes, turn heat to low. After 1 hour's total cooking time, remove from heat and leave rice covered until ready for use.

    Preheat oven to 325°F (160°C). With a sharp knife cut an "X" through to the flesh on the flat side of each chestnut. (This prevents them from exploding in the oven, and provides a place to start peeling.)

    Put nuts on a baking sheet and bake until shells begin to split open (about 20 minutes). Let cool just enough to handle—cold nuts are more difficult to shell. Pull off both the outer shell and the papery brown inner skin. The nuts are now ready to use.

    Now start preparing the filling. Without cutting the inner flesh, remove the papery skin from onions (blanching for 1 minute in boiling water may help). Clean mushrooms. Remove loose leaves of sprouts, then cut an "X" in each stem. (You can do all this a day ahead.)

When ready to stuff the squash, heat 3 tbsp (50 mL) butter in a frying pan. Slowly fry prepared onions and mushrooms until glistening (about 3 minutes).

Steam sprouts in a small amount of water only until brilliant green (about 3 minutes). Refresh in cold water to stop cooking.

In another 3 tbsp (50 mL) butter slowly fry the diced onion, celery, garlic, chili, thyme, sage and nutmeg until onion is lightly browned.

Cut an opening in the squash and remove seeds and membrane. Combine ginger with 3 tbsp (50 mL) butter and rub inside squash.

Combine cooked rice with chestnuts, onion-mushroom mixture, sprouts and onion-herb mixture. Fluff (don't pack too tightly) into prepared squash. It can now sit for several hours. (Any leftovers can be used in a savory strudel—see p. 107).

Preheat oven to 325°F (160°C). Bake stuffed squash until it begins to sag (2 to 3 hours). Carefully slide onto a serving platter and garnish with your favorite trimmings. Carve ceremoniously at table.

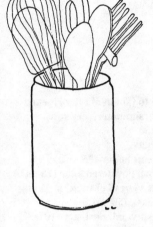

Cranberry Sauce

8 servings
10 minutes preparation

Pick through the fruit, removing any stems and soft berries. Combine with honey, juice and optional flavorings. Bring to a gentle simmer. Simmer only until most of the berries have popped open (about 3 minutes). Remove from heat and allow to cool. Remove zest, nutmeg or cinnamon.

Sauce can be served as is. To remove skins and seeds, push through a strainer. To make it gel, pour into an appropriate container and cool in refrigerator.

2 12-oz (375-g) packages
  cranberries
¾ cup honey (175 mL)
¼ cup orange juice OR water
  (50 mL)

OPTIONAL FLAVORINGS:
1 piece orange zest, 2" (5 cm)
  square
½ nut nutmeg
1 stick cinnamon

103

Thanksgiving Dinner II

Coulibiac is an elegant Russian specialty derived from the simple peasant dish called *pirog*. This version, enriched to make it fit for a czar, is perfectly suited to be the main course of a holiday feast. The rice, crêpes and sauce can all be prepared up to three days ahead of time. Then the final preparation takes only minutes.

Cold Persimmon Soufflé

8 servings
30 minutes preparation
2 hours cooling

Can be kept in the refrigerator for up to a day.

1½ lb (about 5) fully ripened persimmons (very soft) (750 g)
6 eggs
⅓ cup honey (75 mL)
1 tbsp powdered agar (15 mL) OR ¼ oz (8 g) stick OR ¼ cup flakes (60 mL)
2 tsp vanilla extract (10 mL)
pinch salt

Put agar in a pot with ½ cup (125 mL) cold water and soak for 10 minutes. Then slowly bring to a simmer. Meanwhile, cut persimmons in half and scoop out flesh. There should be about 2 cups (500 mL). Purée with egg yolks and honey in a blender or food processor until thick and foamy.

Let rest 10 or more minutes while you tape a 2″ (5-cm) band of waxed paper around the top of a 1-quart (1-L) soufflé dish. Then whisk egg whites to soft peaks.

Put persimmon mixture in a heavy-bottomed saucepan and place on medium heat. Whisk continuously until mixture rises and thickens (about 5 minutes). Then strain agar mixture in and stir well. Whisk in vanilla extract and salt.

Promptly, before mixture has cooled, fold in whipped egg whites and immediately pour into prepared dish. Let set in refrigerator for 2 hours.

Coulibiac

8 servings
1 hour preparation
45 minutes baking

Bring water, butter and salt to a boil. Add wild rice. When it returns to a boil, cover and reduce heat to low. Gently simmer (without stirring) for 1 hour. Remove

RICE:
2 cups water (500 mL)
2 tbsp butter (25 mL)
¼ tsp salt (1 mL)
½ cup (3½ oz) wild rice (125 mL/100 g)

from heat and let rest 10 minutes. Keep grains intact by gently fluffing rice out of pot.

For the crêpes, whisk together eggs, ¼ cup (50 mL) of the milk, and the oil. Whisk in flour. Then add more milk until batter is consistency of whipping cream. Let rest 1 hour or overnight.

Heat a well seasoned frying pan on medium heat. Add ½ tsp (2 mL) oil. Stir batter and pour about 2 tbsp (25 mL) of it into pan. Promptly tilt pan to spread batter in a thin layer. Fry until both sides are lightly browned. Turn out onto a plate. Continue with remaining batter, stacking crêpes on the plate.

For the sauce, purée all ingredients in a blender or food processor until smooth. Let rest at least 1 hour for the flavors to meld and mixture to thicken.

For the choux paste, slowly bring milk, butter and salt to a boil. When it begins to bubble, add the flour and stir vigorously until dough begins to pull away from sides of pan. If after 1 minute it is still sticking, add another 2 tbsp (25 mL) flour.

Cool for 2 minutes, then stir in eggs, one at a time. Beat each until dough is again homogeneous. Stop adding eggs when dough begins to shine and no longer holds its shape.

Preheat oven to 425°F (220°C).

For the filling, heat butter in a large frying pan. Add, one at a time, in this order, shallots, cabbage, mushrooms, dill, vinegar and mustard. When all are softened (about 5 minutes), begin assembling the coulibiac.

Arrange crêpes on an ovenproof platter, overlapping and letting them drape well over the sides. Place cooked rice in the center. Cover with sauce and a layer of sliced hard-cooked eggs. Scoop the fried vegetables on top.

Lift the overhanging crêpes up the sides. Then spoon or pipe (see p. 24) the warm choux paste in an attractive pattern over everything. Don't worry if it doesn't look perfect now—when it comes out of the oven, it will be spectacular.

Bake until dough puffs (about 15 minutes). Then reduce heat to 325°F (160°C) and continue baking until crust is golden (about 35 more minutes). Serve from the platter at the table.

CRÊPES:
2 lightly beaten eggs
¾ cups milk OR beer (175 mL)
1 tbsp vegetable oil (15 mL)
½ cup sifted soft whole-wheat flour (125 mL)

SAUCE:
1½ cups (12 oz) Ricotta (see p. 50) OR cottage cheese (375 mL/375 g)
½ cup plain yogurt (125 mL)
1 clove garlic
¼ tsp mustard powder OR prepared mustard (1 mL)
⅛ tsp salt (0.5 mL)

CHOUX PASTE:
1 cup milk (250 mL)
½ cup butter (125 mL)
pinch salt
1 cup unsifted soft whole-wheat flour (250 mL)
3–4 large eggs

FILLING:
2 tbsp butter (25 mL)
1 cup sliced shallots OR onions (250 mL)
2 cups shredded red cabbage (500 mL)
2 cups sliced mushrooms (500 mL)
¼ cup chopped fresh dill (50 mL)
1 tbsp vinegar OR lemon juice (15 mL)
2 tsp prepared mustard (10 mL)
4 hard-cooked eggs (optional)

Reviving Leftovers

Many foods actually taste better after being reheated. So to save time, money and effort, good cooks often prepare more than one meal's worth, with the distinct purpose of having leftovers.

To minimize bacterial growth, store leftovers either above 140°F (60°C) or below 40°F (3°C). The refrigerator is the best place for short-term (less than one week) storage. Generally it's best to use the food within three or four days, though leftovers that contain a good deal of salt or acid (vinegar or fruit juices) will keep longer.

For longer storage the freezer is best. Although the food will remain safe to eat for many months, the taste and texture deteriorate at a steady rate. So always make a point of consuming frozen leftovers as soon as possible. Clearly label each container with its contents and the date it was packed.

Since most flavors are reduced after even a short stint in the freezer, it helps to add new flavorings before reheating. (Two exceptions are celery and green sweet peppers—their flavors are intensified by freezing.)

Some foods do not freeze well: hard-cooked eggs turn leathery; starch-thickened sauces turn gelatinous; mayonnaise or other high-oil sauces separate; bananas turn mushy; potatoes become dank; and garlic takes on a musty smell. Cooked vegetables, casseroles, stews and pastries generally freeze very well.

Minimize loss of texture in any leftovers by gentle reheating—a hot water-bath is ideal. To add texture to ingredients that have turned excessively soft, combine them with fresh vegetables, nuts or croutons.

To make leftovers more exciting, top with a contrasting sauce. Or serve over toast, French toast, *croustade* (a hollowed-out bun or loaf of bread), waffles, pasta or cooked grain. Alternatively, combine with stock or milk for a soup.

The most elegant way I know to use leftovers is in a savory strudel. It makes a satisfying main course when accompanied with steamed greens (see p. 40) and a boiled vegetable (see p. 168). Finish the meal with a frugtkage—a Scandinavian dessert quickly assembled from leftover fruit sauce and cake or cookie crumbs.

Frugtkage

4 servings
10 minutes preparation

2 cups cake OR cookie crumbs
(500 mL)
3 tbsp butter, softened
(50 mL)
3 tbsp honey (50 mL)
⅛ tsp ground cardamom
(0.5 mL)
4 cups applesauce (see p. 155),
cranberry sauce (see p. 103)
OR rhubarb sauce (see p. 32)
(1 L)

Rub together crumbs, butter, honey and cardamom. In serving dishes, put alternating layers of crumbs and fruit—beginning and ending with crumbs. Garnish each serving with a dab of red currant jelly (see p. 44) or whipped cream.

Savory Strudel

8 servings
15 minutes preparation
30 minutes baking

Use the paper-thin sheets available as strudel or phyllo pastry in the frozen-food section of many stores.

For filling, combine leftovers with chopped parsley or dill and any other flavorings you think will add interest. If mixture lacks texture, stir in the nuts. If it's somewhat soupy, thicken with bread crumbs.

Preheat oven to 400°F (200°C). Remove thawed pastry from package. Place one sheet on a clean dry towel (there should be no tears or holes, since this will become the outside layer). Brush with about 1 tbsp (15 mL) melted butter and sprinkle with crumbs. Repeat with another layer of pastry, butter and crumbs (these interior sheets need not be perfect). Repeat with remaining sheets.

Along one long side brush a 6" (15-cm) band of melted butter (this prevents moisture in the filling from seeping into the pastry). Spread cool filling mixture over the band of butter.

Pull up towel and gently coax strudel to roll into a tube. Fold in ends of roll. Place on a baking sheet, seam-side down. Brush top with remaining butter. Promptly place in oven.

After 10 minutes' baking, reduce heat to 325°F (160°C). Bake until lightly browned (about 20 minutes more). Slice and serve right away.

FILLING:
3 cups coarsely chopped leftovers from a casserole, cooked vegetable(s), OR stuffing for another dish (750 mL)
¼ cup chopped fresh parsley OR dill (50 mL)
¼ cup chopped nuts (optional) (50 mL)
½ cup dry bread crumbs (optional) (125 mL)

PASTRY:
10 sheets (½ lb) strudel (phyllo) pastry, thawed (250 mL)
⅓ cup melted butter (75 mL)
2 tbsp dry bread crumbs OR sesame seeds (25 mL)

Black Beans

Although numerous studies have shown the nutritional benefits of eating beans, many North Americans persist in avoiding them. In Mexico, on the other hand, beans remain an important part of the diet. The spicy Mexican version of baked beans bears little resemblance to the sweet Boston variety. Follow them with a colorful Mexican salad and some tropical fruit.

2 cups beans suggested in recipe (500 mL)
2 tbsp butter OR vegetable oil (25 mL)
½ tsp salt (2 mL)

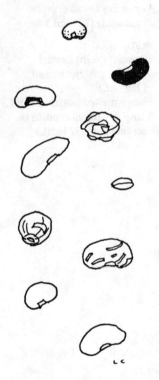

Cooked Beans

5 cups (1250 mL)
10 minutes preparation
1 hour soaking
1 ½ hours cooking

Pick through the beans to remove sticks, stones and misshapen ones. Rinse in several changes of water. Cover with 6 cups (1500 mL) water and soak overnight. (Or, if you're in a hurry, bring to a simmer, promptly remove from heat, and soak for about 1 hour.) Then simmer for the suggested time.

ADZUKI BEANS (2 hours): old ones may require much longer cooking.

BLACK (TURTLE) BEANS (1 ¼ hours): these blacken the pot and anything cooked with them.

BLACK-EYED PEAS (½ hour): presoaking not necessary but improves appearance.

CHICKPEAS (2 hours): old ones may require much longer cooking.

KIDNEY BEANS (1 ¼ hours): to maintain their distinctive colors, cook each type separately.

LENTILS (¾ hour): red ones need no presoaking, but quickly turn to mush; brown ones maintain their shape and cook more quickly if presoaked.

PIGEON PEAS (2 hours): old ones may require much longer cooking.

PINTO BEANS (1 ¼ hours): the pretty ''painted'' pattern disappears when cooked.

SOY BEANS (2 hours): some varieties need significantly longer cooking, and may never soften unless pressure-cooked.

WHITE BEANS (1 ¼ hours): many varieties, all cooked the same way.

When beans have rehydrated, bring to a simmer and skim off any foam. Simmer gently for the recommended number of hours (keeping in mind that old beans may need longer cooking). Beans can be cooked in a pressure cooker for one-quarter of the suggested time, but they will develop less flavor. About half way through the cooking (or at the beginning of pressure cooking) add the butter and salt. They are adequately cooked when the skins split when blown upon.

Cooked beans can be used right away, but their flavor improves if they are cooled then reheated. Keep in refrigerator for up to 2 weeks; in freezer for 6 months (though they will lose some texture).

Frijoles Negros de Olla

8 servings
20 minutes preparation
4 hours baking

Grind all ingredients for chili powder in a spice or coffee grinder or with a mortar and pestle. (For the freshest flavor, use within a week.)

Combine cooked beans with onion, butter, garlic, mustard, salt and half the chili powder. Either transfer the mixture to a crock pot (set on low) or bean pot (in a 300°F/150°C oven); or finish cooking it in a heavy-bottomed pot on top of the stove (on low heat). Simmer slowly until liquid begins to thicken (about 4 hours). If beans seem quite dry add more water; if still runny after 4 hours, cook gently with the lid off until thickened.

Adjust flavor by adding lemon juice and more chili powder. Serve with warm tortillas and salsa cruda (see pp. 16-17) or corn bread (p. 161) and a salad.

CHILI POWDER:
1 tbsp paprika (15 mL)
1 tbsp rubbed oregano
  (15 mL)
1 tbsp cumin seeds (15 mL)
1 hot chili pepper OR ½ tsp
  cayenne (2 mL)
¼ tsp allspice (1 mL)

BEANS:
2 cups cooked black beans
  (500 mL)
1 cup diced onion (250 mL)
¼ cup butter (50 mL)
4 cloves garlic, minced
1 tsp prepared mustard
  (5 mL)
½ tsp salt (2 mL)
1 tbsp lemon OR lime juice
  (15 mL)

Mexican Salad

4 servings
10 minutes preparation

Whisk together oil, lime juice, chili powder and salt. Clean, dry and cut lettuce or cabbage in thin slivers. Cut radishes in wedges so that some red is visible on each piece. Toss dressing with vegetables. Serve as part of any Mexican meal.

4 tbsp olive oil (50 mL)
2 tbsp lime juice (25 mL)
2 tsp Chili Powder (10 mL)
pinch salt
1 medium head romaine lettuce
  OR Chinese cabbage
1 cup red radishes, tops and
  bottoms removed (250 mL)

New Mexico

New Mexico has its own distinctive cuisine—a combination of Mexican flavor and Yankee efficiency. If the thought of Mexican food sets your mouth to salivating but you find it too labor-intensive, try this New Mexican menu.

It starts with a zippy appetizer dip of chili con queso and continues with enchiladas—a popular main course often served with a shredded Mexican salad (see p. 109) and frijoles refritos (see p. 17). Finish the meal with an all-American apple crisp.

New Mexican Enchiladas

4 servings
20 minutes preparation
15 minutes simmering
15 minutes baking

These stacked enchiladas are much quicker to assemble than the rolled Mexican style. You can skip the frying, but the tortillas may turn mushy.

For sauce, heat butter and slowly fry onion, chili and cumin. Meanwhile, whisk together tomato paste and tomatoes. Then add remaining flavorings and heat to a simmer. When onion is softened, add to heating tomato mixture. Simmer 10 minutes.

To prepare enchiladas, preheat oven to 350°F (180°C). Put oil in a small frying pan and heat until a piece of tortilla sizzles as soon as you put it in (375°F/190°C). Quickly fry tortillas to freshen and firm them (about 3 seconds), but don't let them crisp. Drain on paper towels.

Put a tortilla on each of 4 ovenproof serving plates. Ladle on some sauce and sprinkle with cheese, then cover with another tortilla and more sauce and cheese. Continue until there are three or four layers. Wipe rims of plates.

Put in oven and allow the stacks to heat through (about 15 minutes). Set hot plates on larger cool ones and serve right away.

SAUCE:
3 tbsp butter (50 mL)
½ cup finely diced onion
(125 mL)
1–2 hot chili peppers, minced
(wash hands afterwards)
1 tbsp ground cumin seeds
(15 mL)
6-oz can tomato paste
1 cup chopped fresh tomatoes
(250 mL)
1 tbsp lemon OR lime juice
(15 mL)
2 tbsp chopped fresh coriander
leaves (25 mL) OR 2 tsp sage
(10 mL) plus 1 tsp orange
zest (5 mL)
1 tbsp oregano (15 mL)
1 tsp ground cinnamon (5 mL)
4 cloves garlic, minced

ENCHILADAS:
¾ cup oil for frying (175 mL)
12–16 corn tortillas (available
in the frozen-food section of
many specialty shops)
2 cups shredded Cheddar
cheese (500 mL)

Chili con Queso

2 cups (500 mL)
15 minutes preparation

Best made with the large pale-green sweet peppers, but green bell peppers are quite acceptable. Peel the skin with a vegetable peeler (it's usually tough and coated with wax).

Heat butter in small saucepan and fry onion and peppers until onions turn clear and peppers soften. Turn heat to low and add cheeses. Stirring steadily, heat only until cheeses melt. Stir in cereal cream as required to make consistency of thick pancake batter.

Serve right away with tortilla chips or vegetable crudités. If room temperature is cool, keep the dip warm over a low flame.

2 tbsp butter OR vegetable oil
  (25 mL)
½ cup finely diced onion
  (125 mL)
1 cup peeled, seeded and
  chopped sweet peppers
  (250 mL)
1 or 2 hot chili peppers, seeded
  and chopped (wash hands
  afterwards)
½ cup cream cheese (125 mL)
½ cup shredded white
  Cheddar OR Brick cheese
  (125 mL)
cereal cream as required

Apple Crisp

8 servings
25 minutes preparation
35 minutes baking

Just as good with blueberries, cherries, or peaches in place of the apples.

Preheat oven to 375°F (190°C). For the filling, toss together all the ingredients. Put into a buttered 8" × 12" (20 × 30-cm) cake pan.

For the topping, rub together all the ingredients. Sprinkle over the filling. Bake, uncovered, until top is golden (about 35 minutes).

Serve fruit crisp warm or cool, alone or with ice cream or whipped cream (see p. 47).

FILLING:
6 cups (5 large) peeled, cored
  and sliced cooking apples:
  Spy, Granny Smith, Rome Beauty,
  Ida Red, etc.(1500 mL)
⅓ cup unsifted flour (75 mL)
½ cup honey (125 mL)
2 tbsp diced butter (25 mL)
1 tbsp lemon juice (15 mL)
¼ tsp ground cinnamon
  (1 mL)
pinch salt

TOPPING:
2 cups granola OR crushed
  honey-lemon cookies (see p.
  136) (500 mL)
½ cup chopped nuts: walnuts,
  pecans, hazelnuts (125 mL)
¼ cup butter, softened
  (50 mL)
¼ cup whole-wheat flour
  (50 mL)
2 tbsp honey (25 mL)

New Orleans

This Southern menu starts with the same basic ingredients as a Northern classic—baked beans, corn bread and cabbage salad. But the Cajuns traditionally like more color and spice than their Puritan cousins in Boston. Accompany these New Orleans baked beans with spoon bread—a corn bread meant to be served with a spoon—and calico salad, for color and texture. If you want a sweet ending, a platter of sliced oranges would be appropriate.

New Orleans Baked Beans

8 servings
20 minutes preparation
4 hours baking

A hint of rum gives these beans their unique flavor.

4 tbsp butter (50 mL)
1 cup finely diced onion (250 mL)
1 cup seeded and chopped green pepper (250 mL)
1 cup sliced celery stalk (250 mL)
5 cups cooked red kidney beans OR black-eyed peas (see p. 108) with cooking liquid (1250 mL)
1 cup peeled, seeded and chopped tomatoes (250 mL)
1 tbsp lime juice (15 mL)
3 cloves garlic, minced
½ tsp salt (unless cooked with beans) (2 mL)
1 hot chili pepper, seeded and minced (wash hands afterwards)
1 oz rum (optional) (30 mL)

Preheat oven to 300°F (150°C) or slow cooker to low heat. Slowly fry onion, pepper and celery in butter. Meanwhile, put cooked beans and all remaining ingredients in a bean pot or slow cooker. When onions are golden, stir into bean mixture.

Bake until beans begin to thicken (about 4 hours). Stir periodically to prevent sticking. Add more water if mixture seems to be getting dry. If at the end of cooking beans are still soupy, you can thicken them by cooling, then reheating (or, if you are in a hurry, cooking them a little longer with the lid off.) Leftovers are delicious either cold or reheated.

Spoon Bread

8 servings
15 minutes preparation
40 minutes baking

Although this quick bread is a variation on a soufflé, it won't collapse after being removed from the oven.

Preheat oven to 350°F (180°C). Slowly bring milk to a simmer. Meanwhile generously butter a 2-quart (2-L) soufflé dish. Whisk egg whites to soft peaks and lightly beat yolks.

When milk is simmering, remove from heat and whisk in cornmeal. Return to heat and stir until mixture is very thick (about 5 minutes). Stir in corn, butter, honey, salt, pepper and, finally, egg yolks. Then promptly fold in half the whisked whites. Follow with remaining whites. Turn mixture into prepared dish. Place on lower oven shelf.

Bake until spoon bread is firm (about 40 minutes). Let cool about 10 minutes. Serve with a spoon, taking care to include some of the golden crust. Leftovers are best served at room temperature rather than reheated.

2½ cups milk OR water
  (625 mL)
3 eggs, separated
1 cup cornmeal (not coarsely
  ground) (250 mL)
1 cup corn kernels OR diced red
  pepper (optional) (250 mL)
2 tbsp butter (25 mL)
1 tbsp honey (15 mL)
¾ tsp salt (4 mL)
¼ tsp ground black
  peppercorns (1 mL)

Calico Salad

4 servings
10 minutes preparation

Try serving this colorful salad in cups made of cabbage leaves.

Toss all ingredients together. Let sit in refrigerator for up to 1 hour before serving.

1 cup thinly sliced green
  cabbage (preferably savoy)
  (250 mL)
1 cup thinly sliced red cabbage
  (250 mL)
1 cup shredded carrot
  (250 mL)
1 cup whole kernel corn,
  blanched and chilled (250 mL)
¼ cup currants (50 mL)
½ cup mayonnaise (see p. 38)
  (125 mL)

Chili

Chili and Caesar salad are two all-American favorites. For a chewy texture with the beans add some tofu crumbled and fried until most of the water has evaporated. Then continue frying a little of the crumbled tofu until it's crispy brown, and put it in the salad for color and crunch. Accompany the chili and salad with a loaf of crusty bread and some ice-cold beer.

Caesar Salad

4 servings
25 minutes preparation

CROUTONS:
1 tbsp prepared mustard
  (15 mL)
1 tbsp vinegar (15 mL)
1 clove garlic, finely minced
½ tsp oregano (2 mL)
2 slices stale, firm-textured
  bread, cut in cubes
2 tbsp oil for frying (25 mL)

DRESSING:
2 tbsp olive oil (25 mL)
1 tbsp lemon juice (15 mL)
1 raw egg
1 tsp Worcestershire sauce (see
  p. 156) (5 mL)
¼ tsp salt (1 mL)
⅛ tsp ground black
  peppercorns (0.5 mL)

SALAD:
1 clove garlic
6 cups (1 small head) torn
  romaine lettuce, cleaned and
  dried (1500 mL)
1 cup chopped Belgian endive
  (optional) (250 mL)
1 tbsp olive oil (15 mL)
3 tbsp freshly grated Parmesan
  cheese (50 mL)
2 tbsp crispy crumbled tofu
  (see Chili con Tofu) (25 mL)
2 tbsp capers (optional)
  (25 mL)

For the croutons, whisk together mustard, vinegar, garlic and oregano. Toss with bread cubes and let rest 5 minutes. Heat oil in a frying pan and fry croutons until crispy brown. For extra crunchiness, put on a tray in a 250°F (120°C) oven for 1 hour.

For the dressing, whisk together all ingredients. Although the dressing is usually made just before serving, you can prepare it up to 8 hours ahead and keep it in the refrigerator.

For the salad, rub the serving bowl with garlic. Toss romaine and endive with oil. Then whisk and toss in dressing. Sprinkle on croutons, Parmesan, tofu and capers. Toss once again, making sure small pieces are not buried at the bottom. Serve right away.

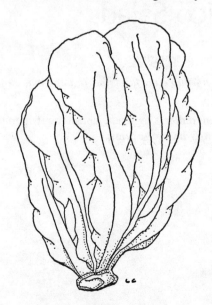

Chili con Tofu

8 servings
20 minutes preparation
10 minutes frying
20 minutes simmering

If you don't have crumbled tofu already on hand, save time by preparing it as the other ingredients are simmering.

Crumble the tofu between your fingers into pea-sized pieces. Drop into an unoiled frying pan. Put pan on medium-high heat, then stir in remaining crumbled tofu ingredients.

As the tofu heats up, whey will slowly exude. If it comes out faster than it evaporates (i.e. the liquid accumulates) increase the heat. If pan seems to be drying out too fast, reduce heat. Continue frying until no more whey exudes (the curds will be about half their original size and the pan dry). For Caesar salad, continue frying 2 tbsp (25 mL) of the crumbled tofu until it turns crispy brown.

For the chili, heat butter in a large saucepan and slowly fry onions and peppers until onions are clear (about 3 minutes). Add crumbled tofu and remaining ingredients and simmer, uncovered, until consistency is no longer soupy (about 20 minutes).

Serve chili as a meal in a bowl with a dollop of sour cream or a sprinkling of slivered lettuce. Leftovers keep well in refrigerator for more than a week—and taste even better the second time around.

CRUMBLED TOFU:
1 lb tofu (500 g)
½ cup cleaned and chopped mushrooms (125 mL)
1 tbsp butter OR vegetable oil (15 mL)
1 tbsp soy sauce (15 mL)
1 tsp cider vinegar OR wine vinegar (5 mL)
3 cloves garlic, minced
1 tsp prepared OR powdered mustard (5 mL)
½ tsp maple syrup OR buckwheat honey (2 mL)
½ tsp rubbed thyme (2 mL)
½ tsp rubbed sage (2 mL)

CHILI:
¼ cup butter (50 mL)
2 cups diced onions (500 mL)
1 cup diced sweet peppers (250 mL)
3 cups chopped tomatoes (750 mL)
4 cups cooked red kidney beans (see p. 108) (1 L)
¼ cup cider vinegar (50 mL)
1 hot chili pepper, minced (wash hands afterwards) OR ¼ tsp cayenne (1 mL)
4 cloves garlic, minced
1 tsp freshly ground cumin seeds (5 mL)
1 tsp freshly ground oregano (5 mL)
½ tsp freshly ground allspice (2 mL)
½ tsp salt (unless already in beans) (2 mL)
black pepper to taste

115

Tempeh

Tempeh, a traditional food of Indonesia, not only offers all the nutritional benefits of tofu—it's a good source of protein, iron and B vitamins, and is very low in fat and cholesterol—but in addition contains fiber, which tofu does not.

Tempeh is formed by cultivating mycologic spores—the same family that gives mushrooms their delicious flavor. Look for tempeh in Indonesian shops or in the frozen-food sections of some natural food stores. Though it keeps for many months in the freezer, once thawed it should be refrigerated and used within a week.

Cubed tempeh is a fine addition to a meatless goulash. While it is cooling prepare the batter for the spätzle, then begin marinating the cucumbers. Finally, reheat the goulash and cook the spätzle. Finish the meal with a poppyseed strudel (see p. 125).

Goulash

8 servings
25 minutes preparation
15 minutes simmering

½ cup butter (125 mL)
2 cups onion crescents
  (500 mL)
4 cups (1 lb) bite-sized pieces
  tempeh OR gluten (see p. 120)
  (1 L/500 g)
2 cups button mushrooms,
  cleaned (500 mL)
2 cups bite-sized pieces red
  potatoes (500 mL)
1 cup diced sweet red peppers
  (250 mL)
¼ tsp caraway seeds (1 mL)
4 tbsp soft whole-wheat flour
  (50 mL)
4 tbsp fresh sweet paprika
  (50 mL)
¼ tsp hot paprika OR cayenne
  (1 mL)
3 cloves garlic, minced
1 cup sauerkraut OR
  shredded cabbage with
  ¼ cup (50 mL) red wine
  vinegar (250 mL)
2 cups stock (see p. 92) OR ¼
  red wine and ¾ water
  (500 mL)
½ tsp salt (2 mL)

The tempeh provides a meaty texture and absorbs the stew's rich juices.

Reserve 2 tbsp (25 mL) butter and melt the rest in a large heavy-bottomed pot. Stirring constantly on medium-high heat, fry onions, tempeh, mushrooms, potatoes, peppers and caraway. When onions are browning, stir in flour, paprikas, garlic and sauerkraut. When hot, stir in stock and salt. Simmer until potatoes have softened (about 15 more minutes). Stew can be served now, but flavor improves after cooling.

When reheating, freshen flavor by stirring in remaining butter. Serve goulash over or beside rice, pasta or spätzle. Highlight the rusty red color with a dollop of sour cream and a sprig of dill.

Spätzle

4 servings
10 minutes preparation
30 minutes resting

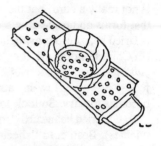

These tiny dumplings are a pleasant change from ordinary rice and pasta. They are traditionally made with a special gadget (available at Eastern European and some kitchen-supply shops) that drips small strands of batter into a large pot of boiling water. An ordinary small-holed colander works well too.

Whisk together flour, milk, eggs, salt, nutmeg and 1 tbsp (15 mL) of the butter to form a runny batter. Let rest at least 30 minutes before proceeding.

Bring a large pot of water to a boil. Place a spätzle-maker or colander over the water and pour in half the batter. With a spätzle-maker you can control the size of the dumplings by adjusting the speed of operation. With a colander, size is determined by the consistency of the batter and the speed with which you push it through with a wooden spoon. Make fine adjustments in consistency by whisking in more flour or milk as needed.

When half the batter is in the pot, reduce heat and simmer, covered, for 10 minutes. Strain out spätzle and repeat with remaining batter. Toss with remaining butter and serve promptly.

2 cups unsifted soft whole-wheat flour (500 mL)
½ cup milk (125 mL)
2 eggs, lightly beaten
¼ tsp salt (1 mL)
⅛ tsp nutmeg (optional) (0.5 mL)
4 tbsp butter, melted (60 mL)

Marinated Cucumbers

4 servings
5 minutes preparation
30 minutes marinating

This salad lightens a heavy meal.

Dissolve honey and salt in vinegar. Toss in cucumber slices and let marinate about 30 minutes. Drain off liquid and serve garnished with chopped dill or parsley.

¼ cup cider vinegar (50 mL)
2 tsp honey (10 mL)
½ tsp salt (2 mL)
1 medium seedless English cucumber, thinly sliced
2 tbsp chopped fresh dill OR parsley (25 mL)

117

Dried Bean Curd

Like tofu and tempeh, dried bean curd is a soy product from the Orient that deserves more attention than it has thus far received. In fact, "bean curd" is something of a misnomer. It is not really a curd, but the skin that forms on top of heated soy milk—not unlike the skin that forms on heated cow's milk.

Dried bean curd is available in two forms—flat beige "sheets" and bunched-up "rope". (In Chinese stores ask for "dried bean curd" or *dao fu choap*; in Japanese stores ask for *yuba*.) It contains most of the soy bean's protein, B vitamins and iron. Like other soy foods, it is very low in fats and cholesterol. It keeps indefinitely, but will shatter if it becomes too dry. So look for a package that is not filled with shards.

To use dried bean curd "rope" in a stew soak it in hot water until it turns white (about 15 minutes). Bean curd "sheets" are generally used for wrapping. (See the tofu-mushroom rolls on p. 145.)

Oden is a popular winter stew in Japan, where it is prepared by street vendors. But you can make your own. While the stew ingredients are heating and soaking, cook the rice, prepare the sesame gomasio and mix up some fresh mustard dip (see p. 7) to accompany the main course. For dessert serve very soft, fully ripened persimmons or juicy Japanese pears.

Oden

8 servings
20 minutes preparation
30 minutes simmering

2 cups stock (see p. 92) OR
  broth (see p. 6) (500 mL)
6" (15-cm) leaf kelp (kombu)
1" (2.5 cm) peeled ginger, cut
  in thin slices
¾ cup dried shiitake
  mushrooms (175 mL)
2 tbsp soy sauce (25 mL)
6' (2 m) dried bean curd
  "ropes" OR 2 cups gluten (see
  p. 120) (500 mL)
8 cups bite-sized pieces stew
  ingredients: carrot, kohlrabi,
  turnip, white radish (daikon),
  lotus root slices, white parts
  of green onion, peeled fresh
  water chestnuts, whole snow
  peas (2 L)
¼ cup naturally sweetened
  mirin OR sake with 2 tsp
  (10 mL) honey (50 mL)
2 tbsp dark sesame oil (25 mL)

You can serve this stew on plates, Western fashion, or present it in a bowl in the middle of the table for diners to help themselves, Japanese fashion. The kelp, shiitake (black) mushrooms, dried bean curd, mirin and dark sesame oil are available in Japanese and some natural food stores.

Slowly bring stock, kelp, ginger, mushrooms and soy sauce to a simmer. Presoak dried bean curd in hot water to cover for 15 minutes. Prepare stew ingredients.

Simmer stock and flavorings 15 minutes. Remove kelp and ginger. Increase heat and add rehydrated bean curd and chosen ingredients, one at a time, in order given. When all ingredients have softened (about 10 minutes), add mirin and sesame oil. Stew is ready to serve.

Leftovers keep well in refrigerator for up to 1 week. Reheat as required.

118

Short-Grain Rice

4 servings
5 minutes preparation
50 minutes cooking

Westerners who eat with forks have a penchant for fluffy rice, but those who use chopsticks need a sticky rice so they can pick up more than a few grains at a time. To make it sticky, use short-grain rice and start the cooking in cold water. Note that no salt is cooked with the rice—this flavor is meant to come from salty condiments. Surprisingly, rice cooked this way makes the fluffiest fried rice and rice salad.

Put water and rice in saucepan and bring water to a simmer on medium heat. Cover pot and reduce heat to low. Gently simmer for 40 minutes. Do NOT uncover or stir, it may burn. Remove from heat and let sit 10 minutes before serving. Use any leftovers in Thai fried rice (see p. 12) or rice salad (see p. 57).

3½ cups cold water (900 mL)
2 cups short-grain brown rice, cleaned (500 mL)

Gomasio

¼ cup (50 mL)
5 minutes preparation

This nutritious, low-sodium, high-calcium condiment is as common in Japan as table salt is here.

Put sesame seeds and salt in a small frying pan and heat until seeds begin to pop. Shake frequently so they roast evenly (about 5 minutes). Pour into blender or food processor and pulverize until most seeds are cracked open (about 3 seconds); or grind with a mortar and pestle.

Serve right away over plain cooked rice or anything else you would normally salt. Use it within a month—the salt and cooking cause the seeds to turn rancid quickly.

¼ cup sesame seeds (50 mL)
½ tsp salt (2 mL)

Gluten

Gluten is the protein that remains after the wheat's starch is washed away by repeated rinsings. In China and Japan, this "wheat meat" has long been used to provide the satisfying texture all too often missing from meatless foods. Though it is very high in protein, the amino acids that make it up are not perfectly balanced. So when planning to use gluten make sure there are legumes or dairy products elsewhere in the meal to provide the complementary amino acids.

Chunks of gluten in a rich stroganoff sauce make a superb main course. With a light salad to start and a cranberry kissel (see p. 132) for dessert, you'll have a complete and delicious meal.

7–8 cups (1 kg) unsifted wheat flour (1750–2000 mL)
3 cups water (750 mL)

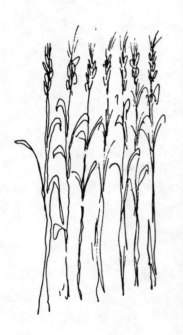

Gluten

about 2½ lb or 5 cups (1 kg/1250 mL)
30 minutes preparation
2 hours soaking
30 minutes cooking

Making gluten is very much like making bread—but even easier. You can use any wheat flour. With no bran or wheat germ, white flour gives a higher yield than whole wheat—and since it lacks the sharp bran particles, it's easier on your hands. Since most of the vitamins and minerals are washed away in the rinse water, there is little advantage in using whole-wheat flour for gluten.

Combine half the flour and all the water in a large bowl. Beat until stringy (about 5 minutes). Then add remaining flour, 1 cup (250 mL) at a time. When it becomes too thick to handle, begin kneading like bread. Knead until dough stretches rather than tears when pulled (about 10 more minutes). Put dough back in bowl and cover with cool water. Let rest at least 2 hours (or overnight).

Now rinse dough by kneading it in the soaking water. Pour out the milky starch that will exude and replace with fresh water. Repeat several times (alternating with cool and warm water speeds the rinsing) until water remains relatively clear (about 10 minutes).

The gluten is now ready to cook, either in a flavorful stew or broth or by one of the following methods:

DEEP FRYING (produces the lightest gluten): cut into ¼" (5-mm) cubes and drop them, one at a time, into 375°F (190°C) oil. Free any pieces that stick to the bottom. Cook until puffs turn golden (about 4 minutes). Drain. Rinse off the oil with hot water so the gluten will more easily absorb subsequent flavorings.

SIMMERING (either in plain water or in a flavorful broth): cut dough in ½" (1-cm) chunks and add to a large pot of boiling liquid. Stir frequently at first so they don't stick together. To be sure the gluten is completely digestible, simmer (boiling toughens it) for 30 minutes to 1 hour. Subsequent frying will give a crispy crust.

BAKING (produces the densest gluten): put ½" (1-cm) cubes on a buttered baking sheet in a preheated 375°F (190°C) oven. Bake until browned (about 25 minutes).

Refrigerate—keeping the deep-fried and baked cubes dry and the simmered ones completely immersed in water or broth—and the precooked gluten will remain fresh for 2 weeks.

Stroganoff

8 small rich servings
20 minutes preparation

This stew is so rich and creamy that small portions are quite sufficient.

In a large pot, slowly fry onions in butter. When clear, add mushrooms and gluten. Fry until heated through. Stir in flour, garlic, mustard, salt and pepper. Finally, stir in beer and sour cream. Simmer gently, uncovered, for 10 minutes.

Can be served right away, but flavor improves if stew is cooled and gently reheated. Serve over freshly baked biscuits, slices of toast or diced boiled potatoes. Accompany with a brightly colored steamed vegetable (see p. 100).

4 tbsp clarified butter (see p. 60) OR ½ butter and ½ oil (50 mL)

2 cups 1" (2.5-cm) onion squares (500 mL)

3 cups whole small mushrooms, cleaned (750 mL)

3 cups gluten chunks (preferably simmered) OR diced tempeh (see p. 116) (750 mL)

2 tbsp flour (25 mL)

2 cloves garlic, minced

1 tsp prepared mustard (5 mL)

¼ tsp salt (1 mL)

⅛ tsp ground white peppercorns (0.5 mL)

½ cup beer, white wine OR stock (see p. 92) (125 mL)

1½ cups sour cream (375 mL)

Cassoulet

Because they live in an exceedingly rich agricultural region, the French have been able to make meat an important part of their cuisine. For this reason it has been difficult to translate many of the great French dishes into successful meatless versions. In the Orient, however, where population pressures have historically limited meat consumption, a variety of "meaty" vegetable-based foods have been developed, among them tofu, gluten and tempeh.

The nutty flavor of tempeh shines in cassoulet—the French version of baked beans that traditionally includes assorted meats. With a few steamed Brussels sprouts, a loaf of crusty bread, a bottle of wine, and a crisp green salad, this adaptation makes a memorable meal. For dessert, enjoy some fresh grapes with a semi-soft cheese such as Oka or Saint-Paulin.

Brussels Sprouts with Walnuts

4 servings
5 minutes preparation
5 minutes steaming

You can substitute chestnuts for the walnuts—to prepare them see p. 102.

1 quart very fresh Brussels
 sprouts (1 L)
½ cup walnut halves (125 mL)
2 tbsp butter (25 mL)
1 tsp lemon juice (5 mL)
½ tsp Dijon mustard (2 mL)
pinch salt

Slice dried ends from stems and remove any loose leaves. Cut an "X" in each stem. Put trimmed sprouts in a heavy-bottomed pan with ¼ cup (50 mL) of water.

Cover and put on high heat. When steam starts to rise, reduce heat to low and steam until sprouts turn brilliant green (about 5 minutes). Drain off any excess water. Toss in walnuts, butter, lemon juice, mustard and salt. Serve right away.

Cassoulet

8 servings
30 minutes preparation
1 hour soaking
1 hour precooking
2½ hours baking

Clean beans and soak in water and wine for 8 to 12 hours at room temperature (or 1 hour in hot—not boiling—water). Tie bay leaf, celery leaves, thyme, marjoram, sage and cloves in a piece of cheesecloth. Simmer until beans have softened (about 1 hour).

Thaw tempeh and cut into ¾" (2-cm) cubes. Combine vermouth, vinegar, garlic, mustard, salt and nutmeg. Put in a shallow bowl with tempeh cubes. Marinate in a warm place for 1 hour or more. (If marinating for more than 8 hours, keep in refrigerator.) Drain off liquid and reserve for another use. Heat oil in a frying pan. Sauté cubes with frequent tossing until crispy and brown.

Preheat oven to 350°F (180°C). Sauté mushrooms and garlic in oil until lightly browned. Remove herbs in cheesecloth from simmering beans. Stir in the sautéed mushrooms and tempeh. Then stir in butter, vinegar, tarragon, salt and pepper. Pour into a shallow casserole dish. Bake uncovered about 2 hours, pushing top crust into beans about half-way through cooking. If top has not crusted, increase heat to 425°F (220°C) and cook until a crust forms.

If beans seem dry, stir in a little white wine. When crusted a second time (about 30 minutes' additional baking), remove from oven and garnish with chopped parsley.

BEAN MIXTURE:
2 cups dried baby lima beans (500 mL)
5 cups water (1250 mL)
1 cup white wine OR dry vermouth (250 mL)
1 bay leaf
1 stalk celery leaves
1 tbsp rubbed thyme (15 mL)
2 tsp rubbed marjoram (10 mL)
1 tsp rubbed sage (5 mL)
3 whole cloves

MARINATED TEMPEH CUBES:
1 lb tempeh (500 g)
1 cup sweet vermouth OR red wine (250 mL)
1 tbsp red wine vinegar (15 mL)
3 cloves garlic, finely minced
1 tsp prepared Dijon mustard (5 mL)
1 tsp salt (5 mL)
½ tsp freshly grated nutmeg (2 mL)
3 tbsp olive oil (50 mL)

OTHER INGREDIENTS:
3 tbsp olive oil (50 mL)
1½ cups small mushrooms (375 mL)
4 cloves garlic, minced
⅓ cup butter (75 mL)
2 tbsp cider vinegar OR white wine vinegar (25 mL)
1 tbsp crushed tarragon (15 mL)
1 tsp salt (5 mL)
¼ tsp ground white peppercorns (1 mL)
2 tbsp chopped parsley (25 mL)

Romania

Ghivetch is a Romanian vegetable stew. Quick to cook, it traditionally includes twelve vegetables—one for each of the apostles. Since the flavor improves with sitting, you could make it ahead of time and simply reheat it while you prepare the cornmeal mamaliga. For extra interest and protein, top each serving of this Romanian "bread" with a poached egg. Poppyseed strudel is an elegant yet easily prepared dessert.

Ghivetch

2 cups stock (see p. 92)
(500 mL)
10 cups bite-sized chunks of
assorted firm vegetables:
carrots, parsley root, potato
(new or red), kohlrabi, turnip
or rutabaga, celery
or celeriac, parsnip,
Brussels sprouts, cauliflower
(2500 mL)
½ cup olive oil (125 mL)
5 cups bite-sized chunks of
assorted tender vegetables:
small onions, fennel, green
beans, small mushrooms,
sweet pepper, okra (1250 mL)
½ cup coarsely chopped fresh
dill (125 mL)
¼ cup lemon juice (50 mL)
3 cloves garlic, minced
2 tbsp sweet paprika (25 mL)
½ tsp freshly grated nutmeg
(2 mL)
½ tsp salt (2 mL)
¼ tsp cayenne (1 mL)

8 servings
20 minutes preparation
15 minutes cooking

Choose your twelve vegetables from the suggestions at left.

Put stock in a large pot and bring to a boil. Add prepared firm vegetables, one at a time, in order given. This way they should all be tender at about the same time.

Heat oil in a frying pan. Add tender vegetables, one at a time, in order given. Fry until brightly colored and nearly tender.

Add fried ingredients to boiled ones, then stir in remaining flavorings. Bring back to a simmer for 5 minutes to help marry the flavors.

You can serve the stew now or cool and reheat it. It's also delicious as served in Romania, cold or at room temperature. For extra color and a refreshing taste, sprinkle with more chopped dill.

Mamaliga

4 servings
10 minutes preparation

Look for freshly ground whole-grain cornmeal, not the de-germinated kind—natural food stores that turn over their stock quickly are the best source. Avoid any batch in which fine flour is mixed in with coarse granules (it is difficult to cook without sticking and burning).

Bring water and salt to a boil. Remove from heat and, stirring constantly, pour in cornmeal in a steady stream. If any lumps form, break them up with a whisk. Return pot to heat.

Stir constantly with a wooden spoon until thick (about 5 minutes). Stir in green onions. Serve immediately, perhaps topped with a poached egg (see p. 169).

4 cups water (1 L)
1 tsp salt (5 mL)
1 cup cornmeal (250 mL)
½ cup chopped green onions
 OR fresh corn kernels
 (125 mL)

Poppyseed Strudel

8 servings
25 minutes preparation
25 minutes baking

To avoid bitterness, be sure to use fresh poppyseeds.

Toast poppyseeds in a dry frying pan until they begin to pop, then put in the boiling water to soften. Remove pot from heat. After 15 minutes, scoop out and discard any floating seeds. Drain off all excess water. Grind soaked seeds in a blender, food processor or food grinder with honey, raisins and lemon zest until thick and smooth. (This filling can be made several days in advance.)

Preheat oven to 400°F (200°C). Lay a clean dish towel on the counter and get out about 10 sheets of phyllo. Lay one sheet of phyllo on the towel and lightly brush with butter and sprinkle on a few poppyseeds. Repeat with remaining sheets. Brush the last layer with extra butter.

Spread poppyseed mixture in a narrow strip along one long side. With the aid of the towel, roll pastry around filling. Fold in the ends. Slide onto a baking sheet and brush top with butter. Bake until lightly browned (about 25 minutes). Cool before slicing.

FILLING:
1½ cups poppyseeds (375 mL)
2 cups boiling water (500 mL)
½ cup honey (125 mL)
¼ cup raisins (50 mL)
½ tsp lemon zest (2 mL)

WRAPPING:
(½ lb) phyllo (strudel) pastry,
 thawed (250 g)
⅓ cup butter OR oil (75 mL)
2 tbsp poppyseeds (25 mL)

Holiday Entertaining

The foods and drinks served at parties are often high in sugars, fats and alcohol. Here are a couple of healthier, equally satisfying alternatives.

Chickpea pâté is an ideal party food: it can (and should) be made several days ahead, it looks impressive, it's easy to serve, and it tastes unusually good. For a non-alcoholic drink, try this punch. The tea gives it a crisp, dry flavor.

Cranberry Punch

25 5-oz (150-mL) servings
10 minutes preparation
1 hour chilling

Serve in stemmed glasses.

3 heaping tsp tea leaves
    (25 mL) OR 3 teabags
2″ (5 cm) stick cinnamon
1 piece lemon zest 2″ (5 cm)
    square
3 cups boiling water (750 mL)
12 oz cranberries, soft and
    discolored ones removed
    (375 g)
2 quarts apple cider (2 L)

Put tea, cinnamon, and lemon zest in a prewarmed teapot. Pour boiling water over and brew for 5 minutes.

Meanwhile put cranberries in a non-aluminum saucepan with about ¼ cup (50 mL) water. Bring to a simmer and cook until all have popped (about 5 minutes). Turn into a strainer and squeeze out pulp with a wooden spoon. Discard skins and seeds.

Whisk tea and cranberry pulp into cider. Chill in refrigerator for at least 1 hour, or overnight, to permit sediment to settle. Decant the clear juice into a pitcher or punch bowl. Garnish with lemon slices and cinnamon sticks.

Chickpea Pâté

1 12" (30-cm) loaf
30 minutes preparation
1 hour baking
2 hours cooling

Whole pistachios and green peppercorns add bursts of flavor, color and texture. Though the list of ingredients is long, the recipe is easy to make.

Melt butter in a frying pan on medium heat. Slowly fry onion, mushrooms, juniper berries and garlic until onions turn clear. Add chickpea cooking liquid and sherry, then simmer until most of the liquid has evaporated (about 20 minutes).

Meanwhile line a loaf pan with bond paper. Butter it lightly, then carefully line with grape leaves, overlapping them and placing the smooth side against the paper.

Preheat oven to 325°F (160°C). Put fried onion mixture, chickpeas, eggs, yeast, lemon juice, sesame oil, nutmeg, salt and pepper in a food processor bowl and blend briefly (leave some texture). Stir in the whole pistachios and green peppercorns.

Pour mixture into lined loaf pan. Cover with additional grape leaves, then cover pan with foil. Set in a larger pan and add 1" (2.5 cm) water. Bake until pâté is just beginning to puff up (about 1 hour). Cool at least 2 hours before serving.

¼ cup butter (50 mL)
1 cup diced onion (250 mL)
¾ cup chopped mushrooms (175 mL)
1 tbsp chopped juniper berries (15 mL)
3 cloves garlic
½ cup chickpea cooking liquid (125 mL)
½ cup dry sherry (125 mL)
1 small jar grape leaves (available in Greek and Middle Eastern food shops)
4½ cups drained cooked chickpeas (see p. 108) (1125 mL)
5 eggs
½ cup good-tasting nutritional yeast (available in natural food stores) (125 mL)
2 tbsp lemon juice (25 mL)
2 tsp dark sesame seed oil (available in Oriental food shops) (10 mL)
½ tsp freshly grated nutmeg (2 mL)
½ tsp salt (none if cooked with chickpeas) (2 mL)
½ tsp ground white peppercorns (2 mL)
½ cup shelled pistachio nuts (125 mL)
1 tsp whole green peppercorns OR capers (5 mL)

Party Snacks

To avoid the inconvenience of dishes and utensils, many people like to serve party snacks that guests can eat with their fingers. A platter of crudités with a dip is an old stand-by. But the world has a vast repertoire of finger foods. Here is a sampling.

Spiced Fava Sprouts

4 cups (1 L)
15 minutes preparation
4 days sprouting
20 minutes cooking

A Chinese specialty, as addictive as popcorn.

1 cup dried fava beans (250 mL)
¼ cup soy sauce (50 mL)
1 tsp ground star anise, anise OR fennel seeds (5 mL)
2 cloves garlic, chopped
⅛ tsp cayenne (0.5 mL)

Soak beans overnight in 1 quart (1 L) water. The next day put them in a quart jar. Rinse and drain twice a day. In about 4 days they will have developed ½″ (1-cm) sprouts. Place in refrigerator to stop further growth.

Bring soy sauce, anise, garlic, cayenne and ½ cup (125 mL) water to a simmer. Add sprouted beans. Simmer and stir periodically for about 20 minutes. Drain. Eat the beans while still warm, sucking out the tender flesh and discarding the skin.

Tikki

12 patties
15 minutes preparation
30 minutes (total) cooking

These spicy patties can be either shallow-fried or baked.

1 lb potatoes (any kind except new or red) (500 g)
3 tbsp butter (50 mL)
1 cup finely diced onion (250 mL)
2 tbsp masala (see p. 10) OR mild curry powder (25 mL)
½ tsp salt (1 mL)
1 cup bread crumbs (250 mL)
oil for shallow frying

Boil whole potatoes until softened (15 to 25 minutes). Meanwhile melt butter and slowly fry onion and masala. Peel cooked potatoes and mash with fried ingredients and salt. While still warm, shape mixture into 2″ (5-cm) patties. Coat both sides of each patty with bread crumbs. Let firm by cooling to room temperature.

To fry, pour oil ⅛″ (3 mm) deep in a frying pan. When hot, add several patties. Fry both sides until crispy. To bake, preheat oven to 350°F (180°C). Bake patties on buttered cookie sheet until lightly browned (about 15 minutes). Serve warm with tamarind relish (see p. 131), yogurt or catsup.

Dry Roasted Nuts

1 lb (500 g)
10 minutes preparation
1 hour baking

Take a tip from commercial roasters and inject steam into the oven as you roast your nuts—it removes some of the bitterness and adds to the texture. Beaten egg whites add even more crunch.

Preheat oven to 325°F (160°C). Put a cake pan containing 1" (2.5 cm) boiling water in oven. Spread nuts on a baking sheet and put in steamy oven. Stir every 10 minutes so they brown evenly.

Continue baking until aromatic (from 30 minutes to more than 1 hour). Smell carefully—over-roasted nuts take on an unpleasant bitterness.

Remove from oven and toss hot nuts in oil, spices, soy sauce or salt, and optional egg whites. If you have used the soy sauce or egg white, place nuts back in oven for 5 minutes to dry.

Freshly roasted nuts are at their best still warm. Since roasting causes them to deteriorate quickly (particularly when salt has been added), be sure to enjoy them within a few days.

3 cups shelled raw nuts:
  natural or blanched almonds,
  hazelnuts, cashews OR peanuts
  (750 mL)
2 tsp butter OR oil (10 mL)
1 tsp ground cinnamon OR
  curry powder (5 mL)
2 tsp soy sauce (10 mL) OR
  1 tsp finely ground salt (5 mL)
1 egg white, beaten until foamy
  but not stiff (optional)

Crostini

18 pieces
10 minutes preparation
5 minutes broiling

For a small gathering, cook these crispy Italian toasts a few at a time in a toaster oven; for a larger party, use the broiler in your oven.

Cut bread in thin 1" × 3" (3 × 8-cm) pieces. Toast until lightly browned on both sides. Spread a thin layer of garlic butter on each piece, then sprinkle on the cheese. (Can be prepared a day ahead.)

Broil toasts until cheese is sizzling (about 2 minutes). Serve crostini warm by themselves, as an appetizer, or as an accompaniment to a bowl of soup.

6 slices bread
2 tbsp butter blended with 1
  clove minced garlic (25 mL)
½ cup mixed shredded cheeses:
  Provolone, Parmesan,
  Gruyère etc. (125 mL)

Indian Appetizers

Fast foods play just as important a role in India as as they do here, and there too frying is one of the quickest and most convenient ways to cook. (For the most delicate flavor and the least detriment to your health, use fresh oil each time you fry.)

These snacks can be prepared a day or two in advance, then cooked on a moment's notice. They're so good, you may be tempted to turn them into a whole meal.

Samosas

12 pieces
30 minutes preparation
5 minutes frying OR 20 minutes baking

These turnovers can be filled with anything. They're especially delicious flavored with amchur (powdered green mango), available in Indian food shops.

FILLING:
2 tbsp clarified butter (see p. 60)
  OR vegetable oil (25 mL)
2 tsp mustard seeds (10 mL)
2 tsp cumin seeds (10 mL)
½ cup finely diced onion
  (125 mL)
1½ cups finely diced potato
  (375 mL)
½ cup peas, corn kernels,
  diced sweet pepper OR
  zucchini (125 mL)
½ tsp amchur (2 mL) OR
  1 tsp lime juice (5 mL)
¼ tsp salt (1 mL)
¼ tsp ground black
  peppercorns (1 mL)

PASTRY:
1 cup whole-wheat flour
  (250 mL)
1 cup white flour (250 mL)
⅓ cup butter (75 mL)

Heat clarified butter on medium-high heat and add mustard and cumin seeds. When they start to pop, add onion and potato. When lightly browned, add peas. Stir in amchur, salt, pepper and 2 tbsp (25 mL) water and turn heat to low. Cover and simmer for 10 minutes. Remove from heat, cover, and let cool.

For the pastry, combine flours, butter and ½ cup (125 mL) water in a bowl. Knead for 1 minute. If sticky, add more flour. Dough can be used right away, but will be flakier if allowed to rest for at least 30 minutes.

Form dough into six equal-sized balls. Roll each into a circle ⅛" (3 mm) thick and about 6" (15 cm) across. Cut each in half. Form a cone by pinching together the cut (straight) side. Fill with about 1½ tbsp (25 mL) cooled filling. Then pinch together the top (curved) side. Twist the two pinched seams into an attractive pattern. Samosas can be cooked right away, kept in refrigerator for 1 day, or frozen for several weeks (thaw before cooking).

For the tastiest and quickest results, deep fry samosas in 375°F (190°C) oil until lightly browned (about 3 minutes). Or bake them on a cookie sheet in a preheated 400°F (200°C) oven until lightly browned (about 20 minutes). Serve right away with tamarind relish, plain yogurt or—as some now do in India—with ordinary tomato catsup.

Tamarind Relish

¼ cup (50 mL)
5 minutes preparation

Try this sweet-and-sour condiment with French fries as well as Indian foods.

Stir together tamarind concentrate, water, ginger, salt and pepper. Relish can be used right away or kept in refrigerator for 2 weeks. To serve, pour into a saucer and garnish with green onion.

1 tbsp tamarind concentrate (available in Indian food shops) (15 mL) OR 2 tbsp (25 mL) molasses with 1 tbsp (15 mL) red wine vinegar
2 tbsp water (none if vinegar used) (25 mL)
2 tsp freshly grated ginger (10 mL)
1 tsp salt (5 mL)
1 tsp ground black pepper-corns (5 mL)
¼ cup sliced green onion tops (optional) (50 mL)

Pakoras

16 "fritters"
10 minutes preparation
10 minutes frying

Chickpea flour (besan—available in Indian and natural food stores) makes the lightest and tenderest batter, but some brands may fall apart when fried. If you aren't sure of the quality, include some wheat flour to prevent problems.

Whisk together flour(s), masala, salt and 1¼ cups (300 mL) water. Batter can be used right away, but coating will be lighter if allowed to rest at least 1 hour (or overnight).

Preheat oil in a deep fryer to 375°F (180°C). Stir vegetables into batter. Scoop up 1½ tbsp (25 mL) of the mixture and drop into hot oil. Loosen any that stick to the bottom. Repeat until surface is crowded. Fry until batter is crispy and lightly browned (about 4 minutes).

Drain on paper towels and serve with tamarind relish or yogurt. Repeat with remaining vegetables.

1 cup chickpea flour (250 mL)
½ cup soft wheat flour OR additional chickpea flour (125 mL)
1 tbsp masala (see p. 10) OR mild curry powder (15 mL)
¼ tsp salt (1 mL)
oil for deep frying
3 cups assorted ingredients: thinly sliced onion, eggplant, okra, zucchini, spinach, green beans, sweet peppers; pomegranate seeds; mung bean sprouts (750 mL)

Sweden

Many people think of cabbage rolls as comfort food—too ordinary to serve to company. But savoy cabbage (the kind with the crinkly leaves) makes especially attractive rolls. Stuffed with buckwheat and lentils and topped with a currant sauce, they're elegant enough for any guests.

Continue the Swedish theme with hasselback potatoes, perhaps some candied or glazed beets with a dollop of sour cream (for color), and a deliciously tart cranberry kissel for dessert.

Hasselback Potatoes

8 servings
15 minutes preparation
1 hour baking

Rich and elegant.

Preheat oven to 350°F (180°C). Make thin (⅛"/3-mm) slices nearly all the way through the potatoes. (Place each one on a saucer when slicing, to avoid accidentally cutting all the way through.) Bake until potatoes open into fans (about 45 minutes). Put a sliver of butter in each slit and sprinkle with salt and pepper. Bake again until golden brown (about 15 minutes). Serve immediately.

8 medium red OR all purpose potatoes, cleaned
⅓ cup butter (75 mL)
salt and pepper

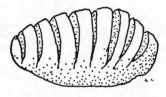

Cranberry Kissel

8 servings
15 minutes preparation
1 hour cooling

This jelly-like dessert can be made with any tart red fruit.

Simmer cranberries, honey, cinnamon and salt in 1½ cups (375 mL) water until the berries have popped (about 5 minutes). Remove skins, seeds and cinnamon by pushing through a strainer.

Bring juice back to a simmer. Meanwhile combine arrowroot with ½ cup (125 mL) cool water. Stir into hot juice. Stir continuously until mixture turns clear and again reaches a simmer. Pour into serving bowls and refrigerate until cool and set.

Serve garnished with whipped cream and a sprinkling of chopped almonds

12 oz cranberries, discolored and misshapen ones discarded (375 g)
⅓ cup honey (75 mL)
2" (5 cm) stick cinnamon
pinch salt
3 tbsp arrowroot OR other starch (50 mL)

Swedish Cabbage Rolls

18 rolls
20 minutes soaking
40 minutes preparation
45 minutes baking

In Sweden the sauce for cabbage rolls is traditionally made with lingonberries, but dried currants are more readily available here. Substitute tomato sauce (see p. 18) if you prefer.

For the filling, soak lentils in hot water, off heat, until doubled in size (about 20 minutes). Bring to a boil and stir in buckwheat and salt. Reduce heat and simmer until water has been absorbed (about 20 minutes).

Meanwhile melt butter on medium heat in a large frying pan. Add onion, celery, mushrooms and caraway. Fry gently until onion turns clear. Then add dill, garlic, thyme and sage. Remove from heat and cover. Stir fried onion mixture into cooked buckwheat and lentils. (If you have more than you need, use it in a savory strudel, p. 107.)

For cabbage leaves, bring a large pot of water to a boil. Break off and reserve outer leaves, then carefully peel off inner ones. Blanch, a few at a time, in boiling water until softened (about 3 minutes). Slice off protruding main ribs.

Preheat oven to 350°F (180°C). Put about 2 tbsp (30 mL) stuffing on the concave side of each leaf. Roll one turn from the base, fold over the sides, then roll to the tip of each leaf. Place in an 8" × 10" (20 × 25-cm) baking dish with tip sides down. When dish is filled, cover with reserved cabbage leaves and ¼ cup (50 mL) water. Place in oven and bake until heated through (about 45 minutes). Discard cabbage-leaf cover before serving.

For currant sauce, slowly heat stock, currants, soy sauce, vinegar and cardamom. Whisk together arrowroot and 2 tbsp (25 mL) water. Stir into hot stock mixture and bring to a simmer. Remove cardamom and serve sauce immediately over cabbage rolls.

BUCKWHEAT STUFFING:
½ cup brown lentils (125 mL)
3 cups boiling water (750 mL)
1 cup (raw) buckwheat OR (toasted) kasha (250 mL)
1 tsp salt (5 mL)
¼ cup butter (50 mL)
1 cup diced onion (250 mL)
½ cup finely diced celery OR celeriac (125 mL)
½ cup finely chopped mushrooms (125 mL)
¼ tsp caraway seeds (optional) (1 mL)
¼ cup chopped dill (50 mL)
3 cloves garlic, minced
2 tsp rubbed thyme (10 mL)
½ tsp rubbed sage (2 mL)

CABBAGE LEAVES:
1 large head savoy cabbage

CURRANT SAUCE:
¾ cup stock OR ⅓ sherry and ⅔ water (175 mL)
¼ cup dried currants (50 mL)
2 tsp soy sauce (10 mL)
2 tsp vinegar (10 mL)
4 pods white OR green cardamom
1 tbsp arrowroot (15 mL)

Christmas Tradition

In Dickens' *A Christmas Carol*, the highlight of the Cratchit family's dinner was the Christmas pudding. This recipe makes a pudding much like the one the Cratchits enjoyed, without refined sugar or artificially colored fruit. If you make up extras to give to friends, you might like to include reheating instructions and the recipe for butter cream.

FRUIT:

3 cups (packed) dried fruit: raisins or currants; seeded and chopped prunes; diced figs, dates and apricots (750 mL)

3 cups liquid: apple cider, orange juice, beer, wine OR sherry (750 mL)

BATTER:

1 cup butter (250 mL)

2¼ cups sifted soft whole-wheat flour (550 mL)

5 cups bread OR cake crumbs (1250 mL)

1 tsp mixed ground allspice, cinnamon, nutmeg AND cardamom (5 mL)

½ tsp freshly grated ginger (2 mL)

½ tsp grated lemon OR orange zest (2 mL)

¼ tsp salt (none if breadcrumbs used) (1 mL)

2 cups finely shredded apple OR carrot (500 mL)

1 cup chopped (preferably roasted) walnuts, almonds, pecans OR hazelnuts (250 mL)

5 eggs, beaten until foamy

2 cups additional liquid: apple cider, orange juice, beer, wine OR tea (500 mL)

1 cup sweetener: buckwheat honey, maple syrup OR malt syrup (250 mL)

2 tbsp lemon juice (25 mL)

1 cup rum OR brandy (optional) (250 mL)

Christmas Pudding

4 quarts (4 L)
45 minutes total preparation
7 hours steaming
1 week resting

A proper Christmas pudding calls for many ingredients and a lot of resting, but it is by no means difficult to prepare. Make it a family event: have each member choose at least one ingredient and for good luck let everyone stir.

The day before assembly, put dried fruit in the first liquid to soak.

The day of assembly, cut butter into flour as for pastry, until the consistency of rolled oats. Toss in crumbs, mixed spices, ginger, zest, salt, apple or carrot, and nuts. Combine eggs, additional liquid, sweetener and lemon juice. Stir this mixture and the soaked fruits (with their liquid) into the tossed ingredients. Cover and let rest overnight.

The following day check batter for taste and consistency. It should be just liquid enough that it mounds, then slowly flows to make a level surface—add more liquid to thin or more crumbs to thicken. Taste, then stir in whatever additional flavorings you want.

Generously butter pudding molds (inexpensive stainless steel bowls work well). Fill three-quarters full with batter. Cover with foil. Set on racks in one or two large pots and fill with cold water until it comes two-thirds of the way up the sides of the molds. On low heat bring water to a simmer (it should take 30 minutes). Simmer, covered, for 6 hours (4 hours for very small molds). Turn off heat and leave puddings in water to cool overnight.

Keep puddings in refrigerator for at least 1 week. (For more flavor, remove from molds, poke holes in them with a knitting needle, wrap in cheesecloth and drench with rum or brandy, then return to molds.)

Before serving remove cloth, return puddings to molds, cover and steam for at least 1 hour. Turn out and garnish with sprigs of holly. For a more spectacular presentation, pour on some fresh rum or brandy and ignite. Serve with whipped cream (see p. 47) or butter cream laced with rum.

Butter Cream

2¼ cups (550 mL)
20 minutes preparation
20 minutes cooling

Use butter cream as a cake filling or as a sauce for warm puddings.

Heat syrup in a heavy-bottomed saucepan to the soft-ball stage (245°F/120°C). Meanwhile beat egg yolks and lemon juice until thick enough to leave a trail when beater is lifted (about 4 minutes). While continuing to beat, slowly pour hot syrup into beaten yolks. Continue to beat until mixture has cooled to about 75°F (25°C). Whisk in butter, and continue to whisk for 5 minutes. Whisk in liqueur.

⅓ cup maple syrup OR honey (75 mL)
4 warm egg yolks
¼ tsp lemon juice (1 mL)
½ cup unsalted butter, room temperature (125 mL)
2 tbsp your choice of liqueur (optional) (25 mL)

Honey-Sweetened Treats

For anyone who likes sweets, the holiday season usually means constant temptation. Fortunately, honey's natural flavor is strong enough that a little goes a long way. Here are three honey-sweetened treats.

1 cup honey (250 mL)
¾ cup unsalted butter
   (175 mL)
3 tbsp lemon juice (50 mL)
1 tbsp ground anise seeds OR
   freshly grated ginger (15 mL)
3 cups sifted soft whole-wheat
   OR triticale flour (available at
   natural food stores) (750 mL)
½ tsp baking soda (2 mL)
pinch salt

Honey-Lemon Cookies

36 cookies
15 minutes preparation
1½ hours cooling
30 minutes baking

If you can keep these cookies from being eaten, they will continue to improve in flavor for some time.

Beat honey and butter until creamy. Beat in lemon juice and anise or ginger. Sift together flour, baking soda and salt. Stir into honey-butter mixture until well blended.

   Place in refrigerator until firm (about 1½ hours or overnight). Shape mixture into 1″ (2.5-cm) balls. Place on a cool shiny cookie sheet, leaving 2″ (5 cm) between them. Press into disks ¼″ (1 cm) thick.

   Preheat oven to 350°F (180°C). Place cookies on middle shelf and bake until lightly browned (about 15 minutes). Bake a second sheet of cookies. When cool enough to move, transfer to a cake rack to cool and dry.

Marzipan

3½ lb (1.5 kg)
15 minutes preparation
20 minutes roasting
1 week chilling

Avoid all the sugar and food coloring in the commercial versions and enjoy the rich flavor of this home-made Romanian-style marzipan. Since you are relying on crystallization to firm it, be sure to use only unpasteurized honey and make it up a week or two ahead, since the process takes some time. It is definitely worth the wait.

Lightly roast almonds in a 300°F. (150°C) oven until aromatic (about 20 minutes). Grind until fluffy, either in a food processor with the fine blade of a shredder attachment, or in small batches in a blender. Knead in remaining ingredients. The mixture should feel like bread dough. If crumbly, add a little more honey; if too sticky, add more ground almonds.

Form mixture into whatever shape you like—perhaps a log, for slicing into wafers. Wrap well in waxed paper and foil and place in refrigerator for honey to crystallize.

After 1 to 2 weeks the marzipan will be firm and ready to serve. It will remain fresh in the refrigerator for weeks and in the freezer for months.

5 cups (2 lb) almonds
   (1250 mL/1 kg)
2 cups liquid unpasteurized
   honey (500 mL)
¼ cup toasted carob powder
   (50 mL)
¼ cup liquor: brandy,
   Amaretto or Grand Marnier
   (50 mL) OR ½ tsp rosewater
   (2 mL)
½ tsp grated lemon zest
   (2 mL)
pinch salt

Creamy Eggnog

4 quarts/25 servings (4 L)
20 minutes preparation

This tastes even richer than it really is.

Slowly heat milk and vanilla bean in a large heavy-bottomed pot. Meanwhile whisk together egg yolks, honey and arrowroot. When milk reaches a gentle simmer, remove vanilla bean (save it for another use). Stir the egg mixture as you pour in half the hot milk. Then stir the remaining milk as you pour the mixture back into the pot.

Return mixture to stove and stir continuously until thick enough to coat the back of the spoon. Immediately strain to remove any curdled particles. Then stir in liquor (or cider) and salt.

This base can be used right away, but the flavor improves if it rests in the refrigerator overnight. Just before serving, beat half the egg whites until soft peaks form and fold into the base. Reserve the remaining egg whites to beat and add for late arrivals and second helpings. Serve in wine glasses or punch cups, topped with freshly grated nutmeg.

2 quarts milk OR cereal cream
   (2 L)
1 vanilla bean
12 large eggs, separated
½ cup honey (125 mL)
1 tsp arrowroot OR other
   starch (5 mL)
1½ cups liquor: rum, brandy
   or whisky OR sweet apple
   cider (375 mL)
pinch salt

Jewish Holidays

Many Jewish holiday foods have particular historic or religious significance. Mushroom and barley soup, for example, is now enjoyed in honor of earlier, harder times when it was daily fare. Latkes, potato pancakes fried in plenty of oil, are a highlight of Chanukah.

Mushroom and Barley Soup

8 bowls
15 minutes preparation
3 hours soaking and cooking

Since the barley swells considerably, avoid the temptation to start with any more than suggested. Pot barley gives the best flavor.

¾ cup pot OR pearl barley, rinsed and cleaned (175 mL)
3 tbsp butter (50 mL)
1 cup diced onion (250 mL)
2 cups diced potato (500 mL)
2 cups sliced fresh OR rehydrated dried mushrooms (500 mL)
½ tsp rubbed thyme (2 mL)
1 cup stock (see p. 92) OR beer (250 mL)
1 tsp salt (5 mL)
¼ tsp ground black peppercorns (1 mL)

Put barley in a large soup pot with 6 cups (1500 mL) water. Bring to a simmer and cook gently for 2 hours, stirring occasionally.

Heat butter in a frying pan on medium heat. Add onion, potato, mushrooms and thyme. Fry until aromatic (about 5 minutes). Add fried ingredients, stock, salt and pepper to cooked barley.

Soup can be served now, but will taste even better after cooling and reheating. Serve with a dollop of sour cream or a knob of butter.

Tzimmes

8 servings
20 minutes preparation
1½ hours baking

Though this casserole filled with sweet golden "coins" is a traditional part of the Jewish New Year, it can be served any time as a side dish or a main course.

3 cups carrots cut in ¼" (5-mm) "coins" (750 mL)
4 tbsp flour (50 mL)
1 cup sliced onions (250 mL)
½ cup pitted and chopped prunes (125 mL)
¼ cup diced butter (50 mL)
1 tsp ground cinnamon (5 mL)
1 cup sliced apple (250 mL)
2 cups sliced sweet potato (500 mL)
2 cups stock (see p. 92) OR white wine (500 mL)
½ cup matzo meal OR bread crumbs (125 mL)

Preheat oven to 325°F (160°C). In a deep 4-quart (4-L) casserole, put layers of carrots, flour, onions, prunes, butter, cinnamon, apple and sweet potato. Pour in the stock and sprinkle on the matzo meal.

Cover and bake for 1 hour. Uncover and continue baking until mixture is bubbly and the top layer is lightly browned (another 30 minutes). Serve right away.

Latkes

12 pancakes
25 minutes preparation

For the laciest pancakes, grate the potatoes into large shreds—best done with the shredding attachment of a kitchen machine or food processor.

Toss together potato, eggs, meal and salt. Heat a heavy-bottomed frying pan on medium-high heat. Melt 1½ tbsp (25 mL) of butter and spoon in enough batter to make three thin 4″ (10-cm) pancakes. Brown on both sides.

Repeat with the remaining batter. Keep cooked latkes warm on a plate in a 200°F (100°C) oven. Serve, the most attractive side up, with sour cream and applesauce (see p. 155).

3 cups shredded potato (750 mL)
3 eggs, lightly beaten
4 tbsp matzo meal OR soft whole-wheat flour (60 mL)
½ tsp salt (2 mL)
6 tbsp clarified butter (see p. 60) OR ½ butter and ½ oil (100 mL)

Hamantaschen

16 pastries
20 minutes preparation
2 hours chilling
10 minutes baking

These triangular pastries are especially good with tea. For a poppyseed filling, see p. 125.

Beat butter and honey until creamy (about 3 minutes). Knead in flours and salt until well blended. Chill in refrigerator for 1 hour.

For the filling, bring prunes, honey and ¼ cup (50 mL) water to a simmer. Remove from heat and cool to lukewarm. Blend until smooth. Stir in lemon zest.

Roll golfball-sized pieces of pastry dough into 3″ (8-cm) disks. Place 1 tbsp (15 mL) filling in the center of each. Fold dough into a three-cornered pouch, leaving some of the filling still visible. Moisten edges and squeeze seams together. Chill pastries for another hour, or freeze until needed.

Preheat oven to 375°F (190°C). Bake pastries on a cookie sheet until crust is lightly browned (about 10 minutes) Serve while still warm

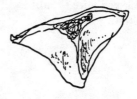

PASTRY:
1 cup butter, softened and diced (250 mL)
½ cup honey (125 mL)
1½ cups sifted soft whole wheat flour (375 mL)
1½ cups sifted triticale OR durum flour (available in natural food stores) (500 mL)
pinch salt

FILLING:
2 cups finely chopped pitted prunes (500 mL)
¼ cup honey (50 mL)
¼ tsp lemon zest (1 mL)

Christmas Breakfast

Christmas morning calls for a special breakfast. One easily prepared treat is nothing more than popovers with lots of homemade sweet butter (see p. 35), assorted jams and jellies and a pitcher of freshly squeezed orange juice. For something more substantial, add a pan of scrambled eggs garnished with caper tapénade.

Popovers

about 20 popovers
10 minutes preparation
40 minutes baking

For the batter to have the strength to rise high, its gluten must be developed. Start with all ingredients at room temperature and beat them vigorously.

2 cups milk (500 mL)
4 large eggs
2 cups unsifted finely ground
  soft whole-wheat flour
  (500 mL)
½ cup white flour (125 mL)
½ tsp lemon juice (2 mL)
pinch salt

Preheat oven to 400°F (200°C). Pour milk into a pitcher and immerse it with the eggs in a bowl of hot tap water. Butter and dust with flour two muffin trays or several custard cups (the heavier the better). Place in oven for 2 minutes to warm.

Combine warmed milk, flours, lemon juice and salt. Spin in a blender or food processor with plastic blade (or whisk by hand) for 30 seconds. While still spinning (or whisking), break in warmed eggs one at a time. If mixture is any thinner than pancake batter, add more flour.

Fill each container ¾ full of batter (and any empty ones with water). Quickly place in oven and bake until puffed up (about 15 minutes). Then reduce heat to 350°F (180°C) and continue baking until tops are golden brown (about 25 minutes more).

Scrambled Eggs

8 servings
10 minutes preparation

Problems arise when you try to cook too few eggs, too quickly, and with too much stirring.

Slowly melt butter in a saucepan on medium-low heat. Meanwhile whisk together eggs and water or wine. When nearly blended, stir in cheese. When butter is melted, pour in egg mixture.

When eggs begin to coagulate on the bottom, push them aside to let raw egg flow down. Don't be tempted to do this more than once every minute—you want the curds to be large.

When eggs have turned to a mixture of tender curds and soft custard, remove from heat. If you have inadvertently overcooked them, stir in 1 more lightly beaten egg.

Serve right away in popovers or on toast (preferably cooked only on bottom side). Top with a dab of tapénade.

2 tbsp unsalted butter (25 mL)
12 large eggs
½ cup water OR white wine (125 mL)
½ cup diced Brie OR other soft cheese (optional) (125 mL)

Tapénade

1½ cups (375 mL)
10 minutes preparation

Since the capers in this recipe are blended smooth, they need not be the most expensive kind.

Combine everything but oil in a blender or food processor. Blend until smooth. While still blending, pour in oil in a stream until thickened (like a mayonnaise).

Serve immediately or keep in the refrigerator for several weeks. (You might consider packing a batch into attractive bottles for gifts.)

½ cup capers (125 mL)
½ cup pitted black olives (125 mL)
1 tbsp lemon juice OR caper pickling vinegar (15 mL)
1 tbsp brandy (optional) (15 mL)
2 tsp Dijon mustard (10 mL)
½ cup olive oil (125 mL)

Christmas Dinner I

B'stilla is a layered pastry with various fillings that in Morocco is often served as the centerpiece of elaborate banquets. But it also makes a terrific main course for a North American holiday feast. Carve this version at the table and serve it with whatever family favorites you want—its flavors and textures combine well with nearly anything.

Orange Salad

4 servings
10 minutes preparation

Navel oranges are best for this Moroccan salad. The radishes traditionally used are black ones (available in specialty markets during winter months). If your onions are too strong, first soak them in lemon juice for 15 minutes.

4 oranges, peeled, sliced crosswise and seeded
½ cup radish (preferably black), peeled and shredded (125 mL)
½ cup onion (preferably red), thinly sliced (125 mL)
2 tbsp olive oil (25 mL)
2 tsp mint (preferably fresh), chopped (10 mL)
1 tsp ground cinnamon (5 mL)
¼ tsp orange-flower OR rose water (available in Middle Eastern food shops) (optional) (1 mL)

Place orange slices on individual salad plates. Sprinkle radish and onion pieces evenly over the top. Splash on the oil and dust with mint and cinnamon. For an authentic aroma, sprinkle on a few drops of the orange-flower water. Serve right away or let flavors meld for up to an hour.

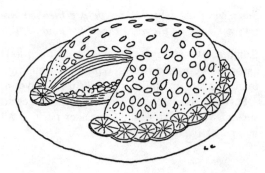

B'stilla

12 servings
30 minutes preparation
45 minutes baking

Stir together cooked rice, butter, cinnamon, salt and pepper. For onion mixture, heat butter and slowly fry onions, olives, almonds and coriander until onions turn clear. Remove water from tofu by wrapping in nylon sheer material and squeezing until volume is reduced by one-third. Knead garlic, cumin, oregano, cayenne and salt into tofu. Cool these mixtures before starting assembly.

Preheat oven to 350°F (180°C). To assemble the b'stilla, take a sheet of phyllo and place on a cookie sheet. Brush on some of the melted butter and sprinkle on 2 tsp (10 mL) ground almonds. Repeat for about 10 layers, rotating each new sheet a few degrees so that a rosette is formed. Cover top sheet with a generous coating of melted butter. Spread with rice mixture. Fold 5 of the phyllo layers over it. Lay on another sheet of phyllo and butter well. Spread with fried onion mixture. Fold remaining 5 layers over top. Cover with another sheet and butter it well. Spread with tofu mixture.

Finish forming your b'stilla by laying on another 10 sheets of phyllo with butter and almonds between them, again rotating each one a few degrees. After the top layer is in place, tuck edges neatly under bottom layer of pastry. For an attractive crust, brush top with butter and sprinkle with ground cinnamon and sliced almonds. Bake until golden brown (about 45 minutes). Serve immediately.

RICE:
2 cups cooked plain rice (see p. 119) OR saffron rice (p. 8) (500 mL)
¼ cup butter, melted (50 mL)
1 tsp ground cinnamon (5 mL)
½ tsp salt (unless cooked with rice) (2 mL)
¼ tsp ground black peppercorns (1 mL)

ONIONS:
2 tbsp butter (25 mL)
2 cups sliced onions (500 mL)
½ cup sliced pitted olives (125 mL)
½ cup chopped almonds (125 mL)
2 tbsp chopped fresh coriander OR mint leaves (25 mL)

TOFU:
1 lb tofu (500 g)
1 clove garlic, finely minced
1 tsp ground cumin seeds (5 mL)
½ tsp ground oregano (2 mL)
¼ tsp cayenne (1 mL)
¼ tsp salt (1 mL)

PASTRY:
1 lb phyllo pastry (500 g)
1 cup ground almonds OR bread crumbs (250 mL)
½ cup melted butter OR almond oil (125 mL)

Christmas Dinner II

The main course of this Christmas dinner is redolent with holiday flavors. Serve it with any of the traditional side-dishes—perhaps wild rice (p. 102), steamed Brussels sprouts with walnuts (p. 122) and cranberry sauce (p. 103). Start with a delicate squash soup (p. 99), and follow the main course with a simple lettuce salad, then finish the repast with a festive apple pie (p. 147) and Christmas pudding (p. 134).

Miso Sauce

1 cup (250 mL)
10 minutes preparation

This soy-based sauce can be used as a light gravy.

½ cup orange juice (125 mL)
2 tbsp light-colored miso or bean paste (available in Oriental and natural food stores) (25 mL)
2 tbsp dry vermouth OR sherry (25 mL)
1 dried hot chili, split open
1 piece orange zest 1″ (2.5 cm) square
1 tbsp arrowroot OR other starch (15 mL)

Slowly heat orange juice, miso, vermouth, chili and orange zest. When liquid reaches a simmer, remove chili and zest.

Combine arrowroot with 2 tbsp (25 mL) cold water and stir into hot liquid. Continue stirring until mixture is thick. Serve right away over sliced tofu-mushroom roll, cooked grains, or vegetables such as parsnips, potatoes or zucchini.

Tofu-Mushroom Rolls

12 servings
45 minutes preparation
30 minutes baking

The almond stuffing provides crunch, the tofu filling richness, and the bean curd covering a satisfyingly firm texture. Dried bean curd sheets are available in Chinese food stores (for more information, see p. 118). Be sure to use unbroken sheets.

For the almond stuffing, heat frying pan on medium heat and add oil. Fry onion, almonds and celery until tender and aromatic. Stir in remaining ingredients.

For the tofu filling, heat another frying pan on high heat. Add oil and mushrooms. Fry until most of the liquid has evaporated. Add garlic and remove from heat.

Put tofu in cheesecloth or a dish towel. Wrap tightly and squeeze out excess liquid (volume should be reduced by about one-third). Scrape tofu from cloth into a bowl. Stir in arrowroot, mustard, soy sauce, lemon juice, honey, and the fried mushroom mixture.

Preheat oven to 350°F (180°C). To assemble, soak the bean curd sheets in a tray or sink of warm water until pliable (about 15 minutes). Place towel on the counter and stack 3 bean curd sheets on it, sprinkling cinnamon between layers.

Along one long side, spread half the tofu filling in a band about 6″ (15 cm) wide. Spread a narrow strip of half the almond stuffing down the center of the tofu band. By lifting the towel, gently coax bean curd sheets around the two fillings (you may need an extra pair of hands). Place on a baking sheet. Repeat to make a second roll. Brush both with oil and sprinkle on more cinnamon.

Bake until filling is set and bean curd is browned (about 30 minutes). Transfer to a platter. Garnish with one or more accompanying vegetables. Slice at the table (using a sharp serrated knife and plenty of sawing action) and serve with miso sauce.

ALMOND STUFFING:
¼ cup almond OR other oil (50 mL)
½ cup diced onion (125 mL)
½ cup coarsely chopped almonds (125 mL)
¼ cup diced celery (50 mL)
3 tbsp chopped parsley (50 mL)
2 tsp rubbed thyme (10 mL)
1 tsp rubbed sage (5 mL)
¼ tsp ground black peppercorns (1 mL)
2 cups whole-grain bread crumbs (500 mL)
¼ cup currants (50 mL)
¾ cup tomato juice (175 mL)

TOFU FILLING:
¼ cup unrefined peanut OR corn oil (50 mL)
3 cups chopped mushrooms (preferably with open gills) (750 mL)
4 cloves garlic, minced
2 lb tofu (1 kg)
4 tbsp arrowroot OR other starch (60 mL)
½ tsp mustard powder OR prepared mustard (2 mL)
1 tbsp soy sauce (15 mL)
1 tsp lemon juice (5 mL)
1 tsp honey (5 mL)

WRAPPING:
6 sheets dried bean curd
1 tsp ground cinnamon (5 mL)

Holiday Pie

Translating heirloom pastry recipes to more natural ingredients is not always successful. But after years of experimentation, I have discovered a number of tricks to ensure tender, flaky pie crusts. The most important points are, first, to start with the most finely ground soft whole-wheat flour you can find (usually a little white flour is needed to compensate for a coarse grind); and second, to measure it by weight rather than volume (to account for variations in percentage of moisture and bran).

You can substitute butter for lard and vegetable shortening (oil will not make flaky crusts—just short tender ones). But keep in mind that butter is about 15% water, which can make pastry tough, and that if it is warm, it will melt too quickly for the pastry to be flaky. To make cold butter pliable enough to work with without raising its temperature, knead it in a towel (the towel will also absorb some of the excess moisture). For tender pastry, work the dough as little as possible, and let it rest between stages. After mastering the basic technique, you can double or triple this recipe.

Whole-Wheat Pie Shell

2 9" (22.5-cm) pie shells
15 minutes preparation
15 minutes resting
12 minutes baking

⅔ cup (5 oz) cold unsalted butter (150 mL/150 g)
1½ cups (7 oz) sifted finely ground soft whole-wheat flour (375 mL/200 g)
1 cup (4 oz) sifted white pastry flour (250 mL/120 g)
1 large cold egg
1 tsp lemon juice (5 mL)
pinch salt
approximately 3 tbsp ice water (50 mL)
1 egg white, lightly beaten

Knead butter in a clean cloth towel. Cut butter into flour with two knives or a sturdy pastry cutter until pieces are the size of oat flakes.

Whisk egg, lemon juice and salt with enough ice water to make ⅓ cup (75 mL).While tossing flour and butter with a fork, sprinkle in the liquid mixture. When all liquid has been added, gather dough into two grapefruit-sized balls. Squeeze each together as you would a snowball. If crumbly, sprinkle in a few drops more liquid. If sticky, use extra flour when rolling out the pastry. Place dough in refrigerator to rest at least 15 minutes.

Place rested dough on a flat surface well dusted with flour. Flatten one ball into a rectangular sheet about 1" (2.5 cm) thick and roll into a 4" × 10" (10 ×25-cm) sheet. Fold sheet in half and roll into a circle by working outwards from the center. (Back-and-forth rolling makes pastry tough and prone to shrink.)

If a tear develops, take a piece of dough from the edge and moisten it with a few drops of water, then press it onto the tear Lift circle of dough over rolling pin and place in an unbuttered pie plate. Gently push (don't stretch) dough into pan.

Prick the bottom in a dozen places with a fork. To keep pastry from sliding into the plate as it bakes, as you trim off the excess dough be sure to leave a little dough falling over the edge. Give the shell a finished touch by pinching the dough around the rim with your fingers, or pressing it with a thimble or the tines of a fork. Let rest in the refrigerator for 15 minutes. Repeat with second ball of dough.

Preheat oven to 425°F (220°C). Cover chilled dough with a sheet of foil and weight it down with a layer of dried beans. Place on a lower oven shelf and bake until lightly browned (about 12 minutes). Remove foil and beans. After cooling a couple of minutes brush the warm crust with egg white. Let dry and cool thoroughly before using.

Apple Pie

1 9" (22.5-cm) pie
20 minutes preparation
40 minutes baking
1 hour cooling

This pie has a fresh apple flavor—the only sweet part is the glaze.

Preheat oven to 350°F (180°C). Whisk together applesauce, eggs and cinnamon. Peel and core apples, then slice them very thinly and toss with lemon juice. Pour applesauce mixture into prepared pie shell and smooth top. Attractively arrange apple slices over it. Promptly bake on an upper shelf until applesauce has set and apples are lightly browned (about 40 minutes).

Completely cool pie on a cake rack (about 1 hour). Slowly melt jelly with sherry, or heat honey to 250°F (120°C). Let cool until the consistency of egg whites. Brush either glaze over apples. Serve the same day, or glaze may melt.

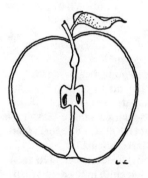

2 cups applesauce (see p. 155) (500 mL)
2 eggs, lightly beaten
¼ tsp ground cinnamon (optional) (1 mL)
2 cooking apples: Northern Spy OR Granny Smith
½ tsp lemon juice (2 mL)
1 prebaked and sealed Whole-Wheat Pie Shell

GLAZE:
⅓ cup red currant jelly (see p. 44) (75 mL) with 1 tbsp sherry (15 mL) OR ½ cup honey (125 mL)

New Year's Eve

The early hours of New Year's Day call for a special meal—something simple to prepare, substantial enough to tame the effects of too much drink, and spicy enough to interest dulled palates.

The Korean dish called bindatuk meets all the qualifications. Cooked with whatever filling(s) your guests choose, these savory pancakes offer a wide range of possibilities, and the flavorful sauces and condiments add even more variety. The batter and condiments can be made up to a week ahead. For a small group the final cooking can be done out of the kitchen in an electric frying pan, but for a large gathering a kitchen griddle is most efficient.

Bindatuk

16 pancakes
30 minutes preparation
24 hours soaking

2 cups brown rice, cleaned (500 mL)
1 cup mung beans, cleaned (250 mL)
2 tsp dry active yeast (10 mL)
1 tsp dark sesame oil (available at Oriental and natural food stores) (5 mL)
2 tbsp sesame seeds (25 mL)
½ hot chili, minced OR ⅛ tsp cayenne (0.5 mL)
1 clove garlic, minced
4 cups trimmed assorted vegetables (see recipe) (1 L)

Soak rice and beans in 3 cups (750 mL) water for 8 to 24 hours.

Pulverize mixture in a blender. If thicker than whipping cream, add a little water; if thinner, add a little flour (any kind). Then stir in yeast, oil, sesame seeds, chili and garlic. Let rest for at least 8 hours.

Before serving, prepare vegetables as described below. (Unusual ones are available in Oriental food stores.) Refresh each vegetable in cold water immediately after blanching in a large pot of boiling water. Then attractively arrange them in mounds on a large platter.

SHALLOTS OR WHITE PART OF GREEN ONIONS: cut into rings and sauté until lightly browned.
MUNG BEAN SPROUTS: break off any brown rootlets and blanch for a few seconds.
CABBAGE: shred and blanch until slightly wilted.
BROCCOLI: cut very small flowerets and blanch until bright green.
CELERY: slice stalks thinly and blanch until just tender.
GREENS (spinach, mustard greens, bok choy or watercress leaves): blanch until bright green and chop.
EGGPLANT (the long, narrow Oriental kind): cut in quarters, slice thinly, then sprinkle with salt and drain for 30 minutes; rinse and pat dry; sauté in peanut oil until softened

SWEET PEPPERS: cut in half and remove seeds; sauté until brightly colored.

ASPARAGUS: peel and slice trimmed stalks diagonally; blanch until bright green.

BAMBOO SHOOTS (canned): cut in thin slivers.

BITTER MELON: cut in half, remove seeds and cut in thin strips; soak in salted water for 1 hour, then blanch until bright green.

BLACK MUSHROOMS: rinse out grit; soak in warm water for 30 minutes, then slice.

TENDER KELP (*wakame*): soak in warm water for 15 minutes, then cut in thin strips.

WATER CHESTNUTS (fresh or canned): peel and dice.

To cook each pancake, put about ½ cup (125 mL) batter on a hot, lightly oiled frying pan or griddle. Sprinkle on about ¼ cup (50 mL) of one or more vegetables, then quickly swirl outward with the back of a spoon to form a pancake ¼" (5 mm) thick. Fry until batter firms. Turn over and brown second side.

Serve right away on a plate (with a fork or chop sticks) or a napkin (to be eaten with hands). Accompany with one or more dipping sauces (see p. 7) and spicy kim chee.

Leftover batter can be kept in the refrigerator for up to 1 week; leftover cooked pancakes can be reheated in a toaster.

Kim Chee

2 to 3 cups (500 to 750 mL)
10 minutes preparation
2 days marinating

This spicy condiment resembles German sauerkraut, but with the addition of chilies, ginger and more vegetables. You can approximate the flavor by adding some of these ingredients to plain sauerkraut and letting the flavors mingle.

Combine sauerkraut, chilies and ginger with whatever optional ingredients you choose. Let marinate for 2 or more days. Serve with bindatuk or other Oriental dishes. Will keep in refrigerator for several weeks.

2 cups loosely packed sauerkraut (500 mL)
1–2 hot chilies, seeded and thinly sliced (wash hands afterwards)
2" (5 cm) fresh ginger, peeled and minced

OPTIONAL INGREDIENTS:
½ cup peeled and slivered white radish (daikon) (125 mL)
½ cup thinly sliced "dill" cucumber (125 mL)
½ cup sliced green onion, (125 mL)

Fiber

The attention now paid to the importance of fiber in the diet is largely the result of the pioneering studies conducted by Dènis Burkitt, MD. A surgeon who practised curative medicine in Africa for 13 years, he noticed that the "old-fashioned" Africans (who did not speak English) were virtually never afflicted with constipation, obesity, appendicitis, diabetes, heart attacks or cancer, whereas their "modern" (English-speaking) cousins were just as susceptible to these problems as anyone in the industrial world. The main difference between the two groups was their diet: those who generally remained healthy ate large quantities of fiber. Dr. Burkitt's work clearly demonstrates that diets high in carbohydrates and fiber, and low in fats and oils, reduce the incidence of many diseases.

For a high-fiber African-style meal at home, you might begin with a peanut soup and follow it with cooked millet topped with a flavorful egasi stew. Fresh tropical fruit makes a fine (also high-fiber) dessert.

Peanut Soup

½ cup smooth OR crunchy
  peanut butter (125 mL)
2 cups stock, beer OR water
  (500 mL)
1 tbsp peanut oil (15 mL)
½ cup diced onion (125 mL)
2 tbsp shelled peanuts (25 mL)
2 tsp cumin seeds (10 mL)
¼ cup minced sweet peppèrs
  (50 mL)
½ cup peeled and chopped
  tomatoes (125 mL)

4 bowls
15 minutes preparation

Whisk stock into peanut butter, a little at a time. Put in a pot and bring to a simmer. Meanwhile, fry onion, peanuts, cumin seeds and peppers in oil.

When lightly browned, add fried mixture to heating liquid. Stir in tomatoes. Simmer until soup has thickened. Serve right away garnished with chopped fresh coriander or thyme leaves.

Cooked Millet

4 servings
5 minutes preparation
20 minutes cooking

Millet contains a nearly perfect complement of amino acids (protein), as well as many vitamins and minerals. Buy the best quality you can find—it should have a slightly green hue.

4 cups boiling water (1 L)
½ tsp salt (2 mL)
2 cups millet, rinsed clean
  (500 mL)

Add salt and millet to boiling water. As soon as water returns to boil, reduce heat to low. Cover and leave to cook. When all water has been absorbed (about 20 minutes) remove from heat and let rest 5 minutes before serving.

Egasi

8 servings
25 minutes preparation
20 minutes cooking

*For authentic red color and mellow flavor, use unre-
fined orange palm oil (it contains no more saturated
fats than butter); for the traditional tartness, use tamarind concentrate. Both are available at stores special-
izing in Indian and Jamaican food, many of which also
carry a variety of starchy root vegetables.*

Bring tomato juice and beans to a simmer. Add starchy
vegetable(s). Meanwhile heat oil in a frying pan on
medium heat and add onion, cumin, chili and ginger.
Fry slowly until aromatic (about 5 minutes), then stir
in the tender vegetable(s) and fry until brightly colored.

When starchy vegetables are just softening, (about
10 minutes) stir in fried ingredients, tamarind, garlic,
thyme and salt. Let simmer 5 minutes, then remove
from heat. Reheat just before serving.

Serve egasi over a cooked grain such as millet, garnished with sliced cucumber, tomato, hot chilies, onion slices, toasted coconut and a chutney. Any leftovers
will keep for a week in refrigerator.

4 cups tomato juice OR whole
  peeled tomatoes (1 L)
1½ cups cooked beans (see p.
  108): pigeon peas, black-eyed
  peas OR kidney beans
  (375 mL)
4 cups peeled starchy
  vegetable(s) cut in 1″ (2.5-cm)
  dice: yam, sweet potato,
  cassava, plantain, breadfruit,
  jicama OR ordinary white
  potato (1 L)
4 tbsp unrefined palm OR
  peanut oil (50 mL)
2 cups diced onion (500 mL)
1 tbsp cumin seeds (15 mL)
1–2 hot chili peppers, diced
  (wash hands afterwards)
1″ (2.5 cm) fresh ginger, peeled
  and minced
2 cups tender vegetable(s) cut
  in 1″ (2.5-cm) pieces: sweet
  peppers, okra, green beans
  OR eggplant (500 mL)
1 tbsp tamarind concentrate
  (15 mL) OR 2 tbsp lime juice
  (25 mL)
3 cloves garlic, minced
2 tsp thyme (10 mL)
½ tsp salt (2 mL)

Whole-Grain Porridge

A nutritious breakfast of hot cereal is a big help in getting through the winter day. And with the variety of whole grains now available, you needn't limit yourself to rolled oats.

There are a number of ways to shorten the cooking time. Thermos porridge makes an instant breakfast, while overnight soaking in cold water permits most grains to be "quick cooked" the following morning. Another time-saver is to cook more servings than you need, and use the rest for fried porridge.

If you like a smooth creamy porridge, start the cooking in cold water; for more texture stir the cereal into already boiling water. To add a nutty flavor, lightly toast the grain before boiling by tossing it in a frying pan over medium heat.

Hot Porridge

4 hearty servings
5 minutes preparation
15 to 45 minutes cooking

4 cups cold OR boiling water (1 L)
¼ tsp salt (1 mL)
cereal grain (see recipe)

The quantities and estimated cooking minutes noted after each grain are only approximations. Vary them as required to allow for differences in starch content, size of kernels, and personal preferences.

BUCKWHEAT—groats or kasha (1½ cups/375 mL; 20 minutes): the raw groats are very mild; toasted kasha has a more distinctive taste.

CORNMEAL (1 cup/250 mL; 5 minutes): for the best flavor look for freshly ground whole-grain meal; coarsely ground grain may take longer to cook.

MILLET (1½ cups/375 mL; 20 minutes): texture is smoother when millet is presoaked overnight.

ROLLED OATS (1½ cups/375 mL; 5 to 15 minutes): rich and creamy; smaller flakes cook more quickly.

STEEL-CUT OATS (1¼ cups/300 mL; 45 minutes): very nutty flavor; especially good if soaked overnight before cooking.

ROLLED RYE (1¼ cups/300 mL; 15 minutes): a somewhat sour flavor and rough texture; best combined with other grains.

ROLLED WHEAT (1¼ cups/300 mL; 15 minutes): similar to oatmeal.

CRACKED WHEAT (1¼ cups/300 mL; 25 minutes): hearty flavor of whole-grain wheat.

BULGAR (2 cups/500 mL; 20 minutes): nutty flavor of preroasted wheat.

SEMOLINA (1 cup/250 mL; 5 minutes): from the white part of the wheat (farina is a slightly coarser grade of the same thing); mild creamy flavor.

Put salt and grain in water (cold or boiling, depending on desired texture) in a heavy-bottomed saucepan. Bring mixture to a simmer, give it a quick stir, reduce heat to low, and cover pot. Stir once every 5 minutes, being sure to scrape the bottom well.

When water is completely absorbed, remove from heat and, for best flavor and texture, let porridge rest for 5 minutes. Serve with milk or cream and your favorite sweetener or nutritional yeast.

Thermos Porridge

2 servings
10 minutes preparation
overnight soaking

Preheat thermos (preferably one with a wide mouth) with boiling water. Heat and lightly toast cereal by putting it in a 250°F (120°C) oven for 20 minutes, or tossing it in a dry frying pan on medium heat for 5 minutes.

Drain thermos. Put in the warm grain and salt. Promptly pour in boiling water and cover. Porridge will be ready to eat in about 8 hours.

1 cup cereal grain: bulgar; cracked wheat; cornmeal; rolled oats, rye or wheat; semolina (250 mL)
¼ tsp salt (1 mL)
2 cups boiling water (500 mL)

Fried Porridge

4 servings
10 minutes preparation

Before porridge cools, pour it onto a salad plate and promptly smooth it into a disk ½" (1 cm) thick. (It will keep at room temperature for 3 days.)

When cooled and set, cut porridge disk in quarters. Melt butter in a large heavy-bottomed frying pan on medium-high heat. Add porridge triangles and fry both sides until lightly browned (about 5 minutes).

Serve right away with maple syrup, a dab of yogurt and sliced fresh fruit.

½ recipe Hot Porridge
3 tbsp butter (50 mL)

Buckwheat

Unrelated to ordinary wheat, buckwheat is a nutritious grain that is especially useful for celiacs—those who are allergic to wheat and its many cousins, including barley, rye and triticale. It is available in two forms: mild, green-hued raw kernels and rust-colored toasted "kasha", which has a stronger flavor. Either can be cooked as a whole grain (see p. 93) or hot porridge (p. 152).

Buckwheat flour is at its best in pancakes. My favorite version, yeast-leavened Russian blini, can be the basis of a satisfying meal. Serve them with the traditional accompaniments—sweet butter, sour cream, cottage cheese, butter-fried mushrooms, chopped green onions, shredded carrot and (black) radish, chopped hard-cooked eggs, eggplant caviar, apple-sauce, and assorted pickles—or such North American favorites as whipped cream, yogurt, chopped nuts, fruit, jam, honey or maple syrup.

Blini

36 3" (7-cm) pancakes
30 minutes preparation
8 hours rising
15 minutes cooking

2 cups warm milk (500 mL)
2 tbsp honey, preferably buckwheat (25 mL)
1 tbsp dry active yeast (15 mL)
2 cups sifted raw OR toasted buckwheat flour (500 mL)
2 tbsp butter, melted (25 mL)
4 eggs, separated
⅛ tsp salt (0.5 mL)

Combine milk, honey and yeast. When mixture begins to foam (about 10 minutes), stir in flour, butter, egg yolks and salt. Whisk vigorously until well blended. Let rest and rise at room temperature for 8 to 12 hours.

Just before cooking, beat egg whites to soft peaks. Fold into batter. Preheat a lightly oiled frying pan and pour in about 2 tbsp (25 mL) batter for each pancake. Fry until lightly browned on both sides.

Serve right away with assorted accompaniments. Cook any unused batter into pancakes, then freeze and pop them into a toaster for instant meals and snacks.

Eggplant Caviar

2 cups (500 mL)
15 minutes preparation
25 minutes baking

Preheat oven to 500°F (260 °C). Poke two holes in each eggplant. Put on a baking sheet and bake until skin is well charred (about 25 minutes). Remove from oven, cool and scrape out flesh. Chop and place in a colander to drain for 5 minutes.

Meanwhile heat oil and slowly fry remaining ingredients. When softened, add chopped eggplant. Fry slowly until most of the excess moisture has evaporated.

Let cool before serving with blini or sliced dark rye bread. Keeps well in refrigerator for 2 weeks.

2 medium eggplants (with fresh green caps)
3 tbsp olive OR other oil (50 mL)
½ cup minced onion (125 mL)
½ cup minced seeded sweet pepper (125 mL)
1 cup minced tomato (250 mL)
2 tbsp chopped fresh parsley OR dill (25 mL)
1 tbsp cider vinegar (15 mL)
½ tsp salt (2 mL)

Applesauce

1 quart (1 L)
15 minutes preparation
10 minutes cooking

Choose the apples and method to create the kind of sauce you want. Red and Golden Delicious are sweet; McIntosh, Empire, Spartan and Cortland are mild; Granny Smith, Northern Spy and Greening are tart. Gravenstein and Jonathon apples give the best texture and flavor.

Simmer apples in ½ cup (125 mL) water until softened (about 10 minutes). Sauce can be used as is. To remove chunks but maintain some texture, use a potato masher or put through a food mill. For the smoothest texture, spin in a blender or food processor.

For a personal touch stir in one or more of the optional flavorings.

Serve either warm or chilled. Keeps well in refrigerator for 2 weeks and can be frozen for up to 6 months.

10 cups (3 lb) cored and chopped (peeled if waxed) apples (2500 mL/1.5 kg)

OPTIONAL FLAVORINGS:
1 tsp ground anise (5 mL)
2 tbsp butter (25 mL)
1 tsp grated ginger (5 mL)
¼ cup honey (50 mL)
1 tbsp lemon juice (15 mL)
½ tsp vanilla extract (2 mL)

Meal in a Packet

If you're involved in an active outdoor sport (or just watching a winter carnival) you'll probably want to have an easy-to-eat meal ready whenever you are. Try a Cornish pasty—it's a whole meal in a packet. The fillings can be made days ahead of time and the pasties assembled the day before, then baked while you get ready to leave (they'll keep warm for several hours).

Worcestershire Sauce

1 cup (250 mL)
15 minutes preparation
1 day resting

If you don't like all the ingredients listed on ready-made bottles, make your own. Tamarind concentrate and palm sugar are available from Indian food stores.

Combine all ingredients and heat slowly. Simmer for 10 minutes, then remove from heat, cover and leave for 1 day. Strain and transfer to a clean bottle. Store in refrigerator for up to 3 months.

¾ cup soy sauce (175 mL)
2 tbsp tamarind concentrate (25 mL) OR 1 tbsp lime juice (15 mL) with 2 tbsp Barbados molasses (25 mL)
1 tbsp palm OR brown sugar (15 mL)
1 tbsp malt OR cider vinegar (15 mL)
1 hot chili, split open
½ nut nutmeg
6 cloves
1" (2.5-cm) square piece lemon zest
1" (2.5 cm) fresh ginger, thinly sliced

Cornish Pasties

6 pasties
1 hour preparation
30 minutes resting
35 minutes baking

Cater the fillings to individual preferences, then prick in each person's initials over the dessert side—that way everyone will get the proper pasty and start the meal at the right end.

For the pastry, combine all ingredients with 1½ cups (375 mL) water and knead on a floured surface only until well blended. Cover and let rest in refrigerator 30 minutes or overnight

PASTRY:
4 cups finely ground soft whole-wheat flour (1 L)
1 cup white flour (250 mL)
¾ cup butter, diced (175 mL)
¼ tsp salt (1 mL)

For the mashed potatoes, simmer whole potatoes and celery in about 1″ (2.5 cm) water until a knife pierces them easily (about 20 minutes). Meanwhile slowly heat milk, butter, honey, salt and pepper. Place cooked potatoes in cold water to cool for handling. Discard celery. Peel potatoes.

Add hot milk mixture to warm potatoes. Mash, whisk, or beat with an electric mixer until smooth. (A blender or food processor makes them too gummy.) Cool before assembling pasties.

Crumble tofu into pea-sized pieces. Fry in a dry pan on high heat until most of the liquid that exudes has evaporated. Add butter, sherry, leek and rutabaga. Simmer, uncovered, until most of the liquid evaporates and vegetables soften. Remove from heat and stir in Worcestershire sauce, garlic, parsley and horseradish.

For the apple filling, peel, quarter, core and slice apples. Stir together arrowroot, honey, butter, cinnamon and salt in a heavy-bottomed saucepan. Add apples and put on low heat. Slowly bring to a simmer, stirring constantly as liquid begins to thicken. Simmer only until mixture is clear and thick. Remove from heat and cool.

Preheat oven to 400°F (200°C). Divide pastry into 6 pieces. On a floured surface, roll out into 9″ (22.5-cm) circles. Put a portion of mashed potatoes in the center, rutabaga-tofu filling on one side and apple filling on the other. If desired, include a dab of chutney or a pickle, or sprinkle on some shredded cheese—perhaps Cheddar over potatoes, or blue cheese over apples.

Moisten edges of pastry. Fold one side over fillings and wrap over the bottom. Press together at 1″ (2.5-cm) intervals with fingers. Bake until crust is lightly browned (about 35 minutes). Serve pasties right away or wrap in a towel to keep warm. Serve with Worcestershire sauce.

MASHED POTATOES:
1 lb (3 medium) potatoes (500 g)
1 stalk celery, sliced
½ cup milk OR cream (125 mL)
2 tbsp butter (25 mL)
1 tsp honey (5 mL)
½ tsp salt (2 mL)
¼ tsp ground white peppercorns (1 mL)

RUTABAGA-TOFU FILLING:
1 lb tofu (500 g)
2 tbsp butter (25 mL)
2 tbsp sherry OR apple cider (25 mL)
1 cup diced leek OR onion (250 mL)
1 cup coarsely shredded rutabaga (250 mL)
2 tbsp Worcestershire Sauce (25 mL)
3 cloves garlic, minced
¼ cup chopped fresh parsley (50 mL)
2 tsp shredded fresh OR prepared horseradish (10 mL)

APPLE FILLING:
3 medium tart apples: Northern Spy, Ida Red OR Granny Smith
3 tbsp arrowroot (50 mL)
⅓ cup honey (75 mL)
1 tbsp butter, melted (15 mL)
¼ tsp ground cinnamon (1 mL)
pinch salt

Winter Barbeque

A crackling fire in the middle of a winter outing can be even more warming with the aroma of food cooking over the coals. So on the next clear, crisp day, why not pack the grill, step out in the snow, and have a winter barbeque?

Tempeh patties can be prepared ahead, ready to take on a moment's notice, and they require only a few minutes' grilling over the fire. Corn chowder kept hot in a thermos or reheated over the fire provides instant sustenance, while a flask of spiced wine or cider will warm the last chilled bone. Granola bars provide quick energy for the journey home.

Blue-Cheese Mayonnaise

1 cup (250 mL)
5 minutes preparation

2 egg yolks
¼ cup crumbled blue cheese (50 mL)
2 tbsp lemon juice (25 mL)
½ tsp dry mustard powder (2 mL)
1 clove garlic
pinch cayenne
1¼ cups olive oil (300 mL)

Blend egg yolks, cheese, lemon juice, mustard, garlic and cayenne in a blender or food processor, or with a whisk. While still beating, slowly add oil—drop by drop at first, gradually increasing to a thin stream. Stop adding oil if mixture begins to lose its shine, or to thin rather than thicken.

Use in sandwiches or thin with a little milk for a salad dressing. Will keep in refrigerator for 2 weeks.

Tempeh Patties

8 patties
15 minutes preparation
1 hour marinating

Look for tempeh (see p. 116) in Indonesian and natural food stores.

1 lb tempeh, partially thawed (500 g)
¼ cup soy sauce (50 mL)
1 tbsp unrefined peanut oil (15 mL)
2 tsp ground coriander seeds (10 mL)
2 tsp vinegar OR lemon juice (10 mL)
1 tsp honey (5 mL)
3 cloves garlic, minced
1 hot chili, minced (wash hands afterwards)

Cut tempeh into patties 2½" (6 cm) square. Place in a pot. Combine remaining ingredients with 1 cup (250 mL) water and pour over tempeh. Slowly bring to a simmer, gently turning the patties periodically. Cool at least 1 hour or overnight. (If hurrying to a barbeque, carry patties and marinade in a tightly sealed container.)

Grill patties over an open fire until lightly charred. (At home, grill under broiler or fry in a lightly oiled frying pan.) Serve in burger buns with your favorite condiments—or try alfalfa sprouts (see p. 98) and blue-cheese mayonnaise.

Corn Chowder

8 bowls
15 minutes preparation
15 minutes simmering

Have this whichever way you prefer: New England cream-style or Manhattan-style, with tomato broth.

Slowly heat cream or juice, stock and bay leaf in a heavy-bottomed saucepan. In a frying pan on medium heat melt butter and slowly fry onion and potato until softened (about 10 minutes). Add flour and corn. When sizzling, add to hot liquid. Simmer 15 minutes. Stir in salt, pepper and celery leaves. Chowder is ready to serve but, like most soups, tastes even better after being reheated.

3 cups cereal cream OR tomato juice (750 mL)
1 cup stock (see p. 92) OR water (250 mL)
1 bay leaf
4 tbsp butter (50 mL)
1 cup diced onion (250 mL)
1 cup diced potato (250 mL)
4 tbsp flour (50 mL)
2 cups corn kernels (500 mL)
¼ tsp salt (1 mL)
⅛ tsp ground white peppercorns (0.5 mL)
2 tbsp chopped celery leaves (25 mL)

Spiced Wine or Cider

1 quart (1 L)
5 minutes preparation
15 minutes heating

If using cider, look for the more flavorful unfiltered, unpasteurized type.

Slowly heat all ingredients in a non-metallic pot. Just before it begins to boil, remove from heat. Strain out flavorings and serve in mugs.

1 bottle (25 oz) red wine OR cider (750 mL)
1 whole orange
4 pods cardamom
6 cloves
1 tsp coriander seeds (5 mL)
1 bay leaf

Crunchy Granola Bars ⌄

12 bars
10 minutes preparation
30 minutes baking

Preheat oven to 350°F (180°C). Butter a 9″ × 14″ (25 × 30-cm) cake pan. Combine granola, honey and flour. Spread mixture into prepared cake pan, patting it down evenly with moistened hands.

Bake until lightly browned (about 30 minutes). Cool slightly. While still warm, cut into bars and place on a cake rack to cool and dry. Keep crisp in a tightly sealed container.

3 cups granola (without any large fruits or nuts) (750 mL)
½ cup honey (125 mL)
¼ cup soft whole-wheat flour (50 mL)

Rutabagas

The yellow rutabaga (sometimes mistakenly called turnip) is often mistreated, but when handled with care it appeals to nearly everyone. Just be sure to use the entire vegetable within 24 hours after cutting it open, so it won't turn bitter, and take care not to overcook it.

Rutabagas can be prepared in just about any way you would carrots or potatoes. They can be eaten raw in salads or as crudités, steamed (see p. 100), lightly boiled (see p. 168), sautéed, glazed, deep-fried, baked, puréed, scalloped—even made into cake. The following recipe for red flannel hash uses rutabaga preserved in the Chinese fashion, by blanching and drying. Serve the hash with corn bread and a steamed green vegetable (see p. 100). Baked apples (see p. 169) would be a good dessert.

Preserved Rutabaga

2 lb dried chips (1 kg)
30 minutes preparation
2 hours marinating
4 hours drying

Use preserved rutabaga with creamed vegetables, egg dishes, salads—anywhere you want some extra flavor and texture.

2 cloves garlic
2 tbsp Szechuan pepper pods
  (25 mL) OR 1 tbsp black
  peppercorns (15 mL)
3 pieces star anise OR 1 tbsp
  anise seeds (15 mL)
½ cup soy sauce (125 mL)
1 tbsp molasses (15 mL)
1 tbsp vinegar (15 mL)
2 tsp mustard powder (10 mL)
6 cups (4 medium) rutabagas,
  peeled and cut in very small
  chips (1500 mL)

Enclose garlic, pepper and anise in a teaball or piece of cheesecloth for easy removal. Add with soy sauce, molasses, vinegar and mustard to 3 cups (750 mL) water. Bring to a boil.

When boiling, turn heat to high and add rutabaga. When the pot returns to boil, remove from heat. Let cool (about 2 hours) with periodic stirring.

Pour off liquid and remove teaball. Spread marinated rutabaga over two baking sheets. Place in a 150°F (65°C) oven and leave door ajar. Every hour or so stir the chips so they dry evenly. When texture is chewy (about 4 hours) remove from oven.

When cool, wrap chips in a plastic bag and store in refrigerator; as long as they remain dry they should keep indefinitely.

Red Flannel Hash

4 servings
20 minutes preparation

Based on a traditional dish from New England.

Melt butter in a heavy, well seasoned frying pan on medium-high heat and fry onions until clear. Add potatoes, beets, preserved rutabaga, thyme and celery seeds.

Cook until bottom crusts (about 2 minutes), then fold over, scraping up crust with a metal spatula. Continue cooking about 15 minutes, turning occasionally. After each turn sprinkle on a spoonful of hot water to generate steam.

When done, remove from heat and cover frying pan. Let rest a few minutes before serving. Garnish each portion with a poached egg (see p. 169), a dab of sour cream, sliced pickles and grated horseradish. Leftovers are good cold or reheated.

4 tbsp clarified butter (see p. 60) OR ½ butter and ½ oil (50 mL)
1 cup onions, finely diced (250 mL)
4 cups shredded potatoes (1 L)
1 cup peeled shredded beets (250 mL)
½ cup Preserved Rutabaga, crumbled cheese crisps (see p. 97) OR chopped mushrooms (125 mL)
1 tsp thyme (5 mL)
1 tsp celery seeds (5 mL) OR 1 tbsp chopped celery (15 mL)

Corn Bread

8 servings
15 minutes preparation
15 minutes baking

For a crunchy crust, preheat the baking pan in the oven.

Preheat oven to 400°F (200°C). Generously butter a 10″ (25-cm) iron frying pan and place in oven. Whisk buttermilk, butter, honey and egg until frothy. Combine cornmeal, flour, baking soda and salt. Sift into liquid ingredients and add peppers. Fold together with as little agitation as possible.

Pour mixture into hot pan—it should be two-thirds full. Bake until top is lightly browned (about 15 minutes). Serve right away with plenty of sweet butter.

1 cup buttermilk OR fresh milk plus 2 tbsp (25 mL) vinegar (250 mL)
2 tbsp butter, melted (25 mL)
1 tbsp honey (15 mL)
1 large egg
1¼ cups cornmeal (300 mL)
¾ cup sifted soft whole-wheat flour (200 mL)
2 tsp baking soda (10 mL)
¼ tsp salt (1 mL)
½ cup red and/or green peppers, diced (125 mL)

Winter Produce

This menu features three of the most familiar produce varieties available in winter: carrots, cabbage and oranges. Prepare the orange upside-down cake first. While it starts baking you can assemble the carrot timbale and put it in the oven to bake alongside the cake. Finally, prepare the cabbage and any other accompaniments you may want.

Carrot Timbale

4 servings
25 minutes preparation
40 minutes baking

A timbale is a drum-shaped molded casserole.

SHELL:
½ lb dried fettucine or other pasta (250 g) OR ¾ lb fresh (375 g)

FILLING:
½ cup finely diced onion (125 mL)
3 cups coarsely shredded carrot (750 mL)
¼ cup chopped hazelnuts (50 mL)
4 tbsp butter (50 mL)
2 tsp rubbed thyme (10 mL)
2 tsp rubbed marjoram (10 mL)
⅛ tsp ground black pepper (0.5 mL)
3 eggs, lightly beaten
¼ cup grated Parmesan cheese (50 mL)

CHEESE SAUCE:
1½ cups (12 oz) Ricotta OR dry cottage cheese (375 mL/375 g)
½ cup buttermilk OR yogurt (125 mL)
1 clove garlic
¼ tsp mustard powder (1 mL)
¼ tsp salt (1 mL)

Cook pasta in 1 quart (1 L) boiling water (less than you would ordinarily use). Use no oil—you want the pasta to be somewhat sticky. Drain and put in a generously buttered 2-quart (2-L) soufflé dish. Press up around sides of dish and hold in position by placing a smaller dish inside. (You can do this a day ahead.)

Preheat oven to 350°F (180°C). For the filling slowly fry onion, carrot and hazelnuts in butter. When soft (about 5 minutes) add thyme, marjoram and pepper. Turn into a mixing bowl and let cool a minute. Stir in eggs and Parmesan.

By now the pasta should be cool enough to hold its shape. Lift out the smaller dish and pour the carrot mixture into the shell. Cover and put in oven. Bake until set (about 40 minutes).

Meanwhile, blend all cheese sauce ingredients to the consistency of whipping cream. You may need to add additional cheese to thicken or buttermilk to thin it. Blend for several more minutes, until perfectly smooth.

Remove baked timbale from oven and let cool 10 minutes. Run a knife around the sides to loosen it, then turn out on a warm plate. Cover with cheese sauce and surround with steamed cabbage.

Steamed Cabbage

4 servings
10 minutes preparation

Quick cooking maintains a fresh, sweet flavor.

Heat a heavy-bottomed frying pan on high heat. Add oil, then cabbage. Toss while sprinkling in spoonfuls of the boiling water. When cabbage has wilted (about 4 minutes), toss in parsley, lemon juice, salt and pepper.

1 tbsp vegetable oil (15 mL)
4 cups shredded cabbage (1 L)
¼ cup boiling water (50 mL)
3 tbsp chopped fresh parsley
OR fresh dill (50 mL)
2 tsp lemon juice (10 mL)
salt and pepper to taste

Orange Upside-Down Cake

1 9″ (22.5-cm) square OR 10″ (25-cm) round cake
25 minutes preparation
60 minutes baking
30 minutes cooling

In the summer use peaches in place of the oranges; in the fall use apples.

Preheat oven to 350°F (180°C). Arrange oranges evenly over the bottom of a generously buttered cake pan (remember that the bottom will become the top).

Sift together flour, baking soda and powder and salt. Whisk together yogurt, ginger and vanilla. In a large bowl, beat honey and butter until pale (about 4 minutes). While still beating, add egg yolks one at a time. Beat egg whites in a clean glass or metal bowl until soft peaks form.

Re-sift half the flour mixture into honey-butter mixture. Add all the yogurt mixture, then sift in remaining flour mixture. Stir for 200 strokes or mix with an electric mixer for 30 seconds. Fold in beaten whites.

Promptly pour batter over oranges and place in oven. Bake until cake begins to pull away from sides of pan (about 60 minutes). Remove from oven. When cake has cooled (about 30 minutes), invert onto a platter.

Serve with whipped cream Any leftovers will remain fresh for up to 4 days if kept well covered at room temperature

2 seedless oranges, peeled and sliced
2¼ cups (11 oz) sifted soft whole-wheat flour (300 mL/ 310 g)
1½ tsp baking soda (7 mL)
½ tsp baking powder (2 mL)
pinch salt
¾ cup yogurt (175 mL)
1 tsp freshly grated ginger (5 mL)
1 tsp vanilla extract (5 mL)
1 cup honey, preferably crystallized (250 mL)
¾ cup room-temperature butter (175 mL)
2 eggs, separated

Stews

Although meatless stews can have plenty of flavor, they frequently lack the firm ingredients that provide a satisfying texture. Yet there are many non-meat ingredients that you can sink your teeth into. Eggplant and mushrooms are two vegetables that maintain a chewy texture; chickpeas are among the few legumes that remain firm after being cooked enough to ensure easy digestion; and nuts, after they have been simmered awhile, lose some of their crunch and become pleasantly chewy. You might also consider adding various Oriental ingredients such as gluten (see p. 120), tempeh cubes (p. 116), dried bean curd "ropes" (p. 118) or crumbled tofu (p. 115).

Olla podrida is a Spanish stew that makes delicious use of several chewy ingredients. Accompany it with a red wine, a loaf of crusty bread and a crisp Spanish salad, and finish off with a smooth egg flan.

Olla Podrida

4 cups tomato juice (1 L)
1 bay leaf
4 cups of bite-sized vegetables to be boiled: carrot, whole onion, potato, Jerusalem artichoke, artichoke hearts (1 L)
¼ cup olive oil (50 mL)
4 cups of bite-sized ingredients to be fried: eggplant, mushrooms, hazelnuts, sweet pepper, cabbage (1 L)
2 cups cooked chickpeas (see p. 108), with their liquid (500 mL)
6 cloves minced garlic
¼ cup freshly chopped parsley (50 mL)
1 tbsp chopped fresh mint (15 mL) OR 1 tsp dried (5 mL)
1 tsp salt (less if included in tomato juice or chickpeas) (5 mL)
¼ tsp ground black peppercorns (1 mL)

8 servings
30 minutes preparation

"Rotten pot"—so called by Cervantes' Sancho Panza, because of the leftovers that were continually added to it.

Bring tomato juice and bay leaf to a boil in a saucepan. Add vegetables to be boiled in order given, letting liquid return to a boil after each addition. Heat oil in a frying pan on high heat. Add ingredients to be fried in order given and cook just until brightly colored. Add fried ingredients and cooked chickpeas to tomato mixture. Simmer until everything has softened (about 10 more minutes).

Add garlic, parsley, mint, salt and pepper. Simmer another 5 minutes. Remove from heat and let cool. Stew will keep for 1 week in refrigerator.

To serve, gently reheat the amount you want and garnish with additional chopped parsley.

Spanish Salad

4 servings
10 minutes preparation

Cut onion, pepper, orange and olives into thin rings and arrange over lettuce leaves. Drizzle some oil and lemon juice over each serving.

1 small sweet onion
1 red sweet pepper
1 peeled orange
12 pitted olives
4 leaves lettuce
2 tbsp olive oil (25 mL)
2 tsp lemon juice (10 mL)

Flan

8 servings
15 minutes preparation
1 hour baking

This variation of crème caramel is traditionally cooked in a ring pan, but you can use custard cups.

Preheat oven to 300°F (150°C). In a heavy-bottomed saucepan on medium heat cook ¼ cup (50 mL) of the honey until it reaches 245°F (120°C) (hard-ball stage). Meanwhile lightly butter baking container(s). Pour in hot honey and let cool.

Stir eggs and egg yolks until smooth and homogeneous, taking care not to incorporate any air (best done by gentle hand stirring). Stir in remaining honey, milk, vanilla and salt. Strain into prepared container. Set in larger pan containing ½" (1 cm) water and put on the lowest oven shelf.

Baking times vary, but you can begin checking after 1 hour (45 minutes with cups). Flan should be set nearly to the center. Turn off heat, leave door ajar, and let slowly cool in oven. If flan begins to puff up, it's overdone and should be removed from oven immediately.

Once cooled, the flan can be turned out of its container—easiest after a day's wait. Serve with fresh fruit.

½ cup honey (125 mL)
6 egg yolks plus 2 whole eggs
2 cups milk OR light cream (500 mL)
1 tsp vanilla extract (5 mL)
pinch salt

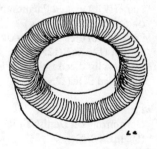

Gnocchi

Gnocchi are little dumplings that, like pasta, come in many forms. The base is usually wheat flour, but it might also be squash, potato, chestnut, ricotta cheese, cornmeal or a rich choux paste. It can be flavored and colored with various fresh herbs or vegetable purées and made into any number of shapes—balls, disks, "corks," "bow ties." You can even serve gnocchi with your favorite pasta sauce.

This menu of squash gnocchi with a rich quattro formaggi topping makes use of a nutritious winter vegetable. Start off with a hearty minestra ceci, an Italian bean soup, and finish with a crisp green salad.

Minestra Ceci

8 servings
15 minutes preparation

You can save time by cooking the chickpeas in a pressure cooker or using canned ones. But for the richest flavor, slow (unattended) soaking and cooking are called for.

4 cups cooked chickpeas
(garbanzos; see p. 108) (1 L)
4 cups chickpea cooking liquid
plus water as required (1 L)
4 tbsp olive oil (50 mL)
1 cup diced onion (250 mL)
1 cup diced celeriac (peeled) OR
celery (250 mL)
½ tsp salt (none if cooked with
chickpeas) (2 mL)
1 tsp lemon juice (5 mL)

Heat oil in a frying pan on high heat and sauté onion and celeriac until lightly browned. Blend with cooked chickpeas and liquid, salt and lemon juice in a food processor, blender or food mill. Reheat and serve garnished with chopped fresh parsley or other herbs.

Quattro Formaggi

2 cups (500 mL)
15 minutes preparation

You need not limit yourself to the "four cheeses" (and alternatives) suggested here. But there should be an old cheese for strength, a middle-aged one for body, a young one for creaminess, and a blue for bite.

¾ cup cereal cream (175 mL)
¼ cup (⅛ lb) grated Parmesan
OR Sardo (50 mL/60 g)
½ cup (¼ lb) diced Fontina OR
Gouda (125 mL/125 g)
½ cup (¼ lb) diced Bel Paese
OR peeled Brie (125 mL/
125 g)
¼ cup (⅛ lb) crumbled
Gorgonzola OR Danish Blue
(50 mL/60 g)
3 egg yolks
2 tbsp white flour (25 mL)
2 tbsp butter (25 mL)
¼ tsp freshly ground white
peppercorns (1 mL)

Put all ingredients in a heavy-bottomed pot or double boiler. Whisking frequently, slowly bring to a very gentle simmer to melt cheeses and thicken eggs and flour. Serve right away over pasta or gnocchi. Leftovers can be gently reheated in a double boiler.

Squash Gnocchi

8 servings
25 minutes preparation
1 hour baking OR 15 minutes steaming
10 minutes poaching

Steaming is quicker, but baking gives the squash a nuttier flavor.

Preheat oven to 350°F (180°C). Cut squash in half, remove seeds and bake upside down until tender (about 1 hour). (Or steam in a pot with ½"/1 cm water for 15 minutes.) Scoop flesh from skin and chop. Purée in a food processor or food mill; there should be 2 cups (500 mL).

Stir in eggs, Parmesan, butter, garlic, salt, nutmeg, pepper and only as much flour as required to hold dough together (it should still be somewhat sticky). Dough can be used now, but will be easier to work with and more tender to eat if it rests for an hour (or overnight) in refrigerator.

With well-floured hands, form dough into marble-sized balls or wine-cork-sized cylinders. Let rest on a floured plate until ready to cook.

Bring to a gentle boil a large shallow pot half-full of lightly salted water. Add only as many dumplings as will comfortably float on the surface (leave enough room for them to swell). Stir gently so that none stick to the bottom. Poach about 10 minutes with lid on.

Lift out with a strainer and serve on a preheated platter. Top simply with melted butter and minced garlic, or more elegantly with quattro formaggi.

1 medium winter squash
2 eggs, lightly beaten
1 cup shredded Parmesan cheese (250 mL)
1 tbsp butter (15 mL)
1 clove garlic, minced
¼ tsp salt (1 mL)
⅛ tsp freshly grated nutmeg (0.5 mL)
⅛ tsp ground white peppercorns (0.5 mL)
about 2 cups soft whole-wheat flour (500 mL)

Old-Fashioned Food

In my restaurant I often served a variety of plain "old-fashioned" vegetables. They attracted many old-timers who enjoyed recalling the days when a meatless meal of boiled vegetables with a poached egg and perhaps a baked apple for dessert was a standard menu item. These days such a combination may seem rather bland, but in the early years of this century eggs really tasted substantial, and the produce was almost all locally grown—still the best kind.

Boiled Vegetables

4 servings
10 minutes preparation
7 to 20 minutes boiling

Cooking vegetables in boiling water has received a lot of bad press recently—often justified. But if it's done properly, boiling is an excellent way to cook.

If you use a small amount of water in relation to the quantity of vegetables, it will stop boiling soon after the vegetables have been added, causing vitamins and minerals to be leached out and the vegetable to become waterlogged. On the other hand, if you add the vegetables to a large amount of boiling water, the intense heat seals in the flavor and nutrients and the cooking is quick enough to maintain the vegetable's texture. Here is a list of vegetables recommended for boiling, with the quantities required for four servings and suggested cooking times.

CARROTS (2 cups/500 mL; 10–20 minutes): peel if skin is bitter, then cut in julienne strips or chunks.

CELERIAC (1½ cups/375 mL; 8 minutes): slice off skin with a knife; cut in dice.

JERUSALEM ARTICHOKE (2 cups/500 mL; 8 minutes): wash well; peeling helps it cook more evenly.

PARSLEY ROOT (1½ cups/375 mL; 9 minutes): peel if desired; cut in even-sized pieces.

PARSNIP (2 cups/500 mL; 7 minutes): peel if desired and cut in lengthwise quarters to slice out any woody core; serve with extra lemon juice to cut sweetness.

POTATO (3 cups/750 mL; 10–15 minutes): peel if desired; cut in even-sized pieces.

RUTABAGA (2 cups/500 mL; 10 minutes): slice off waxed skin and cut in bite-sized dice.

SALSIFY (1½ cups/375 mL; 10 minutes): peel and wipe with lemon juice; cut in even-sized chunks.

Add vegetable(s) to 3 quarts (3 L) boiling water. Whisk together ingredients for sauce. Boil vegetables for time indicated, then drain well. Drizzle sauce over vegetable(s) and serve right away.

SAUCE:
3 tbsp butter, melted (50 mL)
1 tbsp lemon juice (15 mL)
¼ tsp salt (1 mL)
⅛ tsp freshly ground black peppercorns (0.5 mL)
⅛ tsp freshly grated nutmeg (0.5 mL)

Poached Eggs

8 eggs
5 minutes preparation
5 minutes simmering

To prevent streaming, be sure eggs are cold when put in the boiling water.

Heat 1½" (4 cm) water in a shallow pan. Meanwhile break eggs into individual cups. When water reaches a boil, slide them in. Promptly reduce heat to medium and loosen any eggs that stick to the bottom.

8 very fresh cold eggs

When eggs give slightly when pushed with the back of a spoon (about 3 minutes), lift from water with a slotted spoon. If not serving right away, keep in ice water for up to 2 days. Reheat by immersing in hot water for 30 seconds.

Baked Apples

8 servings
15 minutes preparation
2 hours baking

Preheat oven to 300°F (150°C). Cut out apple stems and cores, taking care not to puncture the bottoms. To keep skins from bursting, peel the top third of each apple.

8 large apples: Northern Spy, Granny Smith OR Ida Red
½ cup chopped walnuts (125 mL)
¼ cup maple syrup (50 mL)
2 tbsp butter, diced (25 mL)

Combine walnuts, syrup and butter. Fill each apple with a portion of this mixture. Put in a pan containing ½" (1 cm) water and bake until softened (about 2 hours). Serve with ice cream or zabaglione (see p. 83). Leftovers are good either cold or reheated.

Valentine's Day

When planning menus, it's usually best to aim for a variety of textures, shapes, temperatures, aromas, cooking methods, and colors. But there are exceptions. On Valentine's Day, for example, you might like to build a whole meal around a red-and-white theme.

Cranberry soup makes a refreshing starter before a main course of beet kotlety—mashed potatoes and a steamed green vegetable (see p. 100) would be good accompaniments—followed by raspberry mousse. Both red and white wines are suitable for this meal. All but the final preparations can be done a day ahead of time.

Beet Kotlety

12 small cutlets
25 minutes preparation
1 hour cooling

These Russian "cutlets" can be made with other vegetables too—try carrots, rutabagas or cabbage.

2 cups milk (500 mL)
⅔ cup semolina OR Cream of Wheat (150 mL)
3 tbsp butter (50 mL)
½ cup finely diced onion (125 mL)
1½ cups finely shredded raw beet (375 mL)
1 tbsp chopped dill (optional) (15 mL)
¼ tsp caraway seeds (optional) (1 mL)
3 large eggs, lightly beaten
½ tsp salt (2 mL)
⅛ tsp ground black peppercorns (0.5 mL)
1 cup dry bread crumbs (250 mL)
6 tbsp butter OR oil for frying (100 mL)

Bring milk to a simmer in a heavy-bottomed pan. Whisk in the semolina and stir frequently until thickened (about 5 minutes).

Meanwhile heat butter on medium heat and fry onion, beet, dill and caraway. Stir fried mixture into hot semolina. Let cool slightly, then stir in eggs, salt and pepper.

Line a 10″ (25-cm) cake pan with waxed paper and half the bread crumbs. Pour red mixture evenly over crumbs. Sprinkle remaining crumbs on top. Let mixture cool and solidify (about 1 hour). Cut into hearts (or other shapes).

Heat 3 tbsp (50 mL) butter or oil in a frying pan on medium heat. Fry half the breaded kotlety until crispy brown. Repeat for the remaining cutlets. Serve right away with sour cream. (If necessary, keep warm in a 275°F/135°C oven for up to 30 minutes.)

Cranberry Soup

8 servings
15 minutes preparation
15 minutes cooking

The parsnips counteract the cranberries' tartness.

Put all ingredients in a pot with 4 cups (1 L) water and very slowly bring to a simmer. Simmer for 15 minutes. Remove cloves and bay leaf and purée. Chill soup if desired.

    Serve either hot or cold in large wine goblets, garnished with sour cream.

12 oz cranberries (fresh or frozen), stems and soft berries removed (340 g)
2 cups thinly sliced parsnip (500 mL)
1 cup diced onion (250 mL)
1 cup chopped mushrooms (250 mL)
4 whole cloves
1 bay leaf

Raspberry Mousse

8 servings
20 minutes preparation
2 hours cooling

Agar is a sea-vegetable product available in natural food stores. It works in much the same way as the animal product, gelatine, except that it sets at room rather than refrigerator temperature. For the most reliable results, look for the powdered kind.

Soak agar in 1 cup (250 mL) water in a heavy bottomed saucepan for 10 minutes. Combine raspberries, honey, lemon juice and vanilla. Slowly heat agar until completely dissolved. Beat egg yolks in a heavy-bottomed saucepan over medium heat until warm. Remove from heat. Strain dissolved agar into warm yolks. Return to heat and stir continuously until mixture thickens, taking care not to let it curdle.

    Stir warm egg-agar mixture into fruit mixture. Promptly pour into a (heart-shaped?) bowl. Mousse will set when it reaches room temperature. Serve with whipped cream.

1½ cups frozen raspberries, completely thawed (375 mL)
½ cup honey (125 mL)
1 tbsp lemon juice (15 mL)
1 tsp vanilla extract OR kirsch (5 mL)
1 tbsp powdered agar (15 mL) OR ¼ oz (8 g) stick OR ¼ cup flakes (60 mL)
4 egg yolks

Index